AL PACINO

Also by Lawrence Grobel:

The Art of the Interview: Lessons from a Master of the Craft
Montel Williams: Climbing Higher (with Montel Williams)
Endangered Species: Writers Talk About Their Craft, Their Vision, Their Lives
Above the Line: Conversations About the Movies
Talking with Michener
The Hustons
Conversations with Brando
Conversations with Capote

More on Al Pacino at
www.lawrencegrobel.com

AL PACINO

IN CONVERSATION WITH
LAWRENCE GROBEL

FOREWORD BY AL PACINO

SIMON &
SCHUSTER

London · New York · Sydney · Toronto

A CBS COMPANY

First published in Great Britain by Simon & Schuster UK Ltd, 2006
A CBS COMPANY

1 3 5 7 9 10 8 6 4 2

Simon & Schuster UK Ltd
Africa House
64–78 Kingsway
London WC2B 6AH

www.simonsays.co.uk

Simon & Schuster Australia
Sydney

A CIP catalogue record for this book is available from the British Library.

ISBN 0-7432-9497-1
EAN 9780743294973

Printed and bound in Great Britain by The Bath Press, Bath

For my mother, Estelle,
who danced with him.
And for his children,
Julie, Anton, and Olivia,
who love him.

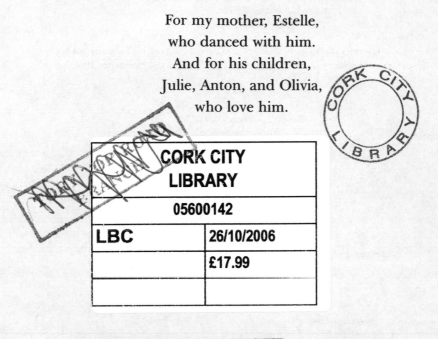
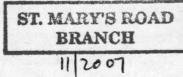

CONTENTS

"I have set my life upon a cast,
and I will stand the hazard of the die."

—Shakespeare, *King Richard III*

FOREWORD

I met Larry Grobel in 1979. I was, of course, mistrustful of him since he was a journalist who came to interview me and, at that time, I had never done an interview. I have since come to know him very well. We've shared many things over this period: successes, failures, encounters with situations both wonderful and unthinkable. Our friendship has survived it all. And for that I am very grateful.

I had not yet said yes to our first interview, but when I read his interview with Marlon Brando on Brando's island in Tahiti, I was impressed. Knowing Marlon as I did, if he liked Larry, if he could speak to him so openly, I felt that I could too. Larry walked into my apartment, which was in shambles. I offered him my half-eaten doughnut. He enjoyed it. We sat down to talk. And what was remarkable about Larry was, at the end of the interview, I knew more about him than he knew about me. I have learned to appreciate his manner, his style, over the years. Some of which is shocking. But you accept it because it's Larry. He persists but never with guile. He has a genuine interest in people, which is why he's such a good writer. He has taken an interest in me for some reason.

Still, I'm trying to figure out why it's so easy to talk to him, to confide in him. That's his talent, I guess.

Larry and I know each other very well (as well as anyone knows anybody). We have forgiven each other many times. I have forgiven him for writing this book. I hope he forgives me for writing this foreword.

—Al Pacino

AL PACINO

INTRODUCTION

Twenty-seven years ago I received a phone call from my editor at *Playboy*, saying that Al Pacino had finally agreed to sit for an interview and was I interested? Of course, I said. What journalist wouldn't be? But there was a catch. I had to fly to New York the next day and meet with him the day after that. I said there was no way I could get ready on such short notice. "You don't understand," my editor said, "he said he would only do this with the guy who did Brando."

Pacino had read the interview I had done with Marlon Brando that had appeared in *Playboy*'s 25th Anniversary issue that month and, apparently, felt that if I was good enough for Brando, then I'd be the right match for him. So I flew to New York and didn't return home for nearly a month.

Before we met, I had an image in my mind: Michael Corleone, of course. Don Corleone's son. The second Godfather. Cold as ice. Someone who could take a gun hidden behind a toilet in a restaurant bathroom and shoot a bullet through the forehead of a corrupt cop. Someone who could tell his wife, Kay, he'd never lie to her, lying to her as he said it. Someone who could give the kiss of death to his older brother Fredo. The other image I had was of Sonny Wortzik, the inept sexually confused Brooklyn bank robber who was brazen enough to pace the sidewalk shouting "Attica! Attica! Attica!" in front of locked-and-loaded cops, TV cameras, and a cheering crowd. These were the guys I was about to interrogate: the cold, calculating mob boss and the wild romantic bank robber with a perverse sense of justice.

The man who answered the door to his brownstone apartment on Sixty-eighth Street between Madison and Fifth Avenue was nothing like either of the men I imagined. Of course, he had those men in him, but it would take years for me to meet them. My first impression of Al Pacino was that he was a somewhat shy and wary actor who happened to be burdened by also being a movie star. His lifestyle brought to mind a line from *Hamlet*: "I could be bound in a nutshell and count myself a king of infinite space." His three-room apartment consisted of a small kitchen with worn appliances, a bedroom dominated by an unmade bed, a bathroom whose toilet was constantly running, and a living room that was furnished like a set for a way-off-off-Broadway production of some down-and-out city dweller. I knew poor people who lived in more luxury than that. Which made me instantly like this man, whose material needs were obviously slight. All around the living room were dog-eared paperback copies of Shakespeare's plays, and stacks of scripts, including one that Costa-Gavras had recently given him based on André Malraux's *Man's Fate*.

Between the apartment, his trailer on the set of *Cruising*, and a few restaurants, we talked every day, often into the early hours of the morning. For an hour or two he would sit or lie on the couch, then jump up and go into the kitchen to light a cigarette from the stove, check the time, walk around a bit. One night I smelled something burning, and we ran into the kitchen to see a pot holder in flames on the stove. Pacino picked up the teakettle and calmly, as if such things happened all the time, put out the fire. On another night I arrived to find him downstairs in the hall, picking up the pieces of a broken Perrier bottle that he had dropped on his way to the elevator. "People wouldn't believe I do this, but I do," he said.

On Waverly Place in Greenwich Village, on location for a scene from *Cruising*, I watched him pace in his camper. While waiting for director William Friedkin to set up the next shot, Pacino tried to relax by reading aloud all the parts from Bertolt Brecht's *The Resistible Rise of Arturo Ui* to his hairstylist, secretary, and makeup man. Down the street, behind the police barricade, he could hear the faint shouts and the shrill whistles of the gay activists who had gathered to protest the making of the film, which dealt with homosexual murders.

"There they go," Pacino said, interrupting his reading. "Sounds like day crickets." The people in his trailer smiled, but no one was laughing, especially

Pacino, who found himself in the midst of a controversy he didn't understand. All his life he had shied away from social movements, political issues,
marches, and protests. Then, the previous summer, he'd done *Richard III* on
Broadway—the first *Richard* done on Broadway in thirty years—and many
of the critics attacked him so fiercely it seemed vindictive. No sooner had that
play completed its run than *Cruising* began. And, once again, the press was
provoked. For an actor who considered himself removed from such furor,
and for a man who had passionately avoided the press, the spotlight had
suddenly been turned strongly his way.

Alfredo James Pacino had traveled a great distance from the South
Bronx of his childhood to the Upper East Side of Manhattan, where he
lived when we first met. The only child of Salvatore and Rose Pacino, of
Sicilian descent, he was born in East Harlem on April 25, 1940, but moved
with his divorced mother to his grandparents' apartment near the Bronx
Zoo in 1942, at age two.

He was nicknamed Sonny, but his friends often called him The Actor,
and, though a prankster throughout his school years, in junior high he was
voted most likely to succeed, mainly in recognition of his acting abilities.
But what he really wanted to be was a baseball player. When they started
teaching Stanislavsky's acting principles (the Method) at the High School
of Performing Arts, which he attended, he thought nothing could be more
boring. He made it through only his sophomore year before the money
ran out and the pressure to get a job surpassed the need to continue his
education.

The succession of jobs brought him in contact with all kinds of characters. He was a messenger, a shoe salesman, a supermarket checker, a
newsboy. He shined shoes and moved furniture. He was an office boy. He
polished fresh fruit. But he also sensed that he could be more, so he auditioned for Lee Strasberg's Actors Studio while a teenager. Rejected but
undeterred, he enrolled in another actor's studio, Herbert Berghof's,
where he met the man who would become his mentor and closest friend,
Charlie Laughton. Not only did Laughton teach acting and direct Pacino
in his first public play (William Saroyan's *Hello Out There*) but Laughton
also wrote poetry and introduced Pacino to poets and writers. Pacino was
accepted by the Strasberg studio four years later.

In the mid-1960s he and a friend started writing comedy revues, which they performed in coffeehouses in Greenwich Village. He was also acting in plays in warehouses and basements. He appeared in numerous plays, including *Awake and Sing!* and *America, Hurrah*. It was on stage when he felt "I could *speak* for the first time. The characters would say these things that I could never say, things I've always *wanted* to say, and that was very liberating for me. It freed me up, made me feel good."

In 1966 he received his first recognition in an off-off-Broadway production of *Why Is a Crooked Letter*. Two years later he won an OBIE for Best Actor in an off-Broadway production of Israel Horovitz's *The Indian Wants the Bronx*. Arvin Brown, who would direct him some years later in *American Buffalo* (1983–84) and *Chinese Coffee* (1992), first saw Pacino in this play and recalled: "He had so much violence in him that he shattered the mystical line that allows the audience to feel comfortable. He scared the shit out of me." Pacino has said that, "In playing it I discovered a kind of explosiveness in me I hadn't known was there." The following year, 1969, he was awarded his first Tony—the legitimate theater's Oscar—for his Broadway performance in Don Petersen's *Does the Tiger Wear a Necktie?*

Like Marlon Brando after his major stage debut in *A Streetcar Named Desire*, Pacino was lured by Hollywood. He was offered a dozen pictures before he and his then manager, Marty Bregman, decided to choose *The Panic in Needle Park* (though he did appear in a bit part in a Patty Duke movie called *Me, Natalie*). *Panic* was a strange and disturbing film about a New York drug addict, which over time picked up a cult following. "The entire cast," Jacob Brickman wrote in *Esquire*, "especially Al Pacino and Kitty Winn in the leads, create intensely real people. Their brand of realness feels close to documentary."

There was something about Pacino, however, that made another newcomer in Hollywood, Francis Ford Coppola, choose him for a film he was about to do on the Mafia. Coppola had big ideas. He wanted not only to have this relatively unknown actor play a major role in his film but also to cast another actor not considered bankable at the time: Marlon Brando. The studio balked twice, but Coppola insisted. When they watched some of the early dailies, they wanted to recast Michael Corleone because they weren't seeing what Pacino was doing. Pacino, however, knew exactly what he was doing. "Michael has to *start out* ambivalent, almost unsure of himself and his place," he said. "He's caught between his Old World family and the postwar American dream." The result was *The Godfather*, a film that reversed the downward trend of Brando's career and that shot Al Pacino into the ranks of stardom. "*The Godfather* belongs to Al Pacino," wrote critic Larry Cohen. "Everyone else is very good, down to the smallest part, but it's Pacino that's great."

Nominated for an Academy Award for Best Supporting Actor, Pacino was insulted (he *was* on-screen longer than Brando, who won—and refused—the Oscar for Best Actor that year) and boycotted the awards ceremony. (He thus didn't get to applaud Joel Grey when he won the statue for *Cabaret*.) For his third movie, *Scarecrow*, Pacino chose an offbeat part in which he played a freewheeling rover on the road with an ex-con, played by Gene Hackman. An unsuccessful picture (different reviewers called the script "phony from word one," and the film "a solemn disaster"), it became one of Pacino's most upsetting experiences with the movie industry.

Still, he responded with another recognized performance in *Serpico*, the New York cop who exposed the New York police force for taking bribes, and almost lost his life for it. "Al Pacino is spectacular," wrote film critic John Simon. "He began on the stage, specializing in vicious psychopaths, and a soupçon of menace still tends to cling to his gentlest moments. But he has now learned how to convert this fierceness into a look of intense moral commitment or zanily lovable passion, and so turn the fuzzy implications of the script into disturbing realities. Pacino has the happy gift of suggesting a mind ceaselessly mobile under a fixed facade, some beast within perpetually coiled for action. . . ." This time he was nominated for an Oscar for Best Actor. (Jack Lemmon got it for *Save the Tiger*.)

His third Oscar nomination came after his strong performance reprising the role of Michael Corleone in *Godfather II*. (Art Carney won the Oscar for *Harry and Tonto*.) The performance was described by critic David Denby in *New York* magazine as "a work of aggressive high intelligence, a bitter and sardonic view of the corruption of America and a frightening embodiment of paranoia as a way of life." (Taken together the two *Godfather* films "come closer to being the great epic of twentieth-century America—or at least American manhood—than any other works of art I can name," wrote

John Powers in the *LA Weekly*.) This was the movie that proved that Pacino was among the rare breed of actors who would leave their mark in American cinema history. (Reflecting on it thirty years later, *Newsweek* said Pacino "gave what is arguably cinema's greatest portrait ever of the hardening of a heart.")

It was a controlled and troubling performance, which put him in the hospital for exhaustion halfway through the production. But when it was completed, he signed to do another controversial and memorable film, *Dog Day Afternoon*, in which he played a bisexual bank robber. Director Sidney Lumet spoke to *GQ* about the actor's intensity: "Everything stems from some incredible core inside of him, that I wouldn't think of trying to get near, because it would be like getting somewhere near the center of the earth. What comes out of his core is so uniquely his own. It's the only thing he can trust. It is quite clear that Al is a loner."

Pacino spent so much time working on the story with Lumet and with writer Frank Pierson, that when they started shooting he realized that he hadn't spent enough time preparing for the character. When he watched some of the opening footage, he insisted that they needed to reshoot it. "When I saw it on the screen," he said, "I thought, *There's no one up there. I was watching someone searching for a character, but there wasn't a person* up there. I came into the bank wearing glasses. And I thought, *No. He wouldn't be wearing glasses. He should forget them at home on the day of the big heist. Because he wants to be caught.*"

Pauline Kael called it "One of the best New York movies ever made," and, for the fourth time, Pacino was nominated for an Oscar. (Jack Nicholson won for his performance in *One Flew Over the Cuckoo's Nest*.)

"All Pacino's best performances are about the paradoxes of power," wrote Ron Rosenbaum in *Vanity Fair*. "In *Dog Day* the powerless briefly take power; in *Godfather II* Michael Corleone becomes a helpless prisoner of his own power."

Hollywood continued to recognize his enormous talent, but he was still an outsider. He refused to move to California, preferring to live in a small, unpretentious apartment in Manhattan; and he refused to consider himself solely a movie actor. Pacino feels his roots are in the theater, and he returns whenever the pressure of being a movie "star" becomes too great.

His next movie was *Bobby Deerfield*, the story of a superstar race-car driver going through an identity crisis. It was also the story of Pacino and his costar, Marthe Keller, who became an item when they decided to extend their relationship offscreen as she moved in with him. But the film didn't work for Pacino or for the public. "If Al Pacino had sent forth his agent to search the world for the role that would call attention to all his weaknesses," wrote Pauline Kael, "the agent could not have come up with an unholier grail than *Bobby Deerfield*." He decided to return to Broadway to do *Richard III*.

But before he did, he completed one more picture, . . . *And Justice for All*, directed by Norman Jewison—a story of an ethical lawyer fighting corruption in the judicial system. Once again Pacino displayed a wide range of acting ability, which earned him his fifth Oscar nomination. (Dustin Hoffman won that year for *Kramer vs. Kramer*, a role Pacino had turned down.)

When *Cruising* came out in 1980, it wasn't the picture Pacino thought he'd been making. Scenes of the killer were truncated; the focus was too one-sided on Pacino's character. All the protests were for naught because the film disappeared quickly. Rex Reed called it "a demented farrago of brutal, incomprehensible, homophobic trash."

Pacino next decided to take a break from the dark side, and tried his hand at playing a single father of five children in *Author! Author!* But he had problems with the director, Arthur Hiller, and felt the end result was a movie that worked better on television. He was itching to find a character he could sink his teeth into, and found it in Oliver Stone's screenplay *Scarface*. Here was a character off the boat from Cuba, who was tough, defiant, reckless, and way over the top. The director, Brian De Palma, had a vision for this remake of the 1932 Paul Muni film, and Pacino's Tony Montana became one of his favorite characters. The critics were harsh when it came out in 1983, but the film built a cult following, and over the years it's been given its due as a heavy influence in the hip-hop world. (Snoop Dogg claimed to watch the movie once a month. "I think any brother watching it can identify with what the main man is going through." The band Blink-182 took its name from the number of times Tony Montana uses the word "fuck.") The movie was Michelle Pfeiffer's first major role, with her playing the trophy moll of the drug lord that Tony

Montana would overthrow, making her his. "I played this appendage, this ice queen, and I was so frightened," Pfeiffer recalled. "I was terrified every single day. I was twenty-four years old. I remember Al and I had dinner one night. It was horrible. We were both so shy. We didn't have one thing to say to each other."

Two years later Pacino appeared in Hugh Hudson's *Revolution*, a film about the Revolutionary War that could have used a few more months in the editing bay before its release. Pacino believed he knew how the film could have been improved—with the proper narration, and with a few scene changes—but the experience (along with such comments as the *New York Times* critic Vincent Canby writing that "Mr. Pacino has never been more intense to such little effect" and *New York*'s David Denby calling it an "epic folly" in which Pacino plays "an alleged Scottish immigrant, but every time he opens his mouth he sounds like Chico Marx with a head cold") soured him on commercial filmmaking for four years. During that time he worked on *The Local Stigmatic*, an independent movie that he financed himself. It was directed by David Wheeler and based on the play by Heathcote Williams, which Pacino had performed off-Broadway in 1969. It was a giant leap away from Tony Montana and Michael Corleone, but Pacino relished working on a Cockney accent and playing opposite Paul Guilfoyle in a tour de force piece about two low-class English outsiders who are drawn to the perversion of fame and to violence. When they see an actor they recognize at a bar, they go to chat him up, and then beat him up. It's a disturbing film that needs to be seen more than once in order to fully appreciate it.

It took Pacino years to complete *Stigmatic*, which *GQ* would call one of his "most brilliant performances," but when it was done, he was hesitant to release it. As Jimmy Breslin observed in *Esquire* in 1996, "He has done everything with it except release it or earn back a nickel of what he's put into it. There is no other recorded case like this in the history of American movie stars." Though he liked to screen it privately, and gave it to the Museum of Modern Art, it would take Pacino nearly twenty years to put it out on a DVD.

In 1989 he returned with a commercial success in *Sea of Love*, directed by Harold Becker and costarring Ellen Barkin and John Goodman. He was back playing a burnt-out detective unsure if the woman he falls for is the killer he's looking for. He seemed to incorporate some of his own dilemmas into the part. "*Sea of Love* was about a guy going through crisis," Pacino said, "which I thought was interesting—to play a cop who's so caught up in his own survival he doesn't realize that his needs are so great they take precedence over his logic." Said Harold Becker, "Al's more than a great actor, he's the human condition walking around. Al doesn't play a character, he *becomes* the character. When he's sitting in a restaurant eating for a scene, he's not acting—he's *eating!*" The reviews were solid, and critics noted that the forty-nine-year-old actor still had his chops.

He followed this with what was the most anticipated film of 1990: *Godfather III*. There had been talk about a third *Godfather* for years, but it wasn't until Francis Coppola felt financially strapped that he set his mind to the story that would complete the trilogy.

Before the production began, Coppola said, "There is a lot of hope in this new screenplay, which I believe is stronger than what Mario and I wrote for the other two. *The Godfather Part III* deals with this kind of American family that functions almost like royalty. Sometimes the younger members are more into the past than the future, and sometimes the older folk are concerned more with the future than the past. . . . Michael Corleone's instincts were always to be legitimate, so it would be odd now, when he's almost in the *King Lear* period of his life, if his prime aim and purpose were not indeed to become legitimate. The result is a very classical piece, in the tradition of a Shakespeare play."

But when Robert Duvall refused to come aboard to revive his consigliere role, and when Winona Ryder, as Michael's daughter, dropped out from exhaustion and was replaced by the director's daughter, Sofia, expectations were lowered. However, while the film didn't come close to the power, intensity, and complexity of the first two, many reviewers agreed with the assessment that critic John Powers made when he wrote, "I'm surprised by how well Coppola's done with a project that could easily have been a disaster. . . . It's still the best and noblest movie that [Paramount] put its name to since, maybe, *The Godfather Part II*."

If the film didn't live up to its great expectations, Pacino's revival of Michael was called "mesmerizing" by Janet Maslin in the *New York Times* and "magnificent" by *Variety*. "Pacino adds the final panel to an extraordinary triptych by an American actor," wrote Jack Kroll in *Newsweek*. Commented David Denby: "The hollow-eyed Pacino performs brilliantly, but he appears to be sinking within himself. . . . Anguished and saturnine and at times deeply funny, Pacino gives a detailed, moving performance. But the emotions that he's playing—self-abnegation, despair—don't fuel a large film." And John Powers wrote: "Michael seems vacant, gutted. And Pacino plays him as a slow, at times shuffling figure—almost comic, yet aching with a desire for forgiveness. . . . Michael's lack of focus is one of the film's boldest and psychologically truest ideas—a harrowingly acute picture of an ambitious man whose inner life has been swallowed up."

If the overall reviews of *Godfather III* were mixed, the reviews were mostly superlative for the next picture Pacino appeared in that year. When Warren Beatty chose to direct and star in *Dick Tracy*, he smartly filled in the comic roles with some of the best actors in the business: William Forsythe as Flattop, R. G. Armstrong as Pruneface, Dustin Hoffman as Mumbles, Madonna as Breathless Mahoney, Glenne Headly as Tess Trueheart, Mandy Patinkin as the piano player, and Pacino as Big Boy Caprice. Pacino took the role as a challenge, and spent months coming up with a look that would totally disguise him. At first he wanted the character to have a huge head, but Beatty vetoed that. Eventually he came up with a character that Vincent Canby called "a mad mixture of *Scarface*, Richard III, and Groucho Marx. He carries on as if his debt to the devil had just come due. He quotes Nietzsche and, when on the run from some nameless terror, moans, 'So many questions, so few answers.'" "What's big about him," Pacino said, "is that he's the world's largest dwarf. . . . He's greedy. Very, very greedy."

As Canby pointed out, Big Boy was no cameo role. "It's of major importance to the scheme of things. . . . [It's] heavyweight hilarity of a high order."

Critics were unanimous in their response to Pacino's way-over-the-top scenery-chewing performance. Sheila Benson in the *Los Angeles Times* called it Pacino's movie. "Al Pacino's Big Boy Caprice has to be one of the screen's most extravagantly funny creations. . . . Who could have suspected that a performance of this hilarity lurked behind Al Pacino's forbidding intensity all these years? *Dog Day Afternoon* may have given more than a hint of it; in

Sea of Love as Pacino fell all over himself to get out of the way of a possibly murderous Ellen Barkin, there was a shutter-quick glimpse of the funniness in the man. . . . Whatever it was, something popped the cork and out spilled this goggle-eyed mobster with a pencil-thin mustache, plastered-down hair and a silhouette roughly like Quasimodo's."

Richard Corliss in *Time* added, "Pacino, as Big Boy, gives *Batman*'s Jack Nicholson a lesson or two in how to play a comic book villain: as part psychotic mastermind, part Hollywood dance director—a Bugsy Siegel who wants to be Busby Berkeley." Roger Ebert said, "Pacino inside that make-up and inside that costume really steals the show. It's a fabulous performance."

The Academy agreed with the critics, and Pacino received his sixth Oscar nomination, but once again it was not to be, as Joe Pesci got the nod for Best Supporting Actor in *GoodFellas*.

Next up for Pacino was the light romantic drama *Frankie and Johnny*, based on Terrence McNally's play *Frankie and Johnny in the Clair de Lune*. The director, Garry Marshall, had wanted Pacino for his previous movie, *Pretty Woman*, and the actor and director enjoyed each other's company (though Marshall's practical jokes, like bringing in the cast of *Star Trek* to Al's dressing room, didn't get the hilarious response Marshall had hoped for, because Pacino had never seen *Star Trek*). "It's strange to talk about vulnerability and innocence with a guy who's played the foremost killers on the American screen," said Marshall. "But he's so pure and honest and artistic, it's a little like Don Quixote walking through Hollywood."

The reviews were mixed, but Pacino enjoyed playing a short-order cook and reuniting with Michelle Pfeiffer, even though she had to ask him to tone down his vegetable chopping so she could hear herself talk.

"Al doesn't like to learn anything pat," Marshall observed. "He likes to wing it at first, improvise until he feels comfortable; and then he locks it down. Michelle is the total opposite. She wants to get every word down perfect and then try some other version. Al likes to try eighty things right away. Despite all that, the two had wonderful chemistry."

Terrence Rafferty in *The New Yorker* wrote: "Pacino's Johnny is a terrifically funny and persuasive portrait of a pesky, in-your-face romantic. . . . This is a wonderful role for Pacino. He brings out the comedy and the ambiguity of a middle-aged man's sense of emotional rebirth: he's exuberant, touching, and a little scary."

In 1992 Pacino appeared as Rick, the supersalesman in *Glengarry Glen Ross*, based on a David Mamet play. It had a strong cast (Jack Lemmon, Alec Baldwin, Kevin Spacey, Ed Harris, Alan Arkin) and received solid reviews. Pacino received his seventh Oscar nomination for his performance, but it was his old *Scarecrow* costar, Gene Hackman, who took home the statue for his role in *Unforgiven*. But that was for Best Supporting Actor. That year Pacino also appeared in *Scent of a Woman*, playing the blind Lieutenant Colonel Frank Slade in a bravura performance that landed him his eighth nomination and his first victory, as Best Actor of 1992.

Pacino's costar, Chris O'Donnell, was just twenty years old when he was cast, and he wasn't at all surprised that Al finally won an Oscar. Intimidated at first, O'Donnell watched as Pacino got into his character (he taught himself to load and unload a .45 in twenty-five seconds, blindfolded), thinking, *The guy is awesome. There's just no way he's not going to win Best Actor for this.* "He's so powerful," O'Donnell observed. "Everything about him. His voice, even on its lowest voltage, still radiates. He's a complete perfectionist. You think he's just a natural, but he works so hard. Every day he was in the dressing room next to me, and I'd hear him working on scenes in days to come, constantly coming up with new ideas. Every scene he wanted to do forty different ways. It was this endless creativity. How did he come up with so many different ideas? It was overwhelming."

Rolling Stone agreed that Pacino was "astoundingly good" but thought "the movie, however, is a crock." The acerbic Rex Reed agreed, writing that "it would be sad if Al Pacino was best remembered in the reference books as a sour-faced blind man dancing the tango. (If you don't believe he won an Oscar for one of the most preposterous performances of his career, you better see the abysmal *Scent of a Woman* again, while sober.) He deserves a better testament." David Denby, on the other hand, watched the same movie—sober, we must assume—and came away believing Pacino "offers the largest, most theatrical and emotional performance of his movie career . . . the character seems both small-minded and magnanimous, abominable and admirable, tyrannical and loving. . . . Technically flawless, the performance has moments of wildness and rage that go beyond anything we've seen from Pacino."

After these two films, Pacino decided to return to the stage, performing in two very different plays on alternate days at the Circle in the Square on Broadway. The first was Oscar Wilde's *Salome*, written in 1893 (two years before *The Importance of Being Earnest*), in which he played a foppish, heavily made-up King Herod, and the second was Ira Lewis's two-man play *Chinese Coffee*, about a down-and-out writer who is owed money from his equally impoverished photographer friend, who feels betrayed by what the writer has written about them. Mel Gussow in the *New York Times* praised the actor more than the plays. "Bejeweled and spangled, Al Pacino swaggers onstage as King Herod in *Salome* and raises his voice almost to a falsetto," he wrote. "He does not edge into this role; he dives headlong. It is a daring performance that flirts dangerously with camp but stays strictly within the character. . . . It is a performance that obscures everything else on the stage."

And: "Just as Mr. Pacino enlivens *Salome* with his presence, he is so intense in *Chinese Coffee* that he almost makes the work seem worthy of his talent."

Linda Winer, reviewing *Salome* for *Newsday*, had this to say: "Try to imagine the meeting that might have seduced Pacino into his own fundraising season for Broadway's Circle in the Square Theatre, a conversation that might have begun: 'OK, Al, what's the strangest thing you ever wanted to do onstage and nobody would let you try?' The result is a truly weird, intense, goofy and mesmerizing performance. . . ."

In 1993 Pacino costarred with Sean Penn in *Carlito's Way*, directed by Brian De Palma, a film that had a lot of preproduction problems. *Entertainment Weekly*'s Owen Gleiberman tried to compare this film to an earlier Pacino–De Palma collaboration: "Scene for scene, *Carlito's Way* is a smoother piece of filmmaking than *Scarface*. . . . But that bloody, lopsided cocaine thriller had a memorable attraction: the itchy hostility of Pacino's performance as Tony Montana, the Cuban crime boss who was such a glowering, paranoid fireball that he was like a walking id. Here, playing a criminal who turns out to be a deeply honorable man, Pacino is trying for something quieter and more emotional."

Director Jamie Foley, who worked with Pacino on *Glengarry Glen Ross*, convinced Pacino to play a dying grandfather in a low-budget film, *Two Bits* (1995). For Pacino it was a chance to go back in time, to think about the man who raised him. "It was the image of my grandfather," he said of the character he portrayed. "That wasn't who my grandfather was, but if I were to paint him, that's how I would paint him. As that character." Though Pacino was praised by the *Los Angeles Times* for bringing sympathy to a man sizing up his life on what he is certain is the day it will end, "It's not quite enough for a fully realized movie."

From that small film Pacino next jumped into a big-budget commercial vehicle that had a lot of heat attached to it. The buzz around *Heat* was that it marked the first time Pacino and Robert De Niro were on-screen at the same time. (They were both in *Godfather II*, but De Niro played the young Brando, so they didn't get a chance to work off each other.) Neither actor wanted to talk about their three scenes together (Al played the cop, De Niro the crook), but director Michael Mann contrasted the way each got into character. "De Niro sees the part as a construction, working incredibly hard, detail by detail, bit by bit building character, as if he were I. M. Pei," Mann said. "The way Al acquires insight into a character is different. It's more like Picasso staring at an empty canvas for many hours in intense concentration. And then there's a series of brush strokes. And a piece of the character is alive."

Mann called Pacino a "genius," and the *Los Angeles Times* praised the director for "helping his actors both uncover and rediscover the core of their appeal, the innate qualities that made them stars in the first place. There is no one in the film, including Pacino, De Niro, Val Kilmer, Tom Sizemore and a ravaged-looking Jon Voight, who does not give the kind of restrained yet powerful performance that ranks with the very best work of their careers."

Critic Manohla Dargis wrote of Pacino, "He's a riot of one, a dynamo charging into the scene of a crime like some demented cross between the Mad Hatter and Hercule Poirot, all sputter, rage and churning gray cells. But if Pacino's Hanna is over the top, he's never out of control."

After *Heat*, Pacino reunited with director Harold Becker, who cast him as the mayor of New York in *City Hall*, costarring John Cusak and written by Bo Goldman. Pacino liked the script, but the critics outside of New York didn't care for the film.

Next Pacino decided to return to his two great passions—the theater and Shakespeare—and invested his time and money producing, directing, and starring in *Looking for Richard*, a docudrama exploration of *Richard III*. As with *Glengarry Glen Ross*, the film featured a strong ensemble cast, including Winona Ryder, Alec Baldwin, Kevin Spacey, Aidan Quinn, Penelope Allen, Kevin Conway, Estelle Parsons, Harris Yulin, and Richard Cox. Pacino also interacts with John Gielgud, Kenneth Branagh, James Earl Jones, and some Oxford scholars, talking about the Bard and his plays.

"*Looking for Richard* was an extension of my vision of something that I wanted to say," said Pacino, who won a Directors Guild Award for it. "I knew I could direct that. Sometimes I'm very inarticulate unless I'm emotional. I can't express myself unless I'm emotional."

Observed *New Times*: "The movie is about Shakespeare, but even more it's about Pacino's bewildered passion for acting. He's like a junkie celebrating the maddening glory of his fix. It's not just the craft of performance that turns him on, it's the whole dizzy realm of the actor's life." Janet Maslin called it "A true revelation! Sharp, funny and illuminating!" *Rolling Stone* wrote that it was "Outrageous fun! Al Pacino's ardor and wit burn steadily on high flame." The *Los Angeles Times* didn't join in the enthusiasm: "Pacino the director can in no way resist shots of Pacino the actor goofing around and so overdoing things. . . . It's hard to imagine this film exciting anyone except Pacino's fans and those who are fatally charmed by celebrity actors."

In 1997 Pacino starred opposite Johnny Depp in *Donnie Brasco*, a true story of an undercover agent who exposed a mob-connected gang by gaining the trust of Lefty Ruggiero, a small-time aging hit man. Director Mike Newell wasn't sure how Pacino was going to play Lefty, a far cry from another Mafia character Pacino had created. "I didn't know whether he was prepared to make himself absolutely absurd," said Newell. "After all, this was the guy who had played Corleone. But he was great, picking some terrible stuff. It was like working with Alec Guinness, who says he starts building a character from the shoes up. All those famous old theater actors see that the externals are very important. And Pacino will always think of himself as a theater actor before he thinks of himself as anything else."

Wrote Kenneth Turan in the *Los Angeles Times*, "Pacino shrewdly underplays Lefty, leaving us with an affecting portrait of an old warrior weary in the service of the dons and hungry for some human contact and appreciation."

The same year Pacino went from sad-sack hit man to a chillingly entertaining Lucifer in *The Devil's Advocate*. Director Taylor Hackford said he was interested in a devil "who was sardonic, fascinating, charming, sexy, and seductive, but not necessarily all-powerful. This devil operates on the power of temptation. He just puts temptation in front of them, and lets them choose."

Pacino played Milton, the devil as senior partner in a major Manhattan law firm, "like a seductive slide trombone," one critic observed.

For Pacino the challenge was deciding how to play that trombone. He looked at how Claude Rains, Jack Nicholson, and Robert De Niro had done it, but it wasn't until he saw Walter Huston's portrayal of Mr. Scratch in the 1941 film *The Devil and Daniel Webster* that he got inspired. "As soon as I saw that, I was going, 'Whoa.' He was giving me wings there. It was just such a brilliant performance. Without him doing anything, he was able to make you feel the devil's power."

There's a scene in the film when Milton rails against God as the father who rejected him, and then breaks into a song and dance, lip-syncing to Frank Sinatra's "It Happened in Monterey." "Al improvised that during rehearsal," Hackford recalled. "It's a moment where Milton feels that Kevin (Keanu Reeves) is coming around, and he's very exhilarated by it. All of a sudden Al just started dancing and singing. I said, 'That's in the movie!'"

Hackford appreciated Pacino's professionalism on the set. "Al is probably the most generous actor I've ever seen," he said. "He could have come to the set arrogant, he could come cool, and he could get away with it. But he doesn't. And Keanu Reeves worshipped Al. They got along great."

Next up was Michael Mann's *The Insider*, based on a *Vanity Fair* feature story about a whistle-blower in the tobacco industry (played by Russell Crowe). Pacino played Bergman, a *60 Minutes* producer. *Los Angeles Times* critic Ken Turan recognized Pacino's performance as "one of Pacino's best, more alive characterizations. It allows him to be natural and powerful, to hold the screen and convince us of someone's sincerity without resorting to mannerisms or well-worn tricks." *New Times* agreed: "Pacino has begun to realize the importance of his legacy and wants to remind us that when the chips are down, he can still deliver on his youthful potential."

That same year Pacino went from the television newsroom to the playing field when he joined Cameron Diaz and Jamie Foxx in Oliver Stone's *Any Given Sunday*. Since *Scarface* was one of Pacino's favorite films, and Stone had written that, he had no qualms about signing on to play a professional football coach before the script was complete. Although Stone had said some negative things about Pacino years earlier for backing out of *Born on the Fourth of July*, he respected the actor's passion and intensity. "Al is sweetness and dark," he said when *Any Given Sunday* was finished. "He's intense and volatile. But very, very, very sensitive. . . . He really listens to the other actors. If you look at five takes of him looking over somebody's shoulder, you will see different expressions each time. Especially on reactive close-ups, which some major stars phone in, he is really attentive. Pacino is an explorer."

Pacino explored the world of science fiction when he signed on to play Viktor Taransky, a fading director who needs to replace a temperamental actress for a film he desperately needs to make. What Taransky does is create a digital actress named S1m0ne, whom he passes off as real. She becomes a sensation, but he must keep his secret from getting out. *S1m0ne* was written (and directed) by Andrew Niccol, who wrote the innovative *The Truman Show*. Like the more serious *The Local Stigmatic*, *S1m0ne* dealt with the nature of fame and celebrity, with reality and illusion, and with success and failure, all intriguing subjects for Pacino. But the critics didn't think it went deep enough, and audiences dismissed it. Though he liked the film himself, he acknowledged that on this one, "The ball didn't go through the cannon."

In 2002 Pacino took on the role of a weathered detective investigating a murder in Canada. Based on a 1997 Norwegian film, *Insomnia* also starred Hilary Swank as a local cop and Robin Williams as the killer. It was directed by Christopher Nolan, whose previous film was the brilliant

Memento, and who would go on to direct *Batman Begins*. Pacino was impressed with *Memento* and was interested in seeing how Nolan would handle the *Insomnia* material. Nolan was unsure how he would direct Pacino. "Before you meet him," he said, "you don't know who he is going to be, because he is so many different people in your mind." The film was successful, and *Newsweek*'s comments were representative of what most critics believed: "Pacino gets deep inside [his character] Dormer's conflicted, burned-out soul—a twilight zone between good and evil where the ends justify the means. . . . Like Pacino's work in *Donnie Brasco*, *Insomnia* reminds you that the actor can play small as rivetingly as he can play big, that he can implode as well explode. . . ." While Robin Williams was noted for his "effectively creepy" character, the magazine pointed out: "Next to Pacino's rich multileveled portrait he seems one-note."

Pacino also appeared in Bertolt Brecht's *The Resistible Rise of Arturo Ui* that year, at Pace University in lower Manhattan. Pacino played the thug Ui in an ensemble cast that included John Goodman, Steve Buscemi, Chazz Palminteri, Charles Durning, Billy Crudup, Paul Giamatti, Dominic Chianese, Linda Emond, and Tony Randall. *Newsday* called Pacino's performance "a hoot . . . first a cadaverous old buzzard, a two-bit Chicago crook who uses the Depression, capitalist corruption, and thugs with tommy guns to control the cauliflower market and, through protection rackets, catapults himself to the top of grocery crime. . . . He's a little man in a big suit—a cross between Pacino's Big Boy Caprice from *Dick Tracy* and an adenoidal Richard III." The *New York Times*'s Ben Brantley enthused that watching Pacino as Ui was like watching him channel most of his more celebrated roles: Tony Montana, Michael Corleone, the Devil, and especially Richard III. "Mr. Pacino has long been fascinated by Shakespeare's nastiest tyrant . . . and puts him to fascinating use here. When you meet his Ui, he walks hunchback-style, with a simian slump. But if Mr. Pacino is doing Ui as Richard, it is the inner pathological Richard, with no courtly camouflage. Here is a purely animal presence, a brute whose hands hang at his sides like deadweights and whose eye sockets register as hungry black holes. This man is all id, and Mr. Pacino's enjoyably audacious performance is about an id in search of an ego. . . . You start to think about how Richard III really is a template for so many of the characters Mr. Pacino has played, of how he has specialized in incarnating either Faust or Mephistopheles and sometimes both at the same time."

Pacino has rarely appeared in cameo roles, and after agreeing to be in one for his *Scent of a Woman* director, Marty Brest, he could only shrug his shoulders and laugh at how poorly Brest's film *Gigli*, starring the romantically connected but soon-to-be disconnected Ben Affleck and Jennifer Lopez, was received.

"I wouldn't have done it if it wasn't for having a history with Marty," Pacino said. "I felt he wrote some nice stuff, and I thought I'd try to do something with this character. But I didn't catch the kind of flavor I wanted. He was a crazy, disjointed character. It's not my style of doing things. I made a mistake. They wanted to increase the part and have me go back for more takes, but I thought best let sleeping dogs lie. I didn't think it would contribute any more to the picture in any way. I feel badly for Marty Brest, because that takes its toll on a director, and he has made some really good and entertaining movies. He's a thoughtful, sensitive person. But he missed with it. Sometimes you miss at the wrong time, and this was the wrong time, primarily because Jennifer and Ben's relationship just caught the imagination of the public. If it wasn't for that, it wouldn't have had that kind of infamy attached."

Pacino hit and missed with his next two films. *People I Know* was a small film about a New York publicist struggling to keep himself going; Pacino gave a tour de force performance that was completely overlooked. And *The Recruit* was a commercial success, about a CIA trainee (Colin Farrell) instructed by his mentor (Pacino) to look for a mole within the organization (which turns out to be Pacino's character).

"*The Recruit* was a movie that I personally couldn't follow," Pacino said. "But I thought [director] Roger Donaldson did a bang-up job with it. A lot of people enjoyed the movie. They took a ride with it. It was not the style movie that I'm usually in, but I like to be in one like that, that's a little more successful than what it's trying to do."

More successful than either of these was his Emmy-winning performance as Roy Cohn in Tony Kushner's Pulitzer Prize–winning play *Angels in America*, which Mike Nichols directed as a two-part six-hour miniseries for HBO. And then came another stage character, Shylock, in Michael

Radford's well-directed *The Merchant of Venice*, which costarred Joseph Fiennes and Jeremy Irons. Pacino brought compassion to a character that was too often played as a caricature.

In the fall of 2005 Pacino took on another role as mentor (to Matthew McConaughey) in *Two for the Money*, playing a bookie who sees in his young recruit a kid with a golden touch for predicting the outcome of sporting events. Like many of the younger actors before him (Cusack, Reeves, Penn, O'Donnell, Pfeiffer, Depp, Crowe, Diaz, Foxx, Swank, Farrell, Fiennes), McConaughey signed on to the project for the chance to work with Pacino and wasn't disappointed. "Working with him made me a better actor for sure," McConaughey said, impressed by how intensely Pacino rehearsed. "It was as vital an acting experience as I've ever had."

On October 21, 2005, the American Cinematheque paid tribute to Pacino at the Beverly Hilton Hotel in Beverly Hills. Jimm Caan, Jon Voight, Ed Harris, Bruce Willis, Charlize Theron, Keanu Reeves, Andy Garcia, Marisa Tomei, and John Goodman were there to offer their words of praise, and Colin Farrell, Meryl Streep, and Robert De Niro taped their remarks. Besides the generous selection of clips showing some of Pacino's memorable moments on film, the Cinematheque also put together a montage demonstrating the poetry of the four letter expletive, as Pacino showed over and over, in film after film, how he could turn the word "fuck" into high art.

Rick Nicita, Pacino's Creative Artists agent, who happened also to be chairman of the board of directors of the Cinematheque, introduced the evening by saying that Pacino "appeals across not only generations but ethnic and social boundaries. Al's audience is truly everyone who goes to the movies."

James Caan remembered how, during *The Godfather*, Pacino was the "weird guy in the corner. I think we all knew at the time that that guy in the corner was mushrooming into probably one of the greatest talents of all time in our industry."

Pacino's *Sea of Love* costar, John Goodman, thanked Al, "for making us proud to be called actors. Thank you for always putting everyone else you work with at ease because whether you know it or not we are stunned, thrilled, and scared to death just to find ourselves in your presence."

Ed Harris, who worked with Pacino in the film version of *Glengarry Glen Ross*, reminded the audience that, though "Al is such a huge film star now, we tend to forget and overlook the fact that he is first and foremost a stage actor."

Jon Voight was moved to self-confession, speaking of a time in the late seventies when he took a long walk with Pacino on the beach in Santa Monica and asked him, "Al, am I a good actor?" Voight described Pacino taking a long time to answer, and when he did, he said, "Jon, you're a great actor." "It made all the difference to me," Voight said.

Colin Farrell, who costarred with him in *The Recruit*, did a hugely funny impression of Pacino and then spoke of what an inspiration he was, "To see that level of commitment and level of passion after so many years [of] putting down some of the most seminal performances on film and on stage."

Robert De Niro said: "Al, over the years we've taken roles from one another. People have tried to compare us to one another, to pit us against each other and to tear us apart personally. I've never seen the comparison frankly. I'm clearly much taller, more the leading-man type. Honestly, you just may be the finest actor of our generation." And then he added, with a smile, "With the possible exception of me, frankly."

Meryl Streep said: "Your acting is just out of the ballpark, darling. There's nobody fiercer. Nobody who burns hotter or chills colder than you do. You are relentless in your pursuit of a character."

When Bruce Willis presented the award, he credited Pacino with changing his life. After seeing *The Godfather* in 1972, Willis related, "I decided I was going to become an actor because I'd seen Al Pacino's work in that movie."

When Pacino came on stage he was visibly moved. "Acting," he said, "miraculously, has taken me far. It's beyond my wildest dreams. My imagination could have never gone there."

In October 2006 Pacino will finally release his independent and very unique films in a four-disc boxed set, *Pacino: An Actor's Vision. The Local Stigmatic* and *Chinese Coffee* had never been released before and it was the first time *Looking for Richard* was issued in DVD form. Pacino provided a prologue, a voice-over narration, and an epilogue explaining what he was thinking while filming each of these plays. The bonus disc is called "Babbleonia" because on it Pacino is seen at the Actor's Studio babbling on about acting—what got him there, what kept him interested, and what keeps him stimulated. It's a glimpse into the mind of the actor one magazine's poll had dubbed one of the two best American actors (along with Robert De Niro) over fifty years old.

While his professional life turned him into a superstar and a wealthy man, Pacino's private life remained somewhat in turmoil. When he was still in his teens, he lived with a woman for a number of years. When they broke up, he lived for short periods with other women, until he met Jill Clayburgh. They lived together for five years. When that broke up (she married playwright David Rabe), he had a relationship with Tuesday Weld, and then with Marthe Keller. That, too, ended. Though he never married, he became involved with other women, including Kathleen Quinlan, Diane Keaton, Lyndall Hobbs, and Beverly D'Angelo. In 1990 he had a daughter, Julie Marie, with Jan Tarrant. In 2001 Beverly D'Angelo gave birth to twins, Anton and Olivia.

During our initial meetings in 1979 for the *Playboy* interview, Al had trouble completing his thoughts—his mind jumped, his sentences dangled, he spoke in dashes and ellipses. But as we got to know each other, his sentences and thoughts became complete. He was fascinated with the actual process of being interviewed. "Nobody ever asked me for opinions," he said.

It was on a Saturday when we finished that interview, and I was scheduled to fly back to Los Angeles the next evening. Sunday morning Pacino called, wanting to know when my plane was leaving. When I told him, he said, "Well, that gives us enough time for one more talk." I put the batteries back into my tape recorders and grabbed a taxi to his place.

After our interview appeared, I continued to talk to Pacino. We talked over the phone, and face-to-face whenever he came to Los Angeles or I went to New York. Over the years I've written about him for different magazines, ranging from *Rolling Stone* and *Playboy* to *Premiere*, *Movieline*, and *Entertainment Weekly*. I've visited him at his homes in New York, and on location in Devonshire, England, and Vancouver, Canada. We traveled together to the desert to escape the aftershocks of the 1994 Los Angeles earthquake. He attended my older daughter's bat mitzvah and my younger daughter's piano recital. We've played cards, chess, baseball, and paddle tennis.

Because of the nature of our relationship, I was always up front with the editors I dealt with, and they were pleased to be able to get an "insider's" take on Pacino. The challenge for me was to not repeat myself with things we had talked about previously. When we returned to some of his films or to his private life, I tried to get him to say something new. I was always looking to keep it fresh, to make it an enjoyable read, and to provide new insights into the actor and the man.

I've had the opportunity to interview hundreds of actors, writers, and politicians. I've been lucky to spend time with artists like Henry Moore, Saul Bellow, Richard Feynman, John Huston, and Barbra Streisand. And what has always attracted me to Pacino is his artistic sensibility. Far more than just an actor, Al Pacino is an artist. He has a great need to do what he does, as well as a great desire. He has turned down huge offers for commercial movies and has instead returned to the stage to do a small play. Brecht, Mamet, O'Neill, and Shakespeare speak to him. Especially Shakespeare. You can throw out the names of most of Shakespeare's plays and Al can quote lines to you. I know, because I've done this with him.

Finally, I'd like to address what this book is . . . and is not. It is a collection of interviews and profiles that I've written over the twenty-seven years that I've known Al Pacino, as a journalist, and later as a friend. Most of them have been reworked and re-edited. This is not a biography of the man, or a memoir of my time spent with him.

I didn't know when I first met him that we would strike up an honest friendship—not one of convenience, where he'd be nice to me hoping I'd write nice things about him. Over the years he and I have had our confrontations and disagreements. But I believe that he respects what I do, as I respect what he does. We come at things from different angles. He has to deal with agents, publicists, studios, and producers who warn him not to trust people like me. I have to wrestle with turning in honest copy whenever I am asked to write about him. It's not an easy position for either of us. He and I both know there will be people he trusts who will hold up this book and say to him, "See, we told you." We've talked about it. We've disagreed over it. I told Al when I wanted to do this that I see it as I see the conversation books I've done with such cultural icons as Truman Capote, Marlon Brando, and James A. Michener. To me Al Pacino is equally fascinating and complex. I've been privileged to observe how such men think and work, how they make choices, and how they deal with their public and private personas.

There are plenty of years left for Al to write his memoirs. If he ever decides to do it, I'll be first in line to read the results.

GETTING TO KNOW YOU

This first interview, over forty hours of taped conversation, turned into two thousand transcribed pages—a lot of talk for a man who was known for his public silence and mystery. "I feel like I have played ball with you," Pacino said as I turned off the tape recorder after our final session in his New York apartment. "Like we know the same candy store or we remember that time when we opened a hydrant or something. It's a good feeling." I smiled and nodded. That was exactly *how I felt about him. And I think some of that good feeling comes through in the interview.*

AL PACINO: Actually, I'd rather you not put the tape on yet—until I get a little bit warmed up here.

Brando had the same reluctance at first. He wanted to talk, but without the tape recorders on.

That reminds me of me.

It's best to just leave them on and forget about them.

Whatever you say. I'm not going to tell you how to do your job. This is so new to me.

Do you feel like this is a coming out for you?

Definitely. It is a huge thing, this interview. There's a certain power in these interviews that I haven't found in profiles—a real power. Like what you did with Marlon Brando. It can be taken seriously. I don't know that *I* can be yet, because I haven't accomplished enough things in my life.

After a lifetime of avoiding the press, what made you finally decide to talk?

I sort of got tired of saying no, because it gets misread. The reason I haven't talked before was that I just didn't think that I would be able to do it. But after a while you just start to feel like, Why not? I'm tired of being too careful, too protective. Actually, look what yes has done to me. I said yes to *Richard III* and to *Cruising*. No wonder I said no for so many years! [*Laughs*]

Want to change your mind?

No, let me try yeses for a while. It's time.

Do you care how you come off in this?

As much as I want to do well in a part, I want to be interesting in an interview.

Good. Hopefully, by the time we're through, we'll have explored some of the public and private sides that make you who you are.

But isn't what I do also who I am? I mean, my work is very consuming; who I am is my work, too.

Part of who you are. We'll get into that. But first, I'm curious: Why do you have Candice Bergen's name on your apartment door and another name on the directory downstairs?

For the obvious reasons—to avoid being hassled. She used to live in this apartment, but it doesn't say Candice Bergen, it says C. Bergen. On the directory I had Goldman for a while, but then a guy named Goldman came in and said, "Stop using my name."

How many people in this building know you live here?

Everybody in the building knows. They are very considerate.

From the looks of things in this apartment, it doesn't appear that your star status has gone to your head.

My lifestyle changes a lot. I've been here five years, but it's like I'm passing through. On your way to Bombay you stop here, stay over, and then you keep going. This is the kind of place I have. It's always been that way. I look around at places I think I should be living in, then I come back and move the couch or the piano and I'm satisfied.

Let's go back and look at the place you came from.

I come from the South Bronx—a true descendant of the melting pot. I grew up in a really mixed neighborhood; it was a very integrated life. There were certain tensions that usually had to do with one's income situation. Being an only child, I had difficulty with competition. I wasn't allowed out until I went to school at about six; that's when I started to integrate with other kids. I was very shy. It wasn't very pleasant going to school at that age and having the feeling that you might get beat up any day. I think a lot of kids suffer from that kind of tension. I didn't know how to protect myself very well, because I had never learned it. I didn't have brothers or sisters, so when I first went to school it was rough. I learned to wrestle, I learned defensive fighting at a young age, because when somebody hit me, I would throw up and fall down. You had to learn how to take care of yourself. I remember one time coming home and this guy called my mother a bastard. I said, "Don't call my mother a bastard." The next thing I knew, we were fighting. That's how it was: You got challenged. I remember saying to one guy, "You can punch me in my right arm five times; I'll punch you once." So he went first. I didn't cry until I got home. Once, I was swinging from the fire steps and I fell off and landed on my head. My friends were laughing, but it wasn't funny. I went home and fell down—I had a concussion. Another time I was doing a tightrope walk on a very thin rail up about five feet. I slipped and fell and the rail hit me right in the crotch. Again, my friends laughed. I got up, walked about twenty feet, fell down. Got up, walked thirty feet, and fell. Then I crawled up against the building, and some of the big guys came and carried me to my aunt's house. My mother and grandmother came over, and there were these three ladies looking at my private parts. I was lying prostrate on my back, and they were all looking and playing with me! I must have been nine.

Then one time I was playing guns in the lots and there was this barbed-wire fence. I caught my lip on the barbed wire. My friend was shooting, "Gotcha, gotcha. You're not falling! I gotcha." I was screaming, and he said, "Yeah, but you're dead! You're dead!" This guy finally runs up and tells my mother that I'm hanging from my lip. She fainted dead away.

You were raised by your grandparents and your mother because your father left the family while you were still a baby. Was it tough?

My mother kept a curfew when I had to be upstairs. I needed that; it gave me a sense of right and wrong, a sense of security. She used to take me to the movies at a very young age; that's how I started acting. My grandfather raised me. He never raised a hand to me. He didn't talk much. He wasn't demonstrative. He didn't display his feelings much in terms of affection. But he was there. I found myself touching him a lot. It was just great to kiss him sometimes. I guess he knew I was an actor, because I used to love to hear him tell me stories about what it was like in New York in East Harlem in the early 1900s. I would bring him out more than anybody else did. I don't think anybody else was interested. He would just string these yarns for hours on the roof. I would spend nights up there, him talking to me. It's almost like a grandfather and grandson on a fishing boat, but we were in the South Bronx, up on a roof.

What were his stories about?

His immigration here, how his mother came first, what it was like. His mother died when he was four. He quit school and went to work at nine on a coal truck. Every time he'd come home from work, I'd be playing in the lot and I'd wait for him to come by. I would ask him for a nickel. He would always kvetch about it, but he'd bend down deep, way down, like he was going into his shoe. And he would come up with this nickel. How *did* he finger the nickel?

Would you say he provided a role model for you?

I imagine he did, yes. My grandfather was a provider. Work, any kind of work, was the joy of his life. So I grew up having a certain relationship to work. It was something that I always wanted.

In . . . *And Justice for All* there's a touching scene in which you visit your grandfather, played by Lee Strasberg, and you say to him, "You cared for me, you loved me, but your son was a shit." Is that getting pretty close to your background?

That was the screenplay. No, I didn't have those feelings when I played the character. There are people whose sense of reality is very strong, who have a sense of honesty. Lee Strasberg is like that, my grandfather was like that. These are the kinds of men I've had close relationships with.

What about that line, though? Was your father, in real life, a shit?

No, no. My relationship with my father wasn't a close one, but he saw me throughout my life. He would come and see me and visit. When I was younger, I stayed with him for a while. Sometimes four or five years would go by before I saw him, but he always tried to communicate with me. [*Puts hand into empty box*] I think I ate the whole box of blueberries.

What was school like for you? Weren't you once put in a class for emotionally disturbed kids?

I was, for a couple of days.

What for?

Pranks. I carried on a lot. I put my teacher's glasses on her seat; she sat on them. I was in a library class, sitting in the back, pushing the books until the bookend would fall and make a noise. I did it once too often, and they threw me out. They put me in what they called the ungraded class, but I wasn't there long.

What did you imagine you'd grow up to be?

I wanted to be a baseball player, naturally, but I wasn't good enough. I didn't know what I was going to do with my life. I just had a kind of energy; I was a fairly happy kid, although I had problems in school. In the eighth grade the drama teacher wrote my mother a letter saying she should encourage me. I used to recite *The Rime of the Ancient Mariner*. And I would read the Bible in the auditorium. That was the first time I heard of Marlon Brando. I was in a play and they said, "Hey. Marlon Brando—this guy acts like Marlon Brando." Isn't that weird. I was about twelve. I guess it was because I was supposed to get sick onstage, and I really did get sick every time we did this play. Actually, the person I related to was James Dean. I grew up with the Dean thing. My mother loved him; I loved him. He had that sense of passing through. *Rebel Without a Cause* had a very powerful effect on me. Remember that red jacket? Everybody wore one. I love that line: "Life can be beautiful."

What encouraged you to attend the High School of Performing Arts?

I went to Performing Arts because that was the only school that would accept me. My scholastic level was not very high. I remember I went to Spanish class, and the teacher started giving a lesson in Spanish.

But you also acted.

I was never very happy with performing; it didn't turn me on much. If I made a catch at third base, I'd do a double somersault and sprawl out on the ground. I was acting—overacting. Instead of OD'ing, I OA'd. They taught Stanislavsky at Performing Arts. That whole thing about the Method and serious acting, having to feel it, I thought it was crazy. What was going on? Where was the fun? So I was kind of bored with it. Once, I was in class and had to act out what it was like when I was in my room alone. Since I never had a room to myself, I had to make it up.

How many slept in your room?

At one point there were nine of us living in three rooms. I lived with aunts and uncles and their children. It was back and forth; it changed. There was some tendency for people to get volatile in those situations. Once, I improvised something at school—I was supposed to be in my room, talking to myself. I hummed, I whistled, I moved around, turned on the radio, picked up this autograph book and started to read it. Then I stopped and started to turn back the pages. The drama teacher, who was into Stanislavsky, said, "Stop! Stop!" She got up and said to the class, "What was he going to do? He was going to tear the page out." Then she said to me, "What were you going to do?" I said, "I was going to tear the page out." She said, "You have the fire of the Sicilian actors!" I said, "What did I do?" I didn't understand. She called my mother and told her that. My mother said that acting was for rich people, and that I should get a job. I left high school after two years to support myself, but I remembered how "natural" the teacher had said I acted. And I went around all the time trying to be natural. I didn't know the difference between being natural and being real. What do I know from Stanislavsky? He's Russian, I'm from the Bronx.

As a kid, what did you learn about sex?

I was wondering when you'd turn that corner. I love work because it keeps sex in perspective. Otherwise it can become a preoccupation.

You mean that's why you work so much?

Yes.

So you can afford it?

So I can afford it. [*Groans*] You said that.

Do you remember your first sexual experience?

My first sexual experience . . . I had an encounter with a girl when I was nine. She took off her blouse, and she actually had breasts. Maybe she was older. Maybe *I* was older. I put my hands on them and she giggled. She was standing in front of a mattress spring, and I pushed her. She bounced off the spring and we repeated that three or four times. I thought that I had been laid. I went right out and bought a pack of prophylactics. You used to carry them around in your wallet. You didn't know what they did, but . . .

You mean you didn't have a friend who knew all about those things?

That would be Cliffy, my closest friend. He looked like a cross between Richard Burton and Marlon Brando. He was a Jewish guy who wanted to turn Catholic. One of the toughest guys I ever knew. He had something we didn't see, like he knew something secret. He was wild. He was ahead sexually, too. He read Dostoyevsky at fourteen and told me how terrific it was. One thing he did, I will never forget, he tried to feel up my mother once. I saw that. He was about fourteen. I thought that was *really* odd.

What did your mother do?

She kind of discouraged him and laughed. She seemed to understand it. Maybe she was flattered. I don't know.

Do you still see him today?

He was on junk and finally died, I heard, at thirty. My other best friend died of drugs at nineteen. My two closest friends.

Did you ever shoot up?

No, I never did. That is when we started separating. They were going into other worlds. I would say my mother kept me alive. I didn't go for the needle at all. I never cared for drugs, because I saw what they did to most people. I thought that was the end of the road. I liked booze every once in a while. I was doing that when I was about thirteen—the way most young guys do. You would get the guy on the street to buy you a bottle because he was older. Drinking and smoking grass were a part of my life as far back as I can remember. I thought everybody drank. I started smoking cigarettes around nine. I chewed tobacco when I was ten. I smoked a pipe at eleven. But it was Cliffy who was always doing something original, something I had never seen.

Such as?

Such as getting off in my bathroom when we were older, after he had told me he wasn't on drugs anymore. Such as hijacking a public bus filled with passengers. Or stealing a garbage truck and pulling up in front of my house with it. He actually got me into trouble once when he kicked in a store window to get me some shoes. A cop caught him at it, and there was this embarrassing scene in front of a crowd. My grandmother got me out of it.

I remember once he got called up in front of the class. He made the teacher so mad that she started to grab and hit him. He was laughing because he was getting a quick feel. So she threw him out and turned to the rest of the class. Naturally I was laughing, so she threw me out too. Those were great times. I often refer to my life back then as a New York Huckleberry Finn, because it was always something else. We would make something out of anything. The time was ours. Were we going to scale a roof? Run as fast as we could around the block?

There was always something going on in that neighborhood. One time I remember going down to where the buses used to be to get some transfers, which we used to use as play money. I was about ten, and this strange kid came up to me with a funny look on his face. He said, "Sonny,"—which was my nickname—"some strange guy just came up and peed in my mouth." I thought, *That was a weird thing to do.* "You'd better go up and tell your mother," I said. Things like that would happen every day.

Sounds like you might have ended up like your friend Cliffy.

I once had this job working for the owner of a fruit farm. My friends were outside playing, and I was separating the green from the red tomatoes. The owner came to me and he actually drew a picture of a countryside on a board. He diagramed the trees and the paths. He said, "There are two paths in life: the right one and the wrong one. You are on the wrong one." I thought it had something to do with the tomatoes. But it had to do with my friends outside. He said, "Stay with them, and you will wind up like them. Jobless and free."

Did you mind working when you were a kid?

Who wanted to work? But I didn't want to go to school. I had to work because it was just me and my mother, nobody else. My grandparents moved out of town when I was fifteen. Then my mother moved with them and they all lived together. I lived alone. I was seventeen. Today that's nothing, but this was twenty years ago.

Your mother died when she was forty-three. How old were you?

I was twenty-two. My mother's death was traumatic to my whole family. She had certain problems with her blood. She was in the hospital with some kind of anemia, and she was suffering so much. It wasn't expected. My grandfather died a year later. I think it was part of the reason why. He was a very strong man. Never sick a day in his life. It makes one a little more fragile when it happens. These are tough things to talk about.

What was your relationship with your mother at the time?

At the time we were having some difficulties communicating. It is always unfortunate when things aren't going well. Especially with your mother. It was the lowest point of my life. It makes one a little more fragile when it happens.

Were you alone at the time?

I was living with someone when my grandfather died. I used to deliver *Show Business* newspapers to newsstands once a week, on Thursdays. That was my job at the time. I was on the route, on Broadway and Forty-eighth Street, and I passed out. I had trouble seeing. The doctor looked at me, took my pulse, said my heart was all right, and said I should go to the outpatient clinic at Bellevue.

After those deaths did you become closer to your father?

No, as a matter of fact, I didn't talk to my father until years later. You know, Brando said something good in his interview with you about guilt.

He said guilt is a useless emotion.

Useless. It is. And when you finally come to terms with that, it gets a little easier. I think I'm beginning to. Because it took a long time before I realized I had it.

[*After a long pause*]

What are you thinking?

I was thinking about forgiveness and guilt. Forgiving oneself. We forgive others.

You've had to live with death at an early age. Do you fear it?

Not consciously. I don't go around thinking about it.

Do you think that you'll die young?

At one point in one's life you get a sense of your own mortality. You view death in a certain way. From that point on you look at your fellow man with a new understanding. I have some feelings for it now. They say it happens in your mid-thirties. Sometimes I have a fantasy of my corpse being carried around in a box, people mourning me. Saying, "We shouldn't have treated him so badly."

I had a bone spur in my left toe recently. I said to the doctor, "Well, it has to get better, right?" He said no. And I realized there's an age where everything doesn't automatically get better. . . . We talk like this, I'll smoke cigarette after cigarette.

We can change the subject.

If I die, you can write my epitaph: "He was just beginning to resolve some of his problems. In about ten or fifteen years he would have been happy. He had made such progress!"

Do you ever go back to your old neighborhood in the Bronx?

How can you go back there? It's not there anymore. The neighborhood is gone. It's over. That world is over.

What were some of the odd jobs you used to do?

I was a mail boy, a janitor, a shoe salesman; I worked in a fruit store, a drug-store, a supermarket; I used to move furniture—that's the hardest work I ever had. The first thing you look at when you're a moving man is the books. Everybody has books, thousands of them. They put them in boxes. It is very deceptive; they have five thousand paperbacks in boxes. I'm the guy who would go to a moving job in a taxi. They'd say, "Al's a little late," and I'd come flying out of a taxi to lug pianos up the stairs for three dollars an hour. I used to move artwork, too. It's wonderful when you're carrying a very valuable sculpture and you walk into a wall. That happened to me— a head came right off its shoulders. A major work of art—and I heard the famous words: You pay for it.

I was also an usher. People would always ask me, "What time does the show start?" "What is the last show that went on?" They ask you all *kinds* of questions. "Is it good?" Finally, I figured, *These people will listen to anything I say.* You're the usher, right? *The Rise of the House of Usher.* So I bet another usher that I could get them to line up across the street. Then I told the people that because of the crowds the line was forming across the street, in front of Bloomingdale's.

And nobody protested?

No, they lined right up.

So you won the bet. Did you get paid?

I got fired. Another time I got fired in midstride—another of my famous usher stories. I was an usher at another movie house, and I suddenly saw myself in a three-sided mirror. I had never seen my profile. I was about twenty-four at the time. I couldn't believe it. Who was this strange-looking person? I had never seen the back of my clothes or the back of my head. So I couldn't stop staring at myself. This manager saw me doing it. He didn't like me from the word go. He just didn't like ushers, I think. He said, "Pacino, what are you looking at?" I mumbled something, and he warned me not to do it again. But I did the same thing a little later as he was coming down the stairs, and he caught me at it and said, "You're fired!" He never stopped, never broke stride, just kept going downstairs. I felt this rush of happiness. I should have been very unhappy, but I wasn't. I went down to the locker room and I began giggling. A couple of my friends asked, "What happened?" I said I had just been fired. "Why?" I said, "Looking at myself too much."

What job did you hold the longest?

The longest stretch was with *Commentary* magazine. I did office work for a couple of years. I delivered things. I enjoyed working there.

Were you acting then too?

I was going to acting school. The Herbert Berghof Studio. That's when I got to meet Charlie Laughton. I was about eighteen and he was around twenty-nine. He was teaching an acting class. I thought there was something about him. I just felt connected to him. Charlie introduced me to other worlds, to certain aspects of life I wouldn't have come in contact with. He introduced me to writers, to the stuff that surrounds acting.

I still remember the time I had fifteen dollars and was sleeping in a storefront, and the night before I must have been a little high, because when I woke up the next morning, I didn't have a penny. I knew Charlie was with his family at the beach in Far Rockaway. It was two fifteen-cent fares you had to pay to get out there, and to get the thirty cents I had to promise this guy who worked with me in the moving company these empty bottles of Ballantine Ale, which he could get nickel deposits on. Then I got on the train and went all the way out to Rockaway. There was Charlie, with his kid and his wife by the water. And he saw me. There I was, trudging toward him, making my way through all the umbrellas, wearing my blacks—my black shirt and my black pants. And he looked at me, and I said, "I don't have any money." He picked out a five, which was probably half the money he had in the world, and gave it to me. I went back through the crowd, up the stairs, and back home. I knew Charlie would take care of me.

We became family—Charlie's wife and daughter. Charlie and I just sort of stuck. A great actor himself, but he never pursued it. In acting class he talked to me like I was a person, not a student. He was responsible for educating me, in a sense.

Would he be for you what Stella Adler was for Brando?

Yeah, he would be that.

Was he also a father figure to you?

I imagine he was. It went from father figure to brother to closest friend. He works with me on everything. I wouldn't have made it here without Charlie. Among many other things, he put me straight about my drinking. He said, "You're drinking. Look at it and recognize it." I didn't know it, and I didn't know that other people knew. It was a powerful moment in my life. Now I find that when I'm around people who do drugs or drink to excess, I become uncomfortable. I'm very sensitive to it and I pick it up.

Was it Laughton who first recognized your star potential?

Absolutely—and it's an incredible story. I was a nineteen-year-old kid living in a tenement in the Bronx. Charlie was coming by as I came down the stairs of my tenement, and he just nailed me: "You're going to be a star." There, in the middle of the Bronx. Weird. And you've got to understand, he doesn't talk that way, I don't talk that way. Neither of us ever mentioned it since then.

Before enrolling at Berghof, didn't you try to get into Lee Strasberg's Actors Studio?

Yeah, I auditioned, got through the preliminaries, and was rejected. I said to myself, *They don't know anything.* I always took a healthy attitude then. There's a certain power, a strength, that comes when you're young. Four years later I auditioned again and was accepted. They even lent me fifty dollars to pay my rent, from the James Dean Memorial Fund. Dustin and I got in the same year. I kept hearing there was this actor, Dustin Hoffman, he's terrific.

Is it true that you've established a fund at the Actors Studio like the one you borrowed from?

Yeah; I don't talk about it.

How important was the Actors Studio for you?

The Actors Studio meant so much to me in my life. Lee Strasberg hasn't been given the credit he deserves. Brando doesn't give Lee any credit— and the Actors Studio has had such a bad name, which is not representative of what it really did for me. Next to Charlie, it sort of launched me. It really did. That was a remarkable turning point in my life. It was directly responsible for getting me to quit all those jobs and just stay acting. It instilled confidence and gave me a place to work out, to connect with people. I could do anything—Shakespeare, O'Neill—it was a constantly active place where actors were coming in. It was a major part of my life. I'll be grateful to the Actors Studio forever. I'd like to marry that place.

Another major part of your life was your first starring movie role, *The Panic in Needle Park*. What did you think when you first saw yourself larger than life?

I was drunk when I saw the first screening, but I was surprised at my bounciness, that I was all over the place. I did say, though, "*That's* a talented actor, but he needs work. Help. And he needs *to* work. And learn. But there's talent there." In one scene we were supposed to be dealing on the corner, and there was a guy actually dealing heroin right there. I looked at him and he looked at me, and I got real confused. . . . I don't like to go on about myself—I feel sometimes that it's not *me* that has something to offer, but, hopefully, my talent.

How selective were you choosing *Panic* as your first big role?

I turned down eleven films before I made my first one. I knew that it was time for me to get in movies. I didn't know what it would be. When *The Panic in Needle Park* came along, Marty Bregman pushed and helped get it together. Without him I don't know what I would have done. He is directly responsible for five movies—a great influence on my career.

How did Bregman become your manager?

He saw me in an off-Broadway show and said that he was willing to back me with anything I wanted to do. I didn't quite know what he was talking about. Then he said that he would sponsor me. I still didn't know what he meant. As it turned out, he acted as a go-between for myself and the business. It was a very important relationship. He acted as an insulator. He got me to work. Encouraged me to do *The Godfather*. *Serpico* was completely his idea. He got me to do *Dog Day*.

Did you have a formal contract with him?

Yes, and it was expensive, but it was certainly worth it.

Are you with him now?

No, our relationship changed several years ago; then it just finally dissi-
pated. He became a producer. It wasn't the same anymore. [*Getting up*]
I'm going to stand and talk to you. Walk around a bit. Is it a competition
thing, an interview? Does it become a battle in a way? Is there an angst
between us? I am going to do this interview, and it's not going to be the
way you want it. Or the way I want it. I am going to make some explo-
sions happen here; make it so that there is a kind of cat-and-mouse thing
that goes on. But it is probably impossible to strip my defenses. How could
I do that with anybody?

Are you feeling very defensive?

I'm in a . . . certain kind of condition now.

Strained?

Stained.

**Why don't we talk about it? It must have something to do with the fact
that you've been filming *Cruising* in New York City and the set has been
picketed and harassed. Gay activists have claimed the story is antihomo-
sexual.**

I feel I don't know what's going on. I don't understand it. It's the first time
in my life I've ever been in this kind of position. I'm baffled. It's a tough
film, there's no getting away from it.

**You play a cop who tracks down a killer of homosexuals, and some of
the protests have been about the fact that the film shows scenes on the**

sadomasochistic fringes of gay life, rather than the mainstream of homo-sexual life.

That's the point! When I first read the script, I didn't even know those fringes existed. But it's just a fragment of the gay community, the same way the Mafia is a fragment of Italian-American life.

What does the film seem to you to be about?

It's a film about ambivalence. I thought the script read partly like Pinter, partly like Hitchcock, a whodunit, an adventure story.

Apparently the gay community in New York sees it differently. Pamphlets were distributed calling the film "a rip-off" that uses gay male stereo-types as the backdrop for a story about a murderer of homosexuals.

How can they say that without seeing the movie?

They say more. They say, "Gay men are presented as one-dimensional sex-crazed lunatics, vulnerable victims of violence and death. This is not a film about how we live. It is a film about why we should be killed."

That is a very strong statement. It's very upsetting.

But how do you react to the charges?

Well, it makes me feel bad. It's actually hard for me to respond at all. When I read the screenplay, the thought of it being antigay never even came to me. It never dawned on me that it would provoke those kinds of feelings. I'm coming from a straight point of view, and maybe I'm not sensitive enough in that area. But they *are* sensitive to the situation, and I can't argue with that. I mean, if you pronounce my name Pakino, Pakano, Picini, or Pokono, like it is often done, I am sensitive to it, I read into it. The only thing I can say is that it isn't a movie yet. It has not been put together as a movie.

Do you think those protests will have an effect on the outcome of the film?

If the gay community feels the film shows them in a bad light, then it is good they are protesting, because anything that raises consciousness in this area is all right. But I hope that's not the case. When I saw *The Deer Hunter*, my only reaction to some of the war scenes in Vietnam was: *War is tough; I don't want to be there*. I was taken up in the horror of war. But I wasn't thinking that the film was racist, as many accused it of being. If I had been pre-conditioned to think it was racist, I probably would have read that into it too.

Then again, if the American Indian had protested, perhaps they wouldn't have gotten as raw a deal as they seem to have in films.

That's true, the Indians were the victims in that way. . . . So who is to know with this kind of film?

Is *Cruising* your most controversial project?

There is no second to it. I thought *Dog Day* was going to be, but nobody bothered us on the set. Nothing else even comes close. I don't like this trouble. I have never stayed in any political arenas. It's just not my thing. The sociopolitical aspects of the films I make are never the front-runner in my mind. It's always the story, the character. This picture is getting international attention, the media is coming up with stories, and it's not me they're talking about. They're talking about the issue. It's such a volatile subject. Still, there is something wrong. This film could be made without me.

Maybe, maybe not. The script was reportedly rejected by three studios before you signed on.

It is not my picture. It is not a film that I originated or got down with. This came to me.

True, but once you agreed it becomes an Al Pacino picture. Don't you feel a responsibility for some of the issues the movie raises?

You're turning this into an Al Pacino movie? Al Pacino is an *actor* in this movie. The way the press focuses attention on something like this is by throwing my name into it. Responsibilities are relative. My responsibility is to a character in a script, to a part I'm playing—not to an issue I'm unqualified to discuss.

But aren't we all ultimately responsible for what we do? Isn't what you're saying something of a cop-out?

I don't think the film is antigay, but I can only repeat—I'm responsible for giving the best performance I can. I took this role because the character is fascinating, a man who is ambiguous both morally and sexually; he's both an observer and a provocateur. It gave me an opportunity to paint a character impressionistically—a character who is something of a blur. My communication with the public is as an actor. Although I'd never want to do anything to harm the gay community—or the Italian-American community or the police community or *any* group I happen to represent on-screen—I can only respond in my capacity as an actor.

Since you're halfway through the filming, what's your sense of the movie so far?

There's a power to it, a certain theatricality. I sensed it when I read it. I hope Billy Friedkin's energy comes off on the screen, because it lifts you. He's a lot like Coppola in that way.

How is that?

I remember that when I met with Francis in a restaurant to discuss doing *Godfather II*, I left absolutely filled with his inspiration; he just charged me with electricity. I wasn't going to do *Godfather II*. There's a funny story about how much they were going to pay me before Francis convinced me. It's about how I got that first big salary everybody talks about.

How *did* you get it?

They wanted to give me a hundred grand on the second picture, and even *I* knew that was. . . . They said, "How about a hundred and fifty?" I said, "Well, I don't think so." They said, "How about if Puzo writes the screenplay?" I said sure. Mario wrote a screenplay, I read it, and it was okay, but it wasn't. . . . So I said no. They went up to two. I said no. Then they went to two-fifty and three and three-fifty. Then they made a big jump and went to four-fifty. And I said no. Then they called me into the office in New York. There was a bottle of J&B on the table. We began drinking, talking, laughing, and the producer opened his drawer and he pulled out a tin box. I was sitting on the other side, and he pushed it over in my direction. He said, "What if I were to tell you that there was one million in cash there?" I said, "It doesn't mean anything—it's an abstraction." It was the damnedest thing: I ended up kind of apologizing to the guy for not taking the million.

He was obviously making you an offer as if you were really the Mafia character you played. What made you change your mind?

Francis told me about the script. He was so wigged out by the prospect of doing it, he would inspire anybody. The hairs on my head stood up. You can feel that sometimes with a director. I usually say, If you feel that from a director, go with him.

Let's finish the story. You didn't get one million for it, you got six hundred thousand, and ten percent of the picture; is that correct?

I think so.

You didn't go to one million until *Bobby Deerfield*, right?

Yeah.

And what did you get for the first *Godfather*?

For the first one I got thirty-five thousand. About fifteen thousand I owed in legal fees.

For what?

I was involved in a movie called *The Gang That Couldn't Shoot Straight* at MGM. I can't talk too much about it, because I don't know the details. My lawyer is taking care of it, but I was supposed to have said yes and signed for it, and then *The Godfather* came along. Nobody wanted me for *The Godfather*; I guess they wanted to cast Jack Nicholson. My agents were telling me to stick with *The Gang That Couldn't Shoot Straight*. I said, "Well, I don't know. Francis keeps telling me not to go with another picture." The first time Francis asked me to go to San Francisco with him, he gave me a haircut because they said I could never look like I was in college. It was very nerve-racking. I remember saying to Francis, "I don't want to be around where I'm not wanted. So please, Francis, no more auditions, no more screen tests. I can live without this picture." He said, "No, you *must* play it."

And then, after the picture was made, MGM got its lawyers after you?

Naturally. After *Godfather II* the MGM people remembered their lawsuit against me and said I owed them a picture. It was a real crazy legal battle that was costing me hundreds of thousands of dollars. There were depositions—"What color tie did he wear when he told you that?" This *craziness*. Reams and reams of paper. I finally said, "There's something really wrong here." So I called the head of MGM and said, "What's going on? This is in the hands of lawyers now; there's no dialogue here, what's up?" He and I talked face-to-face about the situation, and we settled the whole thing. The situation was humanized. Sometimes you're fighting corporations and forget that people can talk to each other.

How did you settle it?

Amicably. If a project comes along, we'll work out something. Any project that I find encouraging that isn't attached to a studio, I can go to them, which I definitely would. There's no more paying the lawyers. There's a time to stay out of your affairs and a time to get into them. You have to take an interest in what you do.

Even when you don't understand what's going on?

What happens is you get an inferiority complex, because you don't feel qualified to deal with those situations, and you just sort of stand there and look around and nod your head. They say, "Right?" And you say, "Yeah." And you don't know what you're saying. You don't even listen. You pretend to listen. But you've got to learn what's going down—it's like the streets, in a sense.

I imagine you didn't stay long with the agents who had told you to forget
The Godfather.

I changed agents. I did it on my own. There was a period where I didn't have an agent and I called William Morris. I said, "Can I speak to the William Morris people? I'm looking for an agent." She said, "Oh? What's your name?" I said, "Al Pacino." She said, "Are you *sure?*"

Getting back to *The Godfather*, Coppola called you self-destructive after your first screen test. Why?

Well, he was expecting me to do *more* in a scene. He took the dullest scene that Michael had, the first wedding scene, which is an exposition scene, and I did it, and he wanted me to do more. I don't know what he expected me to do. He tested people with the wrong scene. At first I thought he wanted me for Sonny. At the time I didn't care if I got the part or not. The less you want things, the more they come to you. If it's meant to be, it will be. Every time I've stuffed or forced something, it hasn't been right.

Yet you always knew you'd get the part, didn't you?

You just get a sense of things sometimes. You just know it. It's kind of simple to assess something if you allow it to happen. It's when the ego and greed get in the way that it's harder to assess what the situation is. But if you step back and you take a look at it, you can sense what's going to happen. If I hadn't gotten the *Godfather* role, it would have surprised me, frankly.

Did Coppola have you in mind before or after he had decided on Brando?

He had Brando in his mind first, I'm sure. We were together at a party, and Francis said to me, "Who do you think the Godfather should be?" I said Brando. Francis is extraordinary in that way. He just feels you out. He's a strange kind of man. He's a voyeur that way. I never saw the likes of him. He can detach like nobody I've ever seen. For a man that emotionally powerful to be able to detach the way he does . . . like Michael Corleone. That's why Francis understood that character.

Did you have Francis in mind when you played Michael?

Partly I did Francis; partly I modeled him from several people I know.

What about any real mob figures? Did you ever meet any of the Mafia?

Yeah. Privately. Somebody gave me a reference.

So you could observe them?

Observe them, yes.

And they let you?

Yes.

And what happened?

Nothing.

Are they all still alive?

I can't answer that.

Is what we saw on the screen styled after what you observed?

Ah, no. It wasn't.

Where did you meet? At a restaurant?

Ah . . . in the sky. Space Station 22.

Right. What were you trying to capture when you played Michael?

In the first *Godfather* the thing that I was after was to create some kind of enigma, an enigmatic-type person. So you felt that we were looking at that person and didn't quite know him. When you see Michael in some of those scenes looking wrapped up in a kind of trance, as if his mind was completely filled with thoughts, that's what I was doing. I was actually listening to Stravinsky on the set, so I'd have that look. I felt that that was the drama in the character, that that was the only thing that was going to make him dramatic. Otherwise, it could be dull. I never worked on a role quite like that. It was the most difficult part I've ever played.

What did the picture mean to you?

Metaphorically, I think Francis was talking about the Italian-American first generation being sacrificed. They came over here and what is the American dream? To have power and money and fame. So they directed all their energies in that area.

There are numerous stories of actors performing with Marlon Brando for the first time. What's your feeling about him?

There's no doubt every time I see Brando that I'm looking at a great actor. Whether he's *doing* great acting or not, you're seeing somebody who is in the tradition of a great actor. What he does with it, that's something else, but he's got it all. The talent, the instrument is there, that's why he has endured. I remember when I first saw *On the Waterfront*. I had to see it again, right there. I couldn't move, I couldn't leave the theater. I had never seen the likes of it. I couldn't believe it.

What was your first meeting like?

Well, Diane Keaton was at that first meeting. We went in and sat at a table, and everybody was pretending that he was just another actor, even though we were all nervous. But Diane was open enough to admit how she felt. She sat at the table, and Brando said hello to me and to Diane. And Diane said, "Yeah, right, sure," as if she couldn't believe it. She really did it. She said, "I just cannot take that."

And afterward?

You can't imagine my feelings during the first rehearsal with Brando. It was Jimmy Caan and Bobby Duvall and me, all sitting around, and there's Brando going on about the Indians. Francis is saying to himself, *This is the first rehearsal, what's going to happen tomorrow? We have two more weeks of this.* And Duvall was making these faces. I had to leave and sit on the bed, because I was laughing and I didn't want to have Brando think we were laughing at him. Duvall finally said, "Keep talking, Marlon, none of us want to work. Just keep talking." With that, Marlon laughed.

I will never forget Brando the first time I did a scene with Keaton. He came and stood right in front of the camera and watched. During the scene at the table, a leaf fell off the tree onto my shoulder. I took off the leaf and tossed it, and later Brando said, "I like what you did with the leaf." Afterward Diane and I just got drunk. But Brando was wonderful to me. He made me laugh, the things he'd do. I'd be playing a scene, and he'd show up off camera, straight-faced, with a silly fake bird in his pocket. His support was so powerful, it helped me a great deal. What can you say about someone that generous? He made it so easy.

People have said that artistically you are Brando's godson.

People have said that. I don't feel anywhere near that. It's meaningless, like saying I have green hair.

There's a rare quote attributed to you about *Godfather*: "They may have come to see Brando, but they left remembering me." Did you say that?

I never said that.

You and Caan supposedly got along well.

Jimmy Caan and I played Tonto and the Lone Ranger. I played Tonto. I'd come and say, "Kemosabe," and he'd say, "Tonto, get my horse. I want you to go to town and this is what I want you to get." And he'd proceed and never stop. He'd say, "I don't like that soap, forget the soap. . . ." People would sit there, then go away and do other things and come back, and he'd still be telling me what to get. Terrific number.

Sounds like you had a good time.

Actually, except for Francis, I really felt unwanted on the set. And except for Al Ruddy, who was incredibly helpful and good. With Francis, although I had personality differences with him, those were his performances, he *made* them. And he knew it. He'd say, "I created you—you're my Frankenstein monster." Another time, he put me in elevator shoes and said, "What's wrong with you? You're walking like Donald Duck." I said, "Get those lifts out of my shoes and I may move straighter."

In fact, you did walk and move differently as Michael, didn't you?

I had to move in a different way than I've ever moved before. All heavy. Especially in [*Godfather*] *II*.

Did you also learn by watching other actors move?

I don't feel I learn anything by watching. I don't like to watch. Even in *The Godfather*, people ask, didn't you watch Brando? I said, "No, I watch him when it's finished and on the screen." I learn better and I learn more when I go through it and make the mistakes myself. Otherwise there's a tendency to avoid mistakes which might lead you someplace. For a while I was influenced and impressed by Jason Robards's performance in *The Iceman Cometh*. It took a while for me to break out of his mold, his way of doing things. I also don't like to be watched when I film.

Do you clear the set as much as you can?

I try to, but I always feel more comfortable when the director does it. It's an unfair way to look at an actor's work. Another thing happens when you see it magnified and photographed. I've been inhibited a lot of times, and it's caused confusion.

It seems much of that confusion happened around the time of *The Godfather*. You became a moodier person. You had had problems with Gene Hackman in *Scarecrow*. You broke up with Jill Clayburgh. You went out with Tuesday Weld. And you had just come from dealing with Brando, one of the world's moodiest actors. Did acting with Brando, and playing the role of the Godfather yourself, have an effect on you?

I imagine it did. In retrospect I see the way I handled my personal life with friends. I went through some bad stuff, and some of the people close to me went through it with me. We were close enough to go through it and survive it. They were right there and called me on anything and faced me off. It was worth it.

I'll come back to your personal side, but let's stay with your role as

Michael Corleone. Do you have a favorite scene in either of the first two *Godfather* **films—a moment you're particularly proud of?**

I have one moment in *Godfather II*. Nobody sees it. Michael and his sad brother Fredo are in Cuba, seeing the Superman show in the nightclub, and Fredo tells Michael, "Johnny always used to take me here." And you see in that moment that Michael realizes his brother betrayed him. That's my favorite moment, but it's subtle. After the scene I was taken to the hospital, the next day.

From exhaustion?

Yeah. We were shooting in the Dominican Republic, and I was being treated like a prince or something. Eight bodyguards and all, which was unnecessary. It was very disconcerting. I got physically ill. I was just overworking in that part.

How would you rate that part against the others you've played?

Of all the parts, I'm most satisfied with *Godfather II*. It was the most important.

Is there a *Godfather III* **in the future?**

There was a scene, which was only half shot, where Michael's son comes back to visit him. The kid talks about how he wanted to join the family business. And I tell him that he should give it more time. But they didn't shoot it all, which I found hard to believe.

Why didn't they shoot it?

We lost the light. Maybe if we hadn't, we'd be hearing about *Godfather III*.

Perhaps it's a good thing, because you followed that with another **remarkable performance in** *Dog Day Afternoon*.

You know, I almost never got to do that film.

Why?

I quit once. Dustin Hoffman was going to do it. I was the original one, and then Dustin, and then it went back to me.

Why did you quit it?

I had just done *Godfather II* and I was tired of films. I just didn't want to make a movie. I found it a hassle. I had done years of stage, and I thought I was one of those actors who couldn't adjust to film, because it was too laborious. I guess I was too tough on myself. I was working in a medium I didn't know, and I felt unsure.

Why did you decide to do it?

Because Frank Pierson wrote a terrific screenplay. And I had strong feelings for that kind of character. See, there're three reasons I take a screenplay: the director, text, and character. If I relate greatly to the director, the text is pretty good, and I think I can do something with the character, I might take it. Or if I can relate greatly to the character, and the text and director are okay, I'll take it too. As long as there's one really strong positive in it. That's how I pick things now. Before, all three had to be great.

Is that how you felt about the script, the character, and the director, Sidney Lumet, of *Dog Day Afternoon*?

Yeah. Pierson had structured it quite beautifully; he really made it sing, it was alive. And Sidney Lumet is a genius in staging; he never tells you a word; just by the way he has you move, the scene comes alive. He pointed me in a direction and said, "Go here and go there." It's extraordinary.

Did you immediately have a sense of the character—a bisexual bank robber?

When I went to the rushes and watched the first day's shooting, I thought, *This is incredible, there's* nobody *up there*. Marty Bregman, who was producing it, said, "What?" I said, "There's nobody up there." He said, "Well, Al's gone. Al's gone." I said, "We're going to have to reshoot this." He said, "What do you mean? It's good, it's terrific. What are you talking about?" I said, "No, no, no. I'll see you later," and I left. I came home, got a bottle of wine, and stayed up all night because I had neglected to work on certain things, and it was very important for me to have seen that day's rushes, because there wasn't a character. I worked through the night. I had to. It was like a crash course. I came back to the set, and that was the character you saw. That's what I worked on all night, to come up with something. We reshot that first day. The guy comes in on the first day with glasses, and I said he would never come in with glasses as a disguise, because he wants to be caught. So we changed it.

There's a truly memorable scene in *Dog Day Afternoon* where you come out of the bank screaming "Attica! Attica!" Did you sense its importance then?

Yeah, I sensed that kind of rush. Sidney Lumet helped me with that. He said, "It's *his* day in the sun, with all those people out there." Charging at windmills, somebody once said to me. But there's another moment that, I think, made it the kind of film that got received universally.

Which moment?

When the delivery boy delivers the pizza and then turns around to the crowd and says, in effect, "I'm a star!" It hit right where we're at—the kind of energy wrapped up in the media and with imagery and fantasy and film. We don't know enough about media yet, we don't know its effect on us. It's new. It's got to do something to us.

Did you sense that *Dog Day* was an explosive kind of picture?

Yes. My friend Charlie Laughton saw the film and said to me, "Al, do you know what it is like? It is like pulling a pin out of a hand grenade and waiting for it to explode." I remember Lumet saying to me at one point, "It's out of my hands. It has got its own life."

Have you felt that with any other picture?

With *Serpico*. It had that kind of pace.

What drew you to that story?

I read the treatment and thought, *Another cop picture*. Then Waldo Salt came over with a screenplay that I could relate to, and I was there. Then I met Frank Serpico. The moment I shook his hand and looked into his eyes, I understood what that movie could be. I thought there was something there that I could play.

Did you prepare for the part by hanging out with him?

Yes. I went out with the cops one night, did about five minutes of that, and said, "I can't do this stuff." So I would just hang around Frank, long enough to sort of feel like him. One time we were out at my rented beach house in Montauk. We were sitting there looking at the water. And I thought, *Well, I might as well be like everybody else and ask a silly question,* which was, "Why, Frank? Why did you do it?" He said, "Well, Al, I don't know. I guess I have to say it would be because . . . if I didn't, who would I be when I listened to a piece of music?" I mean, what a way of putting it! That's the kind of guy he was. I enjoyed being with him. There was mischief in his eyes.

Frank Serpico is living by himself on a farm in Holland. Is the piece we saw together on one of the TV news magazine shows the same man you knew?

No. That was what was so shocking. He looked as if he didn't belong there. Not natural.

He seemed to possess a certain resigned wisdom.

Yes. Resigned wisdom—he would laugh at that. He's a funny kind of guy. He was a loner. A man of intelligence. He'll be back on the police force.

Pauline Kael, in her review of *Serpico*, wrote that as you grew your beard, she couldn't distinguish you from Dustin Hoffman.

Is that after she had the shot glass removed from her throat?

Is that really insulting to you?

Why did you ask me that question? [*Laughing*]

To piss you off.

Really? I'm too good, right. I'm really too nice.

We'll find out.

We got time. If somebody says something like that, I can't retort to it. It has to do with what was going through *her* head at the time. It seems beside the point.

Kael wrote, "Pacino's poker face and offhand fast throwaways keep the character remote."

Are you kidding me, or what? Why was she pissed at me, I wonder? Sometimes the things that piss people off. . . . Well, I piss myself off too, sometimes. When I've seen myself on-screen from time to time, I've said, "Who does he think he is, smirking like that?" Or, "Why doesn't he take a bath?" But that film seemed pretty good to me.

What other films seem pretty good to you?

Bang the Drum Slowly is my all-time favorite film. I saw that three or four times. I'd like to go see it again. The baseball motif. The quality of the relationship between Moriarty and De Niro is beautiful. Maybe I relate to it because I wanted to be a baseball player. For some reason people don't talk about that movie.

You and De Niro are friends, aren't you?

Yeah, I know Bobby pretty well. He's a friend. He and I have gone through similar things. There was a period in my life when it was very important that I get together with somebody I could identify with.

Those must have been strange conversations, since neither of you appear to be very talkative. How did you communicate at first?

Sign language.

That's probably what the press would have to do to interview him.

He's always very quiet; it's an inherent thing. He's really honest about that. I think that the press respects that. They don't push him. He does talk with me, though.

Do you see any similarities between you and De Niro professionally?

I can only judge by what I see on film. I don't see similarities between me and Bobby. The same thing with Dustin; I don't see it, although I think he's great.

What other films besides *Bang the Drum Slowly* do you like?

I liked *Viva Zapata!* I liked Gielgud in *The Charge of the Light Brigade*. I liked *The Loves of Isadora* with Vanessa Redgrave; she's a great actress. I loved Nick Nolte in *North Dallas Forty*. I like going to see Olivier. And Walter Matthau. I go to see all his movies. When I first saw Fellini's *8 1/2*, I liked it a lot. I loved *La Strada*. I wasn't crazy about *Amarcord*. I don't like the Bond films.

What about *Star Wars*?

Didn't see it.

Close Encounters of the Third Kind?

Yeah, I saw that one.

Any reactions? If a spaceship landed in front of you, would you go up in it?

Yeah, but not with Richard Dreyfuss. [*Laughs*]

How did you feel when you saw *Saturday Night Fever* and spotted the poster of yourself—in your *Serpico* beard—on the wall of John Travolta's room?

I ducked. It was upsetting when it happened. Why should they do that? I was watching the screen, and I muttered, "That's not Al Pacino, that's Serpico." Sometimes I talk aloud in a movie theater. Like in *The Goodbye Girl*, with Dreyfuss and Marsha Mason, one of the characters says to the other, "Nobody knew Al Pacino before *The Godfather*," and I yelled up at the screen, "You're full of shit, Marsha. You were in a one-act play with me before *The Godfather!*"

That was during a regular screening at a movie theater?

Yeah. Sometimes I'll do that.

Did people turn and stare at you?

No. I think Dreyfuss looked down at me from the screen and said, "Shush, Al." [*Laughs*]

What other movies have you liked lately?

I liked *Norma Rae. A Little Romance*. I like this new girl, Laura Antonelli, in *Till Marriage Do Us Part*. She's a find, a striking actress.

What actress do you most admire?

Julie Christie is just about my favorite actress in the world. I love her. She's the most poetic of all the actresses.

What about the so-called bankable actresses, such as Streisand, Jane Fonda, Faye Dunaway? Would you like to work with any of them?

They're all exciting actresses, but the fact is, I don't know them very well. And you don't get to know anybody in a movie until after it's over. You work less together in a film than you do onstage. Onstage, you're out there together or you have rehearsal time to develop something. Like, Diane Keaton was talking to me about doing a movie. We'll get together with it, read it a few times, and try to develop something. It needs work, so we don't discuss it. I know Diane from working with her before; we're friends. I think we could maybe do a comedy together. You know, the reason she works with Woody is that familiarity; it takes the edge off.

How do you think you'd go over in a comedy?

You didn't know this, but that's what I did before 1968. I wrote comedy. I directed and acted with revues that I wrote in coffeehouses and like that. I pretty much spent my time doing comedy. But there's a strange thing going on that bothers me. I don't understand it. They're doing surveys: They actually do this at universities, and they ask people what they want to see. They don't want to see me in comedies, they want to see me in certain serious roles. So that's what's going to come my way. There are studio heads who say, "No, no, no, you don't want to put him in this, put him in that." It goes back to the old days, when you had your studio saying, "We have to put him only in romantic parts." So where is the opportunity?

   Maybe I'm being stubborn, but I refuse to look at myself that way, that I'm a commodity. This is such a commercial medium, and I understand and appreciate that. You can't ignore the amount of money you're given for this thing and say you're going to do some kind of art film. But it's disturbing to me when I hear they're taking polls and want me only in serious stuff. It's strange, since I have not done a comedy yet.

There are comic moments in . . . And Justice for All.

But it isn't the kind of comedy that I want to do. I really want to do the all-out Buster Keaton–type comedy. Slapstick. That's what I did, that's what I wrote; we were clowns. I used to think of myself as a comedian, believe it or not. I've always admired comedians. Mel Brooks will have these flashes in his films: You laugh for *hours* afterward. I wonder how he is, what he's like. The same with Woody; I go to see all of his films. Dick Van Dyke is also one of my favorites. Their minds, the way in which they see the world, is so striking, the way they juxtapose things, the way they can see humor in people. There's a liberation in that.

Speaking of liberation, the lawyer you play in . . . And Justice For All seems pretty liberated.

Yes. I sense a certain kind of originality, the way it is done. I have never seen a film like this before.

How do you see it?

It's a simple picture, really. It's about ethics and people; about a guy who is trying to do his job, and his relationship to the law. To say it's about legal systems sounds boring, and that's not what it is. It's funny and poignant.

Have you had any feedback from the legal community?

Most of the lawyers I've talked to are very pro the picture after having read the screenplay. One big lawyer said, "It's just a farce." Others have really enjoyed it. I enjoyed doing it. It was another world to travel in for a while, the world of our courts.

It's being promoted as a lawyer's M*A*S*H.

It doesn't seem to be so farcical. It has certain exaggerations, but it gets real . . . and yet not real. People who are older, who have had dealings with the law, been divorced, might have an interesting reaction to this.

What made you decide to do this one?

Norman Jewison came to me with it. I said, "Well, Norman, why don't I get some actors together and read it for you? Then I will see how I feel after I hear it." We read it aloud, and after I finished, it wasn't halfway bad. I thought it had a nice structure to it. I thought, *If this thing works, what will make it work is that there are so many stories they are juggling*. You could really develop any one relationship out of it. It's a difficult film because it is so verbal; you really have to pay attention to it.

How was Jewison to work with?

He was different from anybody I had worked with before. The thing I like most about Norman is you get a sense of his involvement; he's constantly with the movie. He broods about it. Even after it's over, he's with the picture—he cares about it a great, great deal.

Do you think the film can be seen as *Serpico Takes On the Courts*?

Yeah. Though, in a way, I saw a similarity to George C. Scott in *The Hospital*, which conveyed the feeling I had when I went into a hospital. The similarity to *Serpico* would be the strongest. Although I find this character, Arthur Kirkland, to be less detached, more involved. I like him because of his involvement and his desire to be a part of the system. He liked his work. Only the system drives him nuts. Which creates an ethical question at the end: Is this right or not?

The ending is pretty radical—you sort of watch your character's law career go down the drain in a rather triumphant, perhaps self-indulgent way.

Does the audience have a sense of that? I hope they do. That the guy is giving it all up. You are seeing this guy struggle; it's the last time he's going to be up there. What he's trying to do is expose the system. There was a line that is out of the picture now, where he said, "Did you know that 90 percent of the clients the defense counsel represents are guilty? 90 percent."

How much research did you put into the part?

A lot. I worked with lawyers before filming began, so I felt kind of close to the courts. At one point recently a friend said to me he was having trouble with a contract, and I just instinctively said, "Let *me* see that." You get that feeling that you are able to *do* these things. It's crazy. I literally took it from him and said, "Well, maybe I can help you with this." Can you imagine that? And I looked at the thing, and I thought, *What am I doing?*

Didn't you also do something like that when you played *Serpico*? Like try to arrest a truck driver?

Yeah, I tried to. It was a hot summer day, and I was in the back of a cab. There was this truck farting all that stuff in my face. I yelled out, "Why are you putting that crap in the street?" He said, "Who *are* you?" I yelled, "I'm a *cop*, and you are under arrest, pull over!" I pulled out my Serpico badge. It was a fantasy for a moment. I was going to put him under citizen's arrest, but then I realized what I was doing.

Earlier I asked you what actresses you enjoy watching. Who do you think is the best actor in America?

Among the post-Brando actors—I call it post-Brando. It was about ten years after Brando that a lot of actors . . . There are so many fine actors. . . . I don't know. George C. Scott.

Do you remember that scene of Scott's at the end of *The Hustler*, when Paul Newman is walking out of the pool hall, and Scott is sitting there and suddenly screams—

[*As Scott*] *"You owe me money!"* Very strong movie.

What other actors have you admired?

Gary Cooper was kind of a phenomenon—his ability to take something and elevate it, give it such dignity. One of the great presences. Charles Laughton was my favorite. Jack Nicholson has that kind of persona; he's also a fine actor. Mitchum's great. Lee Marvin, too. And Paul Newman, he's a supersensitive person. I like Warren Beatty, too; I like his style and his mind and his movies. He does a lot of different things—he's much more of an organizer: a producer, leader, director, writer; he's very much a film person. He's involved in film on a deeper level than I am. These guys are terrific actors. I also admire Frank Sinatra. I've been inspired by his singing, although he's a pretty good actor. He's got a nice presence.

What about some of the younger actors, such as John Travolta or Sylvester Stallone?

Travolta's a very talented young actor. Stallone's important; he should be around, he could do a lot of things. He has a sense of comedy.

And Richard Gere?

I never saw Gere's acting. Oh, I saw him in *Days of Heaven*.

Some critics say he's a young Al Pacino.

Young Al Pacino, huh? [*Laughing*] You said that, not me. Talk like that, you're never going to get me to bed. [*More laughter*]

Isn't that what your character says to the girl in . . . *And Justice for All*? Have you ever compared yourself to anyone? To a Nicholson, De Niro, Brando? In the privacy of your room do you look into the mirror and think—

When I look into the mirror, I think of . . . Gary Cooper. Naturally. [*Laughs*] No, I don't think I ever did.

You and Jack Nicholson were both nominated for the Best Actor Oscar for your performance in *Dog Day Afternoon* and his in *One Flew Over the Cuckoo's Nest*. Did you think you'd get it?

No, I never thought I'd get it.

You thought Nicholson would?

Yeah.

Do you feel he deserved it?

Yeah, he did. He'd been out there a while, he's made a lot of different films. He's been great.

Would you have turned the role down?

Yes, I would have turned that down.

Because of *Dog Day*?

No, because I thought *Cuckoo's Nest* was a kind of trap. It's one of those built parts: I don't think it has much depth. Commercially it's very good, but as far as being a really terrific role, I don't think it is.

You still don't?

Yeah, I just don't see much depth in the role.

But you said that you thought Nicholson deserved the Oscar for it.

Who said that?

You did.

When did I say that?

A little while ago.

I'll bet you five thousand dollars I didn't say it.

Five thousand dollars? You said it. Would you really bet?

I'd bet ya five thousand dollars. Yeah.

You would?

Yeah.

Okay. So if you didn't think he did, do you think *you* did?

[*Smiling*] You really want to corner me, don't you?

You've been sitting on it too long. It's got to come out.

You're asking: Do I think I deserved the Academy Award for *Dog Day Afternoon*? Not any less than he did. For that.

Do you think you deserved it *more* than he did?

What do you think? WHAT DO YOU THINK?

Now we're cooking. Did you think *Cuckoo's Nest* deserved to win for Best Picture?

Did it win?

Yes.

It won? Well, I didn't think so. If you asked me, Did I like *Cuckoo's Nest*? I'd have to tell you I didn't. Did you?

Yes.

Finally we disagree on something. Finally.

What the hell.

Get out of my house, then. [*Laughs*]

What about the year before, when you and De Niro were up for *Godfather II*? He got it for—

Yeah, for Supporting.

And you were up for Best Actor. Do you remember who won?

Art Carney.

Well, you can understand that. Can't you?

You really are a wiseass, you know. "You can understand that." Talk about putting words in my mouth.

You felt you deserved it for *Godfather II*?

I think you've got to get your act together about "deserving" Oscars. You really are off there.

It's not the fact that you didn't get it, you mean. It's the fact that someone else did that could disturb you?

Whoever gets it deserves it. Deserves it for what? If you had to get down to the nitty-gritty and say, "If these actors were doctors and I had to have open-heart surgery, which one would I choose?"—*then* we're talking.

But do you care about these things?

Let me say, honestly, I don't care. I do not give a shit. Honestly.

But you did get excited about the Nicholson thing. Enough to forget what you said, anyway. So you care a little bit.

Ah, ho. You're starting to get to me now. If I don't give a shit whether I win or not, what difference does it make?

None at all.

What I mean, basically, is if I won the award, that's terrific. I've won awards. And they didn't make me feel bad winning them, I'll tell you that. They made me feel pretty good. But it also did not make me feel bad *not* winning the Academy Award. I will honestly say I felt . . . the same. I didn't feel as though I was cheated or that I deserved something and didn't get it. That's honest. That's true. Now, if you ask me whether Jack Nicholson deserved it or not—if he got it, he deserved it. Fuck 'em.

Well, you've been nominated four times and you most probably will be again for . . . *And Justice for All*. Would you do anything to subtly campaign for it, as some actors do?

I wouldn't personally, but I can understand somebody campaigning for that. There are certain manipulations that go on, certain favoritisms, partialities. I don't know where, specifically, but I can sense them. I've experienced having lost four years in a row. It's strange. You feel good being nominated, then you get turned into some kind of loser when you don't win it. You've been feeling terrific, and suddenly you've got all these people consoling you. They say, "Oh, sorry," and their heads will bow. I talked to Mike Nichols about that once, and he felt exactly like I do. Those experiences are strange. As Brecht said, People are strange, stinking animals.

Have you ever gone to the Academy ceremonies?

I was at the Oscars once, for *Serpico*. That was the second time I was nominated. I was sitting in the third or fourth row with Diane Keaton. Jeff Bridges was there with his girl. No one expected me to come. I was a little high. Somebody had done something to my hair, blew it or something, and I looked like I had a bird's nest on my head, a real mess. I sat there and tried to look indifferent because I was so nervous. Any time I'm nervous, I try to put on an indifferent or a cold look. At one point I turned to Jeff Bridges and said, "Hey, looks like there won't be time to get to the Best Actor awards." He gave me a strange look. He said, "Oh, really? It's three hours long." I thought it was an hour TV show. Can you imagine that? And I had to pee—bad. So I popped a Valium. Actually, I was eating Valium like they were candy. Chewed on them. Finally came the Best Actor. Can you imagine the shape I was in? I couldn't have made it to the stage. I was praying, "Please don't let it be me. Please." And I hear . . . "Jack Lemmon." I was just so happy I didn't have to get up, because I never would have made it.

Before *Serpico* you were up for Best Supporting Actor for *The Godfather*, Do you feel you were in the wrong category?

Oh, sure. Definitely. That was outrageous. It's things like that that get you a little sour. I decided to pass the ceremonies by. There were certain people around me who wanted to write a letter, who wanted me to announce that I would not accept the nomination. I would always say, "Let it go. Let it go. Don't make waves." But then, even though I didn't go, I watched it on TV. I felt bad. I didn't care for that kind of contradiction.

In the future, will you attend?

I feel a little bit guilty if I don't go. It's more than likely that I would attend. A couple of awards I've won, I was too caught up at that time and had gone through too many strange periods to even understand what they were about. To be able to finally understand what appreciation is, enjoying the moment . . . Take it for what it is.

Do you think you might ever turn down an award, as Brando and Scott have?

I can't foresee that. At one time I didn't see myself doing an in-depth interview, so anything's possible.

Well, having lost four in a row, your chances seem pretty good this time around, don't you think?

It doesn't have to do with the amount of times you've been nominated. When Dustin Hoffman and Jon Voight were up for it and John Wayne won, he won that award for many reasons. Same with Art Carney. He's done fantastic stuff his whole life. I thought Kitty Winn was great in *The Panic in Needle Park*, and she wasn't even on anybody's breath come Oscar time, because the picture didn't do well. The fact is, it comes out of the community. If you don't live there—I'm not saying that they're prejudiced against you—but you're not into it, you can't tap it, you can't feel it. When you're in New York, the intensity of it is not as strong as if you are in L.A. Same thing with the Tonys; I don't think L.A. feels the Tonys as much, although they're not comparable because the Oscars are really huge. It's such an incredibly commercial thing.

We've been talking mostly about your film career, but the fact is you've put a lot more of your time into the theater. Do you consider yourself more deeply involved with the stage?

Yes, I would say I am more concerned with the plays I'm going to do than the movies. I'm more comfortable in a play. In film there's always a certain sense of control, of holding back. The stage is different; there's more to act. There are more demands put on you, more experiences to go through. It is a different craft when it's on the stage. The play is the source, it's orchestrated with words. In a movie you are not dealing as much in that. There are machines and wires. When you're acting for a camera, it keeps taking and never giving back. When you perform with a live audience, the audience comes back to you, so that you and the audience are giving to each other, in a sense. It's an extraordinary thing. It's wild turf up there. In the middle of a speech you turn around and look in the audience, and there's some woman who has a deformed back looking up at you, gleaming; and you say, "Hey, man, we're flying, aren't we? We're moving!" It's hard to explain.

The time I was doing *Pavlo Hummel* in Boston, I made connection with a pair of eyes in the audience, and I thought, *This is incredible; these eyes are penetrating me.* I went through the whole performance just relating to those eyes, giving the whole thing to those eyes. I couldn't wait at curtain to see who it was. When curtain call finally came, I looked in the direction of those eyes and it was a Seeing Eye dog. [*Laughs*] Belonged to a blind girl. I couldn't get over it—the compassion and intensity and the understanding in those eyes . . . and it was a dog. What a profession!

One of your earliest stage appearances was in William Saroyan's *Hello Out There*. Is it true you started to cry because the audience laughed at you?

The audience laughed at my first line. It was a really funny line, and they *should* have laughed, but I had never been in front of an audience doing that play, and I didn't know it was funny. I realized I didn't know the part well. Those days there were sixteen performances a week. Charlie came to me afterward. He had directed it. I was sitting on some stoop in the street, and I just wouldn't go. He said, "Al, you've got to do another one tonight." After I finished that, I stayed in my house for a couple of months and I wouldn't come out.

Backtracking a bit, what was it in your childhood that really decided you on acting?

One of the things that made me want to be an actor more than ever was seeing a Chekhov play, *The Sea-Gull*, when I was fourteen in the Bronx.

This traveling troupe came and performed the play in a huge movie house. There were about fifteen people in the audience. It was a stunning experience.

Another time, later in my life, I was sitting in a restaurant across the street from The New York Shakespeare Festival's Public Theater. The actors were sitting around a table with a red-and-white checkered tablecloth and an umbrella. The sun was coming in from the shade—it looked like a Renoir painting. There were seven or eight of them, talking. I said to my friend, "You see them? I can't get my eyes off that group." It was as though they had existed hundreds of years and you could see their roots, their background, how much like a family they were; how that was something I always wanted . . . I was drawn to them. Maybe that *is* what I want . . . I don't know.

So we can credit Chekhov with igniting you?

Chekhov was as important to me as anybody as a writer. Brecht, as well as Shakespeare, has really helped me in my life. Also Henry Miller, Balzac, and Dostoyevsky. They got me through my twenties, gave me such a *raison d'être*. The relationships that we have with writers are quite a thing; they're different from the ones we have with actors or musicians or composers or politicians. Everything for me is the writer; without him, I don't exist. So he is first. The actor gets all the fame and glory, but I don't know about *endurance*.

What are your three favorite plays?

Forgetting Shakespeare, *The Iceman Cometh*, *The Sea-Gull*, *The Master Builder*. O'Neill, Chekhov, and Ibsen.

Is there ever a time when a play is like a film?

You know what's close to a film? When you're doing a play and the critics come. One wishes that they would come when you do not know it, then they would be able to see a process. When I know somebody is in the audience, I want to say, "See how wonderful I am. Look how terrific I'm doing here." And everything goes right out the window. I blow it. It takes away from a certain spontaneity.

You tried to prevent that from happening when you refused to have an opening night for your *Richard III* on Broadway earlier this year. But it didn't seem to work; you got clobbered pretty badly by some of the press.

I knew that we were going to get hit. It was unavoidable. You figure, well, if you spread it out, it would be easier. All it wound up being was instead of one opening night, four. I thought, *Well, gee, this isn't working right,* you know?

How did you know you were going to get hit?

The *Richard* I did was different, it was a departure. We did it in 1973 at the Loeb theater in Boston, but it wasn't very good. So we moved to a church . . . and the thing took off. Something happened. Three hundred people would come. I came out of the pulpit and put my head out and talked through a microphone. The concept had continuity and consistency. The *Times* came and *Time* magazine, and the reviews were encouraging. So I thought of doing it again. But when we took it out of the church and put it into the theater, things changed. Before, it had a concept; now it didn't.

Have you seen Olivier's film of *Richard III*?

I never saw anyone do it, and I didn't want to see anyone do it. Although I would imagine seeing him would naturally widen my understanding of it.

There aren't many stars of your caliber willing to take the risk of doing Shakespeare on Broadway. Why did you do it?

To stop smoking. For what other reason? You can't smoke when you do *Richard III.* Are there reasons for people doing things? What is a risk? It's a risk *not* to take risks. Otherwise you can go stale, repeat yourself. I don't feel like a person who takes risks. Yet there's something within me that must provoke controversy, because I find it wherever I go.

What did you think of Richard Dreyfuss's comic interpretation of Richard III in *The Goodbye Girl*?

[*Sardonic smile.*]

Richard Eder, in the *New York Times*, wrote, "The stage bristles with cross purposes, crossed purposes, dim purposes, and Mr. Pacino's purposes."

Yeah, I imagine it must have been true, what he said. It's what it was. It had flaws. It wasn't great, but it wasn't bad, either. There was something going on, and the people were coming. The main thing was that people felt the connection with Shakespeare. I've always felt somewhere within me some connection to the Elizabethan temperament. It excites me, it serves me.

But do poor reviews also discourage you from doing it again?

You know, there *were* some good notices. But there's too much going on to really dwell on that. Kitty Winn once told her grandmother how affected she was by the criticism of *The Panic in Needle Park*. Her grandmother said, "Well, that's awful. You should quit." Of course, she didn't, but that's your alternative. Or you can lament about it. The thing is in doing it, that's what it's about. Not in the results of it. The one I love is what Wallenda said. You know the [trapeze artists] Flying Wallendas? The accident they had? He was up there, and they said, "How can you go up again after that tragedy?" And he said, "Life's on the wire. The rest is just waiting." That's where life is for me. That's where it happens. And it does.

In a lot of ways the controversy over *Richard* has only made me feel like I want to do it again. It has encouraged me. I don't mean that as a back-lash. The critics certainly weren't encouraging. I guess one of the great pleasures in my life was just going through this *Richard III* sequence. It opened the door again to say, "Well, I'm doing things. I survived this," you know, having worn through it, having watched and learned. I'm glad I did it. It was very valuable to me. The next time I would have more of an idea, a concept.

Would you be more specific about what you learned from the *Richard* experience?

Something challenging—where you get hit hard, when it's not smooth— often illuminates what other people think and alters your own perspective. And that kind of metamorphosis is a positive, cathartic experience. After seventy performances of *Richard* something started to happen. A scene that I thought I would never get or understand, I began to understand. I knew that there was a lot I had to learn. That's why I can't wait to get back on the stage. See, repetition is a big thing with me. That's technique, repeating. Someone once said, "Repetition keeps me green." I like that saying. Also, doing a play like *Richard III* is being involved with worlds, with where we're from. Four hundred years ago people were saying and going through those exact same things. You feel that connection. You get that sense of universality, of being a part of things.

As an actor, though, can you really make those connections? Or do you feel like an outsider, an interpreter?

Actors are always outsiders. It's necessary to be able to interpret—and that gets distorted when you become famous. Our roots were always outside— we're wayward vagabonds, minstrels, outcasts. And that may explain why so many of us want to be accepted in the mainstream of life. And when we are—here's the contradiction—we sometimes lose our outsider's edge.

One would think that you'd be more hardened to criticism than sensitive to it, after spending most of your life in the theater.

It used to worry me what people said about me. I'm learning not to worry as much. Sometimes you feel critics are wrong all the time, but I don't take objection to it, because that's the way it goes. They can be wrong, they can be right. They can be cruel, they can be kind. For instance, Walter Kerr, who is now the top reviewer for the *New York Times*—I dislike what he believes. There is no doubt about his knowledge, but he hurt me. Two things he said hurt me. It was the only time in my career that I felt that I would confront him on a couple of things he said.

What were they?

What he said about *Pavlo Hummel*. There was something in what he said that profoundly scared me. He said that a character like that was unimportant, that nobody would be interested in a person like that, nobody cares, why do a play like that? Just because he comes from a broken home and, needing to express himself, goes into the army, that doesn't make him a meaningless character. Pavlo Hummel is about as unimportant as Willy Loman in *Death of a Salesman*.

What was Kerr's criticism of *Richard*?

He said I didn't belong in Shakespeare. But Shakespeare is one of the reasons I've stayed an actor. Sometimes I spend full days doing Shakespeare by myself, just for the joy of reading it, saying those words. . . . I do Shakespeare when I am feeling a certain way. Sometimes I will sit here for a day and a night acting out parts. I can go for ten hours straight. Maybe it goes back to the way I worked things out in my subconscious when I was very small, when I went home and acted all the parts in the movies I'd seen. People are always asking me to do Shakespeare—at home, at colleges, on film locations, in restaurants. It's like playing a piece of music, getting all the notes. It's great therapy.

Is that what acting is for you?

More than that; I have a need to do it. My favorite line in *Richard III* is, "Nay, for a need." *For the need!* The need is everything. That is what it is about. Appetite and need. Someone once said to me in the back of one of those big cabs, "You really want to make it." I said, "I really do." He said, "How did you?" I said, "Well, I acted. I had to. I had the *need* to." [*Pacino takes a cookie from a bag on the floor and dips it into his Perrier water.*]

Do you know what you just did?

[*Looks down, laughs*] Now I'm dipping my cookies in water. Next thing you know, I'll be sitting on the windowsill.

There's a box of cookies on top of your refrigerator, the majority of which are half-eaten. Is it that you don't expect many visitors or you don't care if you offer them half-eaten cookies?

Half a cookie? I have to see that to believe it.

You mean you don't know you do it?

[*Pacino gets up, goes into the kitchen, discovers the box of half-eaten cookies.*]

Okay, tough question: What's your favorite cookie?

My favorite cookie? Lavagetto. Cookie Lavagetto played third base for Brooklyn in 1940. I once knew a bartender I used to call Cookie. "Hey, Cookie, let me have a couple of beers."

What's your favorite food?

Now you're sounding like Barbara Walters. Spaghetti and meatballs. There is no second to that.

Not even the head of lettuce and celery sticks that you've been eating for dinner as we've been talking?

[*Laughs*] I'm usually stuffing things down my mouth. I can get something in the kitchen, and on the way to the living room it's gone. [*Takes a new box of blueberries from the refrigerator*] Now I'm going to start eating blueberries again.

Back to your early years. For a while you supported yourself as a building superintendent, right?

I was about twenty-six. My friend told me about this job with a rent-free apartment and fourteen dollars a week. So I went down and got a boiler's permit and came back, and I was a super. It was my first real place that was not a rooming house or sharing with a girl—I had lived with a girl before that. Now I had my own little home. I had no money, hardly anything to eat, but I had a roof over my head. I was a super for eleven months. I drank, actually, but I hung in there and came out of it. It was a very fruitful time and, at the same time, it was the lowest time in my life. I used to hang an eight by ten glossy of me on the door.

Did it help you meet women?

Well, this girl moved into the building. I couldn't believe someone that beautiful existed. I thought I should meet her, but I couldn't wait for something; I wasn't working, and sex was not in the right perspective. So I thought I would blow her lights out, then that would get her to come downstairs for a fuse, and she would—

Blow *your* lights?

You said that. Why did you have to say that? You spoiled everything. [*Laughs*] So I went down to the basement, and I had to find the fuse box. I had been the super for six months, and I didn't know where the fuse box was. I turned the fuse I thought was her apartment's, ran through the building and out into the yard, to see if I'd gotten it right. But it was the wrong person. By the time I got to her apartment, I was exhausted. She came to the door, and I blew it. I was just too overanxious. I went up to her apartment, and I said, "I can fix your lights, and do you want to see the Village?" She was fresh from out of town; she didn't know what I was talking about. I came on a little too strong and I said, *I'm blowing this. I know I'm blowing it.*

Have you ever been afraid of women?

Yes, I have been.

In what way?

You can depend on them for certain things, but you cannot invest anybody with that much power; it's not fair to yourself or to the person. It's hard to know that, because you *did* invest it in your mother. Momma doesn't leave you.

What you're saying is relationships break up. You've had a number of relationships; who's the one who usually leaves?

It's been mutual. I guess I probably have an intense fear of being left.

What do you look for in a woman?

I like women who can cook. [*Grins*] That's first. Love is very important, but you've got to have a friend first—you want to finally come to a point where you say that the woman you're with is also your friend. There's some connection with trust. That takes time. Love goes through different stages. But it endures. Love endures. Shakespeare said, "Even to the edge of doom. If this be error and upon me proved, I never writ, nor no man ever loved." You know, it bears it out even to the edge of doom. "Love's not Time's fool." Romantic love can be a lot of crap, though, let me tell you. And it can hurt you.

How often have you been in love?

I've been in love twice. Once in '69 and once in '76. The first time, because of my career, I wouldn't have any of it. The second time, I found some other reason. I knew the first time that it was promising, but there were a lot of things happening with my life, and I could not deal with it at that time.

Were those times with Jill Clayburgh and Marthe Keller?

I won't tell you who they were. Sorry about it.

You were with Jill for five years, weren't you?

I was, yeah. I don't like to talk about things like that.

Do you still see her?

I will see Jill occasionally. She's a friend. She's married to David Rabe, who's a brilliant playwright.

When did they meet?

He fell in love with Jill when I was with her.

Did Jill know that then?

I don't know. She didn't tell me. I guess she didn't know.

Do you see David as well?

Even professionally, I don't see him.

What did you think of Jill in *An Unmarried Woman*?

She was excellent, wonderful. She came out. She became one of us, in a sense.

At the time you were with her, in your early thirties, you felt too wrapped up in your own career?

I wasn't very aware of things at thirty-two. At thirty-two I was, like . . . swimming. Trying to get out of a barrel. I remember one time with Jill, I was in the bathtub. I had been on a three-day . . . And she came into the bathroom and sat down and said, "I suddenly feel lonely. But you are drunk." I was pickled. It was as though there was a fog on my glasses. The windshield wipers weren't working.

What's the longest you've ever lived with one woman?

Five years.

That was a long time ago. Have you juggled a lot of women around?

Yes. Well . . . if you go with three or four different women, you don't necessarily juggle *them*. They could be juggling you, going with three or four different guys. There was a time in my life when being dishonest with women was the natural way to be. I finally said, "Hey, I have to stop this silliness." . . . I never talk like this—to men or to women. I just don't. I never had occasion to.

I thought I was being gentle with you about this.

I think so—you have been very gentle. If you want to open up with me on that, come on, I'm ready.

Okay. Susan Tyrrell said that "Al was like an animal, like a stallion with his reins pushed too tight. He needs to have his freedom more than most performers. When Al is free, he flies."

That's a real compliment. I really like Susie. She's a great talent, so she may be talking about herself there, but still I'm glad she gave me the credit for it.

Do you like being called a stallion?

A stallion? Oh, yeah. I didn't read that into it. I just thought flying, that's the way I read it.

Sally Kirkland said that women find you fantastically sexy. You're obviously aware of that, aren't you?

[*Smiles*]

I can't verbally record a smile.

Yes you can. You just did.

And Jill Clayburgh is very complimentary about you; she said you projected power because of your lack of egocentricity. "He can turn acting into poetry."

Keep 'em coming!

No reaction, eh? Then let's talk about the women's movement for a moment.

[*Sings*] "The girl that I marry . . ."

Would you consider yourself a feminist?

[*Continues singing*]

All right, have you changed your attitudes toward women since you were a kid?

Naturally, just by experiencing life. I used to say I wanted to genuflect to a woman, put her up on a pedestal higher and higher, way up beyond my grasp. . . . Then I'd find another one. But as an actor I haven't felt that way. Women have always had equal importance onstage, and working with them must have altered my sensibilities. I've never felt sensitive to the whole issue, because being *macho* has never been a problem with me. But, objectively, sure, I can sympathize with the aims of the movement.

Does breaking up with women affect you differently each time?

Let's save that for some other time.

Five minutes ago you said you'd go with me on these questions. Now you say save them.

That question doesn't make sense to me. You mean, is there a pattern in breaking up?

How has it affected you emotionally each time? Have you been devastated once, glad the next time, free, sad, neutral? There are different ways to feel.

Yes, that's true, yes.

You're letting my question be your answer.

Because I know someone who has all the answers when I see him.

Now *you're* playing cat and mouse. How long were you with Tuesday Weld?

Close to a year, I guess.

She was a taboo subject to talk about then; is she still?

I imagine that I wouldn't really talk about any of the women I've been with. I just *couldn't* do it.

I'm just running down the stories I've heard. What about Carol Kane; were you ever with her?

I was never with Carol Kane. She's a friend of mine.

And Liza Minnelli?

Just an acquaintance. I happened to be at her birthday party, and she sang a simple song, like "My Funny Valentine." It was a transcending experience.

How might it affect your acting to be in a film or a play with a former lover?

Well, there needs to be a hiatus, a twenty-year hiatus. I think I can handle it. [*Laughs*] Yeah, it can be fine. You can be friends with them.

Have you remained friends with all your lovers?

Yes, yes, I have.

Since you often live with women you're seeing, have you ever considered having a contract with them, to prevent possible palimony suits down the line?

No, I would not. The women I've known, frankly, I would never expect that from any of them.

But what if, after six months, she said, "You've ruined part of my life. I helped you make two million dollars that year. I want half."

I'd say, [*screams, imitating George C. Scott*] *"You owe me money!"*

Shouldn't you give it some thought?

I will. But it's a little premature.

Do you ever experience guilt when a relationship is over?

No. I am not aware of it. When I think back on some that I really withdrew from, I feel there are certain things I had to resolve that still haven't been resolved. In order to take a relationship further, in order to be fair to the relationship, you have to feel like a complete person toward her. It was like half of me was here, but the other half was . . .

In the Bahamas?

Yeah. Unexplored turf. There were problems stopping me. There were relationships in my life that I didn't pursue, because I consciously knew that they wouldn't last. I remember in 1970 sitting with a woman friend . . . I was half in the bag. I said, *My professional life is going to go fine. That's clear. But the personal stuff*—that relationship wasn't going to last. In a particular point in a relationship, I understood that there was something in myself that was lacking, that was not there.

Did you get a sense that it was closing in on you? That you needed more space?

That is simple, but I guess that would be it. That is the key phrase: the feeling it is closing in on me. And it has to do with you. The *woman* isn't closing in on you. It's crazy. What does that mean? Why would she want to close in on you? Why?

That comes when a relationship is getting deeper.

That's right. You don't feel in control. You think if you let go, you will fall off. You know, we talk about this . . . this hurt . . . and we're not quite able to take it any further. When you write, you are able to do it, and when I act, I am able to do it, to go to those parts in our unconscious that are unleashed. But when we sit here and talk about these subjects, it's like you can see it exhausting itself.

Have you thought of having children?

I haven't had a wife! . . . Yes, I wanted to have a child once. You forget the realities around you. You love the person so much you want to . . . For that moment you say yes. Fortunately, or unfortunately, it didn't happen. I knew it wasn't the time for it. I'm glad. Now I can. I could have, fifteen years ago. A couple of times I regretted it.

Do you have a strong desire to be a father?

Yeah. I will wait until it gets stronger. But there is something about it that wasn't there before. I figure I'll get the dog first. Then the kid.

Sounds like you're ready to get married.

It would mean something to me to have some kind of focus, something that is solid and there all the time. Something you can count on and that is regular. Like Meryl Streep got married. I thought that was very interesting. She has got a very strong sense of herself. I admire her greatly.

So a family structure is beginning to make more sense to you?

Yeah, it is. One understands its relationship to life. Too much of the time there is a pretended commitment. That is where we get in trouble.

Well, there is certainly no shortage of women who would be interested in testing your commitment. You are aware that you're one of the more publicly desirable men in the world, aren't you?

What did you do, consult a poll?

People say there's a magnetism you get across on the screen that has turned you into a sex symbol. Does that make real-life romance harder for you?

I think that is fucking crazy. What are you asking me?

About the nature of being considered a sex symbol and what it does to you.

I don't have that sense. I just sense that they are looking at me because I am someone they know. I am famous. I don't go any further with it.

You don't run into situations in which a woman will come up to you and give you her number?

Oh, yeah, yeah, sure.

Do you keep the numbers?

[*Laughs*] I was in a swimming pool a couple of years ago, and this girl was giving me the eye. I was with some friends and I thought, *Well, she recognized me, and that was it.* But there was something about this girl. She *didn't* know who I was! I didn't talk to her or come on to her in any way. I just sat there. But it was a great experience, one that I hadn't had for years. It was delightful. I didn't pursue it in any way, but it was very exciting. It made me feel alive.

How did you know she didn't know who you were?

She met me afterward and started talking to me. Either she was the greatest actress that ever lived—that has happened before, a woman pretends she doesn't know me—but this was genuine. And it was very moving.

Why didn't you respond to her?

I did. I gave her a picture of me. [*Laughs*]

Oh, great. Did you sign it?

I did. I signed it "Robert Redford."

Has that ever happened in reverse? That you've met somebody famous you used to like from afar?

When I was a young man, there was a certain celebrity I had a crush on. Some years back I was at a party and this girl actually approached me and tried to seduce me. I didn't want her to. I couldn't tell her, "A good part of my young adult life I've had these fantasies with you, and now here you are." She probably would have said, "Let's get married," or something.

The picture that deals with reality and fantasy more than any of your others is *Bobby Deerfield*. **You and the character you play are both celebrities obsessed by your professions, not easily communicative, and you don't readily relate to outsiders. Would you agree with your costar and former lover, Marthe Keller, that, of all your roles,** *Deerfield* **is the one closest to you?**

It was probably closest to me at the time.

Did that scare you at all?

Sometimes characters you play help you work things out in real life. It was a move away from anything I had done before. I'm very grateful to Sydney Pollack for having wanted me to do it. Coming at that time in my life, it was very important for me personally. It certainly wasn't a career triumph.

It was reported that you and Pollack didn't get along very well.

We didn't. It's because we're different. Sydney had a genuine idea for the movie; it meant something to him. We had different views, and in a movie like that you need to be together on it. It was a very delicate subject. On that film it was necessary to be in sync with each other, and we were just a mess. Maybe we would have been better off had I listened to him more; it would have been consistent. I didn't quite understand his point of view. There are aspects in the picture that are really good, but it was one that missed for me.

Can you give an example of how you differed?

In a scene that takes place in the shower, I'd say, "Let's have it in the bathtub with steam." I meant something by that. He meant something by the shower. It's a different thing. Then there was an interesting moment when [Deerfield] was alone in the room. He makes this phone call, hangs up. It's seven o'clock at night and he doesn't know what to do next. It's a moment of indecision that I thought was crystallized at that moment—of pain and confusion. But it's not in the picture. It was cut. We couldn't get together; we just couldn't. It's unfortunate, because he's such a good director.

What were you trying to achieve in *Deerfield*?

I was after the other side of narcissism. That something that happens to a superstar who is left and is idolized, a kind of loneliness I was after, narcissistic detachment, depression. That's what it was about—about breaking that depression, that self-absorption; opening like a flower. In my own life I have not gone into or resolved many things: Many things I've avoided. That is what *Bobby Deerfield* is about. About avoiding—knowing when to duck, when to move, when to hide, when to go in, when to roll with the punches. That is what I call my way of survival. I've had a lot of selfish incidents in my life. One day I just turned around and said, *I am a selfish bastard, and I don't have to be.*

Marthe Keller perhaps sensed that. She said that there was something about that part in you that scared her.

That's complicated.

Were you living together?

Yeah, we were.

When did you break up?

About a year ago.

Is that relationship over?

I don't want to talk about it. I can't talk about that experience. Why are you asking me?

Because there was a lot of publicity about it before and after you made the film.

There *was* a lot of publicity about that. It's hard to have a relationship with someone who does what you do. I've managed to move away from all that stuff—you never saw anything quoting *me*.

***People* magazine did put the two of you on its cover.**

I didn't pose for that. There's damage being done by that. The relationships become crazed by it. Could we not talk about that? I really have to say I cannot talk about it.

You obviously aren't comfortable with your name in the gossip columns.

I think we're so overstuffing ourselves with this kind of thing that any kind of gossip doesn't last but a few minutes, and then on to the next thing. People have said such outlandish things—things I have done, where I have been—I finally said, *I'll do whatever I feel like because it doesn't matter. I can't control it; they're going to say what they say.* I'm starting to relate to gossip in a certain way that I never have before. I'm starting to understand it. It's kind of liberating.

Do you ever miss just being a face in the crowd?

There's a wonderful thing about anonymity that I really don't have, to be just pounding the streets like everybody else. It's a really important thing to be able to go into the streets. I miss it, and at the same time . . .

You're willing to pay the price?

Yeah; it's a crazy thing. There are problems. These guys gave me tickets to a Yankee game. I was in a box seat, when suddenly I looked up and my name was on the big board, AL PACINO IS HERE. And then I was on the giant TV. I had to leave the game. The last thing I wanted was to be on that board.

So how do you adjust to fame?

When I first became famous, it was as though, to paraphrase Pasternak, the lights were pointing in my face and I couldn't see outward. People treat you differently. So you learn to see only a certain side of people. And one loses touch with the way people really are with each other. Not that they are mean, but they carry a lot of weight with each other, they sniff each other. There is that whole thing that takes place between people. Nobody is that accessible or ready to do something for anybody. So what happens is, when you are constantly treated like this, you forget. And the idea is not to forget. People are basically heavy. Sometimes you start to get a little light-headed. I love the line Brando said, "You're a one-eyed Jack in these parts, Dad. I've seen the other side of your face." I often feel like saying that.

How did your sense of perspective about the world around you change?

The world is a different place for me. That's all there is to it. The world got smaller, and the block got bigger. Somebody said to me once, on the street, "You're Al Pacino?" I said, "Yeah." He said, "Well, congratulations, you look like you oughta." [*Laughs*] Another time I was with Charlie in a delicatessen. I was standing outside. A girl said to him, "Is that Al Pacino?" He said yes. She said no. He said, "It *is*." She said, "Al?" I turned around and said, "Yes?" She said, "Oh, my." Charlie said, "Somebody's *gotta* be him." I love that.

Robert Redford said that fame is a two-edged sword: It gives you leverage to do what you want to do, but it's also like a plague. How plagued do you feel?

You should ask him that question. He didn't answer it. You give me the boring part. Next question.

Do people who recognize you get nervous around you?

They go strange, that's what I call it. I see very normal, sometimes highly intelligent, together people who present such an aura of power and sensibility. Then you walk in front of them and it all *goes*. They recognize you, they get silly. Only for a moment. It passes, and they're back to themselves again. But it's a funny kind of thing.

The whole thing of being a star . . . like, you're up there and you're a star, then a *super*star. What it implies is that you're out of it, you're up there and you're away. That can be sad. One time this guy said to me on the radio, "How do you feel being a superstar?" I said, "This is my last interview." That was the answer to that.

In spite of your wrestling with the nature of fame and celebrity, it is your name that brings people to the theaters.

I remember one thing that upset Toscanini very much about Caruso. He was having difficulty with a Beethoven thing. Caruso pointed out the window and said, "See those lines? They're here to see me, not Beethoven." You know, I've seen a lot of actors so crazy about fame, they worry about it *before* they become famous. They enjoy going through the preliminaries: "What will we do? Will we have to move out of the neighborhood?" They love it. That kind of thing can turn me off.

Sounds like a good idea for a TV sitcom: people preparing for fame.

Yeah, it is sort of like looking at your casket.

Would you ever consider doing television?

Sure. I don't get TV scripts. If I do stage, I would do TV.

That's surprising. Most of the major stars—Hoffman, De Niro, Streisand, up to now yourself—don't do TV.

George C. Scott does TV specials. Olivier does television and movies. It depends on the property. If they were to do a TV version of a play I did, and if I felt it would translate, I would do it. They wanted to do *Pavlo Hummel* on television, but I thought that the experience of the stage production wouldn't translate to TV. Same thing with *Richard III*. But I'm going to do that again, so maybe the next time it'll be filmed for TV.

Why not do *Hamlet*?

Nobody asked me to.

If somebody asked you, would you do it?

Yes, of course.

Don't you like to instigate these things?

I really don't. There is never a part that I want to do. An actor basically likes to be asked to do something, no matter what position he's in. It feels more natural. Sitting and waiting is more gratifying.

For things to fall into place?

Yeah. The fruit falls off the tree. You don't shake it off before it's ready to fall.

Then there are always the missed opportunities, the fruit that rots on the ground.

I can't *believe* I'm having this conversation!

You have a reputation for being a workaholic. Do you like working most of the time?

Most things I don't want to do.

Really? What percentage of the scenes you do would you say you don't look forward to doing?

Ninety percent of the time.

Let's get that straight. Are you saying that 90 percent of the scenes you do you don't want to do?

That's right.

You obviously reject a lot of scripts that eventually become films. Are there any pictures that you've turned down that you later thought were really good?

Yes. I've turned down a lot of them. If I told you the parts I turned down, you would laugh. They were really biggies. I can name three right now that were Academy Award nominees. Probably more.

What films were they?

I can't tell you. It's not fair to the persons who played the parts.

That's ridiculous. Everybody knows that scripts go to certain people like you first.

I know when you're after something. Your legs start shaking. Maybe I'm just too nice to be interviewed, that's all it comes to.

Can't you just do it as a game—how you might have played a certain role? Some actors will go down a list of what they passed up.

Well, that's not really very nice. I just don't like it; it grates me to minimize anybody in any way, to move on anybody else's territory. When I talk about this, it puts other actors in another light, in a lesser light, and it just isn't true. Can you understand that?

Absolutely. Now let's talk about it. Let's take something like *Kramer vs. Kramer*. Were you offered that?

See, we've had a long period of decent talk, but now you're back to, "How long a prick do you have?" I just wait for it, and it comes.

I don't want to keep you waiting.

There were times in my life when I didn't even read what was being offered me. Sometimes I can smell something that's not right for me.

You obviously felt that with *Kramer vs. Kramer*.

It was a great book; it wasn't a screenplay yet. I didn't get into the book. I had a feeling it was not for me.

You mean because it's about a married man and his son?

And the divorce courts and stuff. I didn't feel, at this point, it would be useful.

What other films caused conflict for you?

I don't know. *Days of Heaven*. I love Terrence Malick, and I love the picture. And *Coming Home*. I was hoping to make *Born on the Fourth of July* at that time. It was too close.

Whatever happened to that project?

That was a go project. Billy Friedkin and Oliver Stone wrote a terrific screenplay, but Billy couldn't do it for some reason. Apparently there was a studio that wouldn't let him out of a commitment. When a director is taking on a picture of that size and dimension, it's his picture. I had an interest in making it with Billy. So, suddenly, Friedkin is out of the picture—now what? I wasn't going to make that movie.

Would you ever consider directing a movie yourself?

Everybody seems to be doing it. Jimmy Caan, Dustin, Burt Reynolds, Robert Redford, Paul Newman . . . I'll bet you Bobby De Niro does it. Stallone did it very successfully. It's very hard to do. I've directed plays, but only when I felt strongly about the play. And I did it all: I did the sets, the costumes. If I wanted to make a movie and really take over, I would do it. But I believe very much that directors are directors and actors are actors. I'd very much like to keep maintaining the independence I have as an actor: You pay me a salary, I come and do a job. The last three pictures I've made have been that kind of thing.

Did Francis Coppola come to you for *Apocalypse Now*?

Yes, he wanted me to do it. I told him I hadn't been in the army and I didn't intend to go in the army now—and if I were to go, I wouldn't want to go to war with him. He said to someone later, "Al would do the film if we could film it in his apartment."

Speaking of the army, how did you stay out?

The first time, I was made 1-Y. That meant I had to go back in a year. I guess I wasn't ready then.

What do you mean you weren't ready?

I failed the tests. Who knows?

Do you know or don't you know?

Look, I might have gone into the army at eighteen or nineteen, but by the time they called me up, I was twenty-three—and too much had already happened to me. Among other things, I had just lost my mother and my grandfather in the same year. I certainly wasn't ready for the army, and the army wasn't ready for me.

That was before Vietnam, right?

Yes. It was peacetime. I guess that's why they were so lenient with me.

So it wasn't that war you were against but the system's telling you where to go for the next two years.

Yeah; that was the most impossible thing. You know, I still have a thing about that. I feel they could somehow call me up again—at the age of thirty-nine. I *know* I'll pass my physical, and I *know* they'll take me into the army. [*Laughs*] But, as Charlie said to me, "Al, don't worry about it, they don't *want* you. Believe me, they don't *want* you."

Enough about traumatic matters; let's talk about money. In 1972 you said that you've done a lot of things in your life for money, but the one thing you haven't done for money is act. Would you retract that now?

I won't act for money. I don't think I ever will. The big item when I do off Broadway is the fact that I'm getting only $250 a week. In that area you can anger people to no end—you start talking about how you don't care about money, and there you are, pulling in a million or whatever. I feel kind of funny about that, because it really can grate on people's nerves. When you're dealing with money, people change. They go a little strange. I know because I've been there. I asked this guy once for five bucks. Before that it was, "Hey, how're ya doing? Haven't seen you for so long. Fantastic." I say, "Pretty good, you know," and finally I ask for the five dollars. He goes, "See you tomorrow, man, we'll meet at this time." He makes arrangements, and you get there and he's not there. People go crazy with money.

How was it for you to adjust to being rich?

You learn about detachment. You have to learn about this new thing that's entered your life. I never had money before, so you learn to understand it. That's a full-time thing to devote yourself to, before you can recognize it and have any kind of relationship to it. Rich people know about money, they understand it, they relate to it in another way. If you never had it and you have it, you have to learn about it. How many steaks can I eat?

Do friends borrow from you now?

Naturally. But there's nothing like that to ruin a relationship. If friends need some money, I'll lend it to them, sure. When I'm lending it, I preface it by saying, "Look, if this affects the relationship in any way, forget it." Invariably it does, though.

You have a lot of musical instruments in your living room. Do you play them?

Here? I have my conga drums and guitars and a piano. I like it when people come over and we jam for an hour. There is nothing more joyful than coming together with somebody through music. It's contact. I used to play conga drums and the piano. I went through a time when I thought I was Beethoven or something. I had this feeling I was this untapped genius, so I got the piano and played for hours. What it was, really, was that I felt a need to express myself, and I wasn't doing it in my acting. I wrote my own music. I would sit for hours and just touch the piano keys until finally the rhythms would come out, tunes would come, and I taped them. I put together two tapes, which I was really excited about. Then I lost them.

How'd you lose them?

Don't know, but they're missing. I have suits all over the world. You know how it is when you're traveling. I go to Europe, I just take an overnight case. I will find things. In the South Bronx when I left my apartment, I would go out the door and say, "See you later." And I was gone. That's the way I feel about things. But getting back to music, I always fantasized myself being in a jazz combo or in the midst of a Beethoven quartet. Just the feeling of getting so far into something. It hasn't happened in acting, that kind of feeling. Acting is so fleeting and so vicarious. I went and heard Woody Allen play his clarinet once. It was terrific. He's very fortunate to have that kind of talent. I wish I had that. As a matter of fact, I'm going to start taking piano lessons. I love to be around people who are musically talented. I was doing *Scarecrow*, and me and Gene Hackman's brother used to go to nightclubs—they'd let us sit in to play with the band. I would do that until three or four o'clock in the morning and get up at seven to go to work.

Speaking of *Scarecrow*, what did you think of that film?

I didn't think it made it. *Scarecrow* was the saddest experience of my career. That was a definite example of negligence. It was the greatest script I have ever read. Garry Michael White wrote it. There were people involved in that who were really screwballs. Because people wanted to come in below budget, we sacrificed the movie. There were scenes deleted. I mean, who comes in seventeen days early? I never heard of such a thing.

You also reportedly didn't get along well with Gene Hackman.

It wasn't the easiest working with Hackman, who I love as an actor. It's the old thing of not knowing who the other person is until after you've done the movie.

Are there any projects now you'd like to do that you haven't signed up for yet?

There's one thing I'd like to do, and that's the life of Modigliani. Paris in that time, the changing of the Romantic period, I thought that would make a good movie. I had a friend who went to Paris to write a first-draft screenplay. It's a little subjective. I've given it to Coppola. If he doesn't like it, I'll give it to Bertolucci or Scorsese.

What about plays?

I will do *Richard III* again, naturally. And Brecht on Broadway.

Your stage breakthrough was in *The Indian Wants the Bronx*. Did it do for your career what *A Streetcar Named Desire* did for Brando's?

What did *Streetcar* do for Brando?

It made him a star.

I don't think it did that for me. It didn't have that kind of impact or make that kind of impression. Brando set the theater world on its head. No one had ever seen anything like that before. It was an innovation. There was a certain style of acting—Montgomery Clift came and had a certain thing; before that it was John Garfield—but to come onstage with this kind of voice . . . That's what it was, the voice. A new voice.

What do you think of this Brando quote: "We put to sleep our notions about ourselves that are real and dream others."

Who writes his lines? Where does he get his dialogue from?

After your successes in film you returned to the theater. Was that a way of coping with what happened to you?

I went back to the stage because it was my way of dealing with the success I had, my way of coping. It was a way of escaping the responsibility of what was happening. What I used to say was it was my love of the stage, but I don't think so. I think it was my need to say, "This is what I am. This is what I do. This other thing I am unfamiliar with, it scares me. It's too much."

Have you ever felt threatened as an actor?

I used to feel that. I would be in a play and somebody would come, and I would say, *That guy looks a little like me; I guess they are going to replace me.* Insecurity.

Do you ever dream about your characters when you are playing them?

All the time. Acting is hard work. At times it's very energizing and invigorating. It's childish. It's also responsible. It's illuminating, enriching, joyful, drab. It's bizarre, diabolical. It's—exciting. Eleonora Duse said it's such a horrible word, "acting." It makes you feel bad just saying it. It's more trying to get at some certain truth, some common denominator, some exchange, some connection, that makes us feel a certain truth in ourselves. The way of acting that you really try to finally learn is how *not* to act. That's where it's at. Acting is *not* acting.

What are the qualities that make up a good actor and a good director?

There are all kinds of good actors. There are actors who are strong in suggestibility. There are actors who are intellectually attacking material. There are actors who are very instinctive and operate completely on tremendous believability in situations. There are actors who are able to find the humor of a situation immediately, get right to the essence of something.

As for directors, basically great directors can understand staging in such a way that can make a scene come alive. Others have a certain way of pacing the scene. Others have a way of setting a kind of ambience around the set that makes everybody creative around them.

Have you ever considered your image on-screen? At the end of *The Godfather, Serpico, Dog Day Afternoon* and now . . . *And Justice for All*, you appear all alone. You are the loner.

Well, most of the successful characterizations that any actor does seem to be those kinds of characters.

But have you ever thought about it?

Never.

That you're always alone.

That's why I can't wait for you to leave. [*Laughs*] See, as our relationship develops, you get hurt. That's wonderful.

Just a few more questions. What was it that Marlon Brando's makeup man once said to you?

I said, "*I'm* not going to go to California." He said, "Don't worry, I heard Marlon say that. You'll be out there in three years." Well, I haven't moved yet. I haven't moved out of this *apartment*.

What do you think of Los Angeles?

I like parts of L.A. But after a while I can't help but feel that need to be around people. I can't take it in a car anymore. I need to be on the ground with people walking by me, crisscrossing. California gets you slaphappy.

Spoken like a true New Yorker.

It's my turf. I really love New York. You can imagine how I know it, having come here when I was sixteen from the Bronx. I was a city messenger when I was sixteen, on a bicycle. I worked eleven hours a day just riding the streets of the city. I watched this city. I've walked it, lived in it. I know it in all kinds of times of my life. It's home. I know it all, from Battery Park right up to Harlem. I know lights—I can time myself so I never get a light. I used to walk from Ninety-second Street and Broadway right up to the Village and back again, bopping along the street, thinking of parts. I worked out a lot of my role in *Godfather I* that way. I still get out there in the streets as much as I can. Watch a guy put forty packs of crackers in his soup.

You sound like a permanent resident.

I've already been here too long, I want to get out.

What about the museums: Ever go to the Modern?

Sometimes. I go to look at Picasso's *Woman in a Chair*. I know every time I go to the museum that I'm going to come away feeling different. It's almost like going to the Y.

Is there anything that upsets you?

The thing that can get you a little upset is when people say other people are better than you. That can bug you.

What about fears?

I have normal ones. I have a fear of electricity.

Do you have a philosophy?

I believe in one day at a time; you've got *today,* that's what you've got.

What about analysis?

I dabble from time to time. I mean, *this* is analysis. By the time we're finished, I will be empty and your tape recorder will be full. It's a crazy feeling. I get the feeling when you leave I will be interviewing myself.

What makes you cry?

The end of this interview. [*Laughs*] I had a fantasy the other night that this interview is so great that they no longer want me to act—just do interviews. I thought of us going all over the world doing interviews—we've signed for three interviews a day for six weeks. . . .

That's what you think. Enough is enough.

What? You've just put me through something—and it's over? Where are your whips?

Any last words?

Yeah. YOU OWE ME MONEY!

Not after you read this.

THE DEATH OF AN ACTOR AND THE BIRTH OF A CULT CHARACTER

At 6:30 on Tuesday morning, November 8, 1983, the phone rang in Al Pacino's apartment, waking him up. The news was shocking: Jimmy Hayden, the young actor who had played the junkie Bobby, opposite Pacino's lowlife Teach in David Mamet's **American Buffalo,** *had been found dead of a drug overdose in his apartment. The news devastated Pacino, who had grown to love Hayden as they worked together in the three-man play, which ran intermittently between 1980 and 1983. The play was a highly praised American drama.*

The night before, Pacino, Hayden, and J. J. Johnston had appeared in **Buffalo.** *(Over the years they had taken the play from out of town to off Broadway, and finally to Broadway, where it was in the third week of its run.) Johnston, a burly actor who plays the owner of the junk shop where the play takes place, was also devastated when he heard the news, and said he couldn't go on that night. Pacino understood his feelings but disagreed. The show would go on. Not out of show business bravado, but as a tribute to Jimmy. Also, Pacino knew that he had to keep busy, to keep the depression from overwhelming him.*

That afternoon Pacino drove up to his country house, forty minutes from the city along the Palisades Parkway, where I waited for him with a small film crew. Universal Studios had asked me to shoot Pacino at home for an electronic press kit, talking about his latest film, **Scarface,** *fooling around with his two dogs, playing stickball at the nearby park, walking with his live-in girlfriend, actress Kathleen Quinlan. A shy man under normal circumstances, he was in no mood to do an interview. But rather than cancel it, he drew his anger over Jimmy's death deep inside him and mocked for the cameras in a way that defied his loner image. But* *before he sat for the on-camera interview, Arvin Brown, the director of* American Buffalo, *arrived, his eyes swollen. Pacino stood up, and the two men embraced. Brown was sobbing. Pacino took him up to his bedroom and closed the door.*

Forty-five minutes later he came down, and asked me not to ask him about Jimmy, who had recently worked in his first film with Robert De Niro, in Sergio Leone's Once Upon a Time in America, *and had starred in another Broadway play, Arthur Miller's* A View from the Bridge. *Al believed Hayden was on the verge of stardom. "I loved him, you understand? It's just too soon to talk about it. He was the best young actor I ever saw."*

When the cameras shut down, he didn't wait around to say good-bye; he was on his way back to the city to do Buffalo *once again. Before going on that night, Al felt frozen with despair. His legs couldn't move. He was thinking of Jimmy. J. J. Johnston was in no better shape. But Al, J. J., and the understudy, John Shepard, gave magnificent performances. The audience knew they'd experienced something special and gave them a long standing ovation. The actors took their bows but didn't smile. Jimmy Hayden was dead.*

A few days later we sat down again by the fireplace in his country home to continue our conversation, this time for Rolling Stone. *From the window the view was of the swimming pool and the paddle-tennis court, strewn with yellow-and-rust-colored leaves. Through the branches of the nearly bare trees was the Hudson River, picturesque and quiet. In the game room below one of his drivers watched an old movie on the enlarged TV screen, while his secretary made some calls at a desk in a corner opposite the pool and Ping-Pong tables. The emotions of the week had taken their toll, and Al, now forty-two, was suffering from a fever, a stuffed nose, and a feeling of exhaustion. When Kathleen Quinlan returned from rehearsing the play she was preparing to do in New Haven, his eyes lit up. She brought him some hot tea mixed with lemon, honey, and cayenne pepper. They embraced, and I could see that they had true and tender feelings for each other.*

"I know you're going to write about all this, aren't you?" he asked. I was glad he didn't ask me not to. He'd been a loner long enough.

The *New York Post* **blasted your name across its headline:** AL PACINO MOURNS PAL. **Did that bother you?**

I accept it. These things sell papers. Someday it really won't. When most of the people in the world are famous, there won't be any more of this shit.

That's what I'm waiting for. For a time when the not famous will become famous just because they're not famous!

You didn't want to talk about Jimmy on-camera, but you've had a little while to reflect. How good an actor was he?

Jimmy was the best young actor that I've seen. I remember one time reciting to Jimmy a lot of Shakespeare stuff I knew verbatim, and I saw he needed that, he wanted that. There was a sense of a Jimmy Dean about him. In my life I've never seen anything like the way people who knew him, even briefly, responded to his death.

Do you think the role of a junky that he was playing in *Buffalo* had an effect on him?

I've known nonactors who've done hard drugs; it had nothing to do with the role. He was a child of the streets, Jimmy. And an extraordinarily sensitive individual. He was always taking everything in, his eyes were swallowing images . . . In a sense maybe that's why he maybe needed drugs or alcohol . . . to slow things up.

Did you know he had a habit?

That's the single thing that gets me the most—that I didn't know. Jimmy had a way of keeping things. I knew he had a drinking problem; we discussed it.

Can you understand his taking his life?

It's always hard to understand when that kind of thing happens to anyone close to you. . . . You can develop an allergy to it. I guess that's what happens when you get older. You have to live through it.

You've lived through it before with some childhood friends, and you've wrestled with the problem of alcohol yourself.

I don't like to talk about the drinking, because it's something I don't quite understand. I wish I understood it more. We sometimes live a life and do things and are not aware that we're doing them. My friend Charlie made me aware of that: that I was indulging myself in a pattern of work and drink, which is sort of classic, in a way. After recognizing it, it took me about a year to understand it and another year to get off it.

You haven't touched a drink in years, have you?

No.

Do you think you'd be where you are today without Charlie?

No.

Do you think you'd even be alive?

I don't know.

Do you reflect on that much?

All I know is, if you're alive, everything is enriching.

Should be, but it's not always so. There's a lot of depressed people out there.

Me included.

Why do you get depressed?

I don't know. Is depression the realization we've got a one-way ticket? I'm in the car, I look out, I see all these people, and I say, *People don't want to be here.* So they use drugs or alcohol or stuff to get away from it. Anything not to be here. It's very understandable.

Do you think people would be surprised to hear you talking like this?

How would I know what people think about me? I'm not tapped into the way in which I come off as a personality. I sort of concern myself with the work I do.

Let's, then, talk about the work. Several of your pictures—*Panic in Needle Park*, *Dog Day Afternoon*, the two *Godfather*'s, *Serpico*, *Cruising*, now *Scarface*—have created a good deal of controversy. Do you choose films for their controversial nature?

No. I usually do them because I feel there's something I can relate to in terms of the character or the character's dilemma.

***Scarface* seems like a throwback to the gangster pictures of old. Do you think it should be taken seriously, or should people suspend disbelief and treat it as a roller-coaster ride?**

More like a ride. I think that's evident when you see it. But people react differently to it. Some people don't like rides. It's somewhere between naturalism and opera. I know at one point, while screening it with Kathleen, I turned to her and said, "You want to dance?"

After seeing it, did you at all get a sense that the character you play, Tony Montana, borders on caricature?

You're always afraid that you may go over the line into caricature. I hope I haven't. I once saw John Gielgud in a play, *No Man's Land*. He was magnificent. I went backstage to see him, and he said, "Oh, I hope it's not caricaturish." He was worried about that. And indeed it wasn't. It was great.

What made you want to do a remake of a movie that was originally done over fifty years ago?

I had heard about *Scarface* for a long time. It was the model for all gangster pictures. I knew that Bertolt Brecht was very interested in gangster movies. I remember when I was working in *The Resistible Rise of Arturo Ui*, we were looking at old thirties movies, and the one we were trying to get hold of was *Scarface*, and we couldn't get it. Then I was making a movie in California, and there was this little theater on Sunset Boulevard playing *Scarface*. I just went in and saw this great movie: It had a real feeling in it, a grand feeling, and it had a great performance by Paul Muni. He did something different. I thought it would be interesting to make a remake of this, in another way. So I called Marty Bregman, and he saw it and got very excited.

Who thought of turning it into a modern story?

At first I was caught up with the idea of recapturing the thirties. But when I talked to some writers, we found it was very hard, because it was so melodramatic. I didn't want to do a copy of it, I was looking for a style. You see, what Muni had done was a base for me to start from; he gave such a solid foundation to the role, it was like a canvas. I knew it was a characterization I wanted to continue. Then Sidney Lumet came up with the idea of what's happening today in Miami, and it inspired Bregman. He and Oliver Stone got together and produced a script that had a lot of energy and was very well written.

Why was Brian De Palma brought in to direct? What happened to Lumet?

I don't know the intricacies of that. I wasn't involved. Sidney, I think, felt a certain way about the first draft and had some difficulties with the next step. De Palma had a different vision, a way I hadn't thought about at all. I thought he was an interesting choice. He brought a definite style to it, almost Brechtian in a way. He knew what he wanted to do with it right from the start. Brian approaches things—situations, sensibilities, relationships—from another angle, another place than me. We both understood that; and so we were able to get along.

Did you know how the movie would look as you were making it?

I never know what the movies I do are going to look like. I don't know what I'm going to look like, until I see it. I think it has to do with my theater background.

How did you "get" this particular character? It's really unlike anything you've done before, playing a Cuban with a heavy accent.

At first it was almost a potpourri, using everything I knew. Coming from the South Bronx, being, in a sense, Latin myself, I have a certain connection to the Latin feeling, although the Cuban thing is different.

I didn't do it alone; I had a lot of help.

How?

When I started, I met with the lady doing the costumes, and the makeup person, the hair person. We would have long discussions out at my house about what the guy I was going to play would be like. It was the first time I opened the character up to a lot of people, which was helpful for me. I worked with my friend Charlie Laughton on the part, and with Bob Easton, the dialect coach, intensively. I worked with an expert in knife combat, with a phys ed guy who helped me get the kind of body I wanted for the part.

Did anyone in real life inspire you?

Well, I used the boxer Roberto Duran a little bit. There was a certain aspect of Duran, a certain lion in him, that I responded to in this character. And I was very inspired by Meryl Streep's work in *Sophie's Choice*. I thought that her way of involving herself in playing someone who is from another country and another world was particularly fine and committed and . . . courageous. It was very inspiring.

You worked with some young actors who haven't had too much film experience, like your costar, Steve Bauer. How was he to work with?

We worked together closely, especially in our off-hours. Being Cuban, he helped me with the language; he taped things for me, he told me things I wouldn't have known.

Did you know Michelle Pfeiffer before the movie?

No, I met her doing the picture, and she was extremely good to work with. Sometimes that's the case with young actors; they're just starting and there's more of a desire to get in there and really care about what they do. Sometimes, as actors go on, they get a little blasé, only because it becomes repetitive.

How do you keep from getting blasé? Do you try to act as if you're doing it for the first time?

I try to do that. I've been doing it for twenty-five years now, and the more I do it, the more I realize how much I don't know.

How much do you know about the drug trade in this country, and what do you think *Scarface* says about it?

That there's a lot of coke around. [*Pauses*] And that Tony Montana's doing it. [*Laughs*] He's doing all of it!

Do you think the excessive use of drugs depicted in the film is accurate?

I don't think you feel like you want to have coke when you leave that movie. It doesn't seem to be pro-drug at all.

It's a long movie, almost three hours. Were you concerned about its length?

Length is a funny thing. You can look at a movie for three-and-a-half hours and the thing goes by, then they take it down to two-and-a-half and it's much longer. A good idea is to just get a sense of what the film is and try not to reduce it *until* you feel it's living.

You've been nominated five times for an Oscar. Do you think that this will finally be your year?

I felt that way when I received a Tony award once; I had a feeling that was going to happen. And that was very pleasant. With the Oscars the only thing that bothers me is the feeling of feeling like a loser, when you're really not. You've been honored by being nominated. But I remember when I went there for *Serpico*, I thought I might have a chance. Then afterward there was this sense of feeling as though you lost. It's the way it's set up.

Bregman's gone from discovering you to managing you to now producing *Scarface*. How would you describe your relationship with him today?

I have a relationship with Bregman that I don't understand. It's almost primitive. On certain levels we have this connection. In other areas we couldn't be further apart.

He can get you very angry?

Yes.

Bregman was never a teacher the way Charlie Laughton and Lee Strasberg were for you. What did Lee teach you?

That's a very personal thing. You respond to someone on a personal level, and he can influence you and help you with your work without ever formalizing it in a classroom or anything. But Lee was someone I was so close to as a friend. We listened a lot to music together; we talked together.

How involved are you now with the Actors Studio? Aren't you the artistic director?

Yeah, well, it was really out of a special need that I accepted the position. But I'm not interested in being an artistic director, and I'm not interested in going to the classes there and moderating them. I'm not interested in that aspect of the Actors Studio. I'm interested in its endurance. It's an institution of great value to me, and I have very good feelings about the place. But it's without a leader. What's going to keep it going now, I don't know. They've got Ellen Burstyn. If she can develop into a leader . . . She certainly has the commitment and the desire and may very well have the ability. I don't know. Time will tell.

There's recently been a court battle over the ownership of Lee's tapes made at the Studio. His wife, Anna, feels the tapes are Lee's legacy for his two sons. The Studio feels it owns the rights to them. Where do you stand?

I went to court. I testified. I'm not for or against anybody. I just think we should settle the bloody thing in a simple way. Give Anna the tapes, work out a little trade, put the tapes in the archives. Why are we getting all excited over tapes? I don't know why it had to become such a public issue.

You going to court keeps the issue in the public eye. That's the price of fame. Did your own life change drastically when you became famous?

Radically, not necessarily drastically. I don't want to be naïve and say I don't recognize the fact that my whole world has changed: It has. I used to love to go to the Y and play full-court basketball, but as I started to get more and more known, the energy spent just dealing with that, with people's way of treating you—which is only natural—became exhausting. I was forced to go to a place that's more private.

How does success and fame affect your choice of roles and the risks you may or may not take?

It's difficult. You have to accept the place you're in. A lot of the times you're in a position of a certain kind of power. Even though your name has sometimes very little to do with what you're capable of doing, you're in this position where people are deferring to you. So you have to walk that line. You have to learn to somehow cope with this power you're given. The more successful you get, the more difficult it becomes to maintain that success and, at the same time, maintain the original enthusiasm. It's the work, the craft, the getting out there every day, doing roles that aren't necessarily right for you or that you don't have an immediate connection with, that gives you the strength. You don't want to lose that. Still, there's that other side: As you become well known, you become bankable, you can get a picture made. And sometimes the filmmaker wants you for that reason, while you want to be wanted for what you can do, not because you're bankable. So it can get confusing. That's why sometimes you get involved in situations you shouldn't normally be involved in.

Was one of those situations working under the direction of Arthur Hiller in *Author! Author!* You had reported problems, where you supposedly walked off after arriving late when he—

Reported problems?

Stories did appear in the press.

Gets funny when you have to get it from reported problems.

What happened?

What happened is we made the movie together. There it is. That shouldn't have happened. [*Laughs*]

Is it a long story?

I don't think it's such a long story, I think it's a very short story. Sometimes people who are not really meant to be together get together in this business for a short time. It's very unfortunate for all parties concerned. It was just one of those situations where all I needed was to have someone tell me what was going on and I would have responded.

What made you do a lightweight comedy like *Author! Author!*

I thought I would enjoy making a movie about a guy with kids, dealing with New York and show business. I thought it would be fun.

Was it?

No, although I enjoyed working with the kids. *Author! Author!* did very well on cable; it works better on television because it's about the home—you can go into the kitchen, come back, and watch it. We should be able to recognize that. Why don't we make movies just for cable and movies only for the theaters? Keep the big screen going, keep those theaters alive.

One of the movies that doesn't work on the big or small screen is *Cruising*, the film you were making when we first met. What was your reaction when you saw the completed picture?

"Where do I go now? What do I do?" I thought I had reached the bottom, but . . . it's really not so bad down here. [*Half laughs*] I don't believe Billy Friedkin shot the entire script. He went and stripped scenes. He took the meat out of them.

Of all the roles you've played, the character you portrayed in *Bobby Deerfield*—an inward, unrevealing, somewhat distant star race-car driver—is often said to be closest to who you really are—

Who said that?

It's been said—we've talked about it.

It's known around your house, maybe, in your neighborhood. [*Broad smile*] Yeah, there is a closeness there. It made it hard to play for me, actually.

The critics weren't very kind about that one . . . nor about some of the other films we've been talking about. Have you developed a thicker skin over the years toward criticism?

No. It still hurts. You're affected by them because you want to be liked.

Do you find that directors welcome your suggestions while you're making a movie, or do they prefer that you just hit your mark and say your lines?

When I did the first *Godfather*, I was unknown. I went to Francis Ford Coppola with a list of things that I had to say after seeing the movie. He read the list, he considered it, he made some changes.

I once talked to a director who was very strange with me. I told him that the script originally had another kind of ending. And he said, "Well, I'm not used to actors talking to me about scripts." So I said, "Well, I think it's something that you should consider. If I spent twenty years working on scripts, I must have learned something about that."

The actor has something to offer; after all, that's his trade. He may know just a little bit more about dialogue than the director, since that's what he does. Maybe he doesn't know as much about structure and stuff. That's a whole other thing.

Is it true that Coppola wanted an upbeat ending for *Godfather II* and you talked him out of it?

[*Laughs*] He wanted Michael to dance naked with the housekeeper.

The structure of the two *Godfather*s was altered when Coppola decided to add footage and make a longer version of them for television. What did you think of that?

That wasn't what it was meant to be. I reject the sequential order of *The Godfather*. I have rejected it from the moment I saw it. It doesn't play. *Godfather II* is meant to be seen as it was made, with the intercutting of the De Niro section. It was in the blend, that mesh, that Francis found the metaphor for *Godfather II*. When you take that out, you have a linear picture, one I object to.

Over the years you've rejected quite a few films—like *Kramer vs. Kramer*, *Absence of Malice*, *Prince of the City*—that have become decent successes. Have you ever said, "Gee, maybe I should have done that one"?

There's one film that I wanted to do, but because George Roy Hill was doing it, I couldn't do it. That was *Slap Shot*. I should have made that movie. That was my kind of character—the hockey player. Paul Newman is a great actor, it's not a matter of that. I read that script and passed it on to George Roy Hill that I wanted to talk to him about it, and all he said was, "Can he ice skate?" That's all he was interested in, whether I could ice skate or not. That was a certain kind of comment. He didn't want to talk about anything else. It was like he was saying, "What the hell, it could work with anybody." The way in which he responded said to me that he wasn't interested.

What about *Lenny*, which Dustin Hoffman did so brilliantly?

I was removed from that at the time they offered it to me. I've since got some idea of comics and what they go through and who Lenny Bruce was. Dustin did a great job, so I was happy about that . . . but that's one I feel I would have enjoyed doing that I didn't do.

Who are the directors you respect and would one day like to work with?

John Huston and Robert Altman. I love Altman. I don't know about his career, I just know he's a guy with a vision. When he makes a movie, you can feel something's going on. *McCabe & Mrs. Miller* is a wonderful movie. Another guy I love is Peckinpah. I don't know what happened to him, but I'd like to work with him.

You've only made ten movies in fifteen years. Would you like to be working in more films?

I wish I could play one or two movies a year, but unfortunately, you sort of put your career in jeopardy. The success syndrome can be very debilitating, very tiring. It hurts growth, it really does. I would like to see Robert Redford in a movie once a year, but you wait four years to see him in a picture. Or Warren Beatty. I don't understand that.

Who are some other actors you like to see?

I always go to see Meryl Streep. It happens once in a while—somebody like her comes along who has that kind of alacrity. I've always liked Julie Christie. And Diane Keaton—she's just the greatest. I look at Barbra Streisand and I wouldn't mind doing something with her. And Gérard Depardieu, I love that guy; he's probably one of my favorites. I can't think of an actor who isn't good.

What about Richard Gere, whom you didn't really respond to the first time I asked about him, when I mentioned he was being called a young you.

When I saw him for the first time, I knew he was a movie star; it's written all over him. He has an unusual charisma.

William Hurt?

Bill Hurt does theater work and he's got it, he's really got it. He's a major actor. The same way Kevin Kline is.

John Travolta?

I haven't seen that much of what he's done. I saw him in *Saturday Night Fever*. He was good. He's also a wonderful dancer.

What about some of the younger actors coming up: Tom Cruise, Matt Dillon, Timothy Hutton, Sean Penn, Eric Roberts, and Mickey Rourke?

That's a very impressive group.

Are you aware of them?

Very much aware of them. I don't know their work that well. I don't go to the movies that much. I should go more. I went to see *Risky Business* not knowing anything about it, and had such a good time. It was a wonderful movie, and the kid [Tom Cruise] was wonderful. I just would like to see these young kids coming along work on the stage more. It's important.

Brando is often critical of other actors. Aren't you being a little too nice here?

I think Marlon likes actors. I felt that when we made *The Godfather*.

Would it bother you if an actor said something negative about you?

It always bothers me. I know Burt Reynolds said something about me. I was upset. I don't know why he said it.

Do you feel you've accomplished all you should at this stage of your life?

Sometimes I fantasize about going out to the Guthrie Theater [in Minneapolis] and living a life in rep. But when I do it, it isn't what I want. What I'm doing is what I want.

Do you see yourself as a stage actor who makes movies more than a film actor who also does plays?

I don't consider myself one or the other. I like the movies in some ways as much as I like the theater. But my preference for the theater is simply because it's the life that I was most familiar with, the life that attracted me to being an actor, where I feel the most like I am enjoying the lifestyle of it. It's not just the acting; if you're involved in the theater, you're involved in everything that goes with it: the life, the hours, the way you relate to people, the energy.

And film is a lot slower and out of sequence?

I remember the first film I made, it was just a walk-on. I started at seven in the morning. I had two lines. We were dancing the whole time, and by seven at night we were still dancing, saying the same two lines. It was a couple of years before I made my next movie.

Can you get to a point in acting where you feel you're not acting?

That's what you try to do the whole time—to get to a point where it's instinctive.

There's a lot of talk about a national theater lately. How do you feel about that?

It's becoming increasingly obvious that it would be very practical and very important to engage our actors and directors in an ensemble kind of thing. It would mean experimenting with directors and writers in theaters that could reach the people who can't afford your Broadway theater. I think it should be based in New York City, maybe Lincoln Center, because you need three theaters. But more than anything you need a leader. Joseph Papp is a great man of the theater; someone like him could lead it. See, it needs someone like that, like an Orson Welles, who would be able to generate that kind of excitement. Welles did that kind of thing in the thirties.

The idea needs stars to get it going, doesn't it?

Absolutely. You've got to permeate the air with all this stuff, keep the ambiance fluttering, and something will happen. Right now a lot of these energies gravitate toward movies.

Because there's a lot more money in movies. How have you dealt with money as a means of measuring worth?

Your face gets so . . . precise . . . when you ask those things. It's so . . . directed.

Money questions; what can I tell you?

Talk to my agent; he's the one who asks for money.

He's not the one being interviewed.

Do I believe that because I'm getting more money with each picture that

I'm doing a better job? I've never believed that. You have to ask Picasso about that. It's all relative.

Have you ever felt guilty about the millions you're paid to do a picture?

Never. I feel guilty about a lot of things but not about that. And I don't really care if someone gets twice as much money as I do. See, when I was starting out in the theater, I was getting $125 a week. When I was twenty-six, twenty-seven, I started to get a salary. Before that I never knew where my next meal was coming from. When I started to make money, I didn't find myself that much happier. It felt good to eat; it felt good not to go hungry. I was fortunate not to get caught up in the materialistic side of things. It took me a long time before I had a house in the country. I know that if I went and looked at the room I lived in as a kid, at the life I lived then, it would all of a sudden have an effect on me.

Let's go back to your childhood for a while.

Wonderful . . . Well, it's been nice talking to you.

It's not like going to the dentist.

Why do we want to go into all this?

You obviously don't. Nonetheless—you're a product of a broken home, and you lived much of your youth with your grandmother. How old is she now?

I don't know. She's up there, though.

Is she well?

She's very well, very alert; I take her to plays, and she comes to see all my plays. Sometimes I meet her in a restaurant afterward with her daughter, my aunt.

Is she a very Italian grandmother?

No, not particularly. As a matter of fact, she has blond hair and blue eyes.

What does she think of all that's happened to you?

It's very meaningful to her.

Does she criticize you at all?

No, never. The only thing she may talk about is what I wore. She some-times would like me to dress a little nicer for a part.

Besides your grandmother and aunt, do you have any other living relatives?

I have a father in California.

Do you see him very much?

No.

What happens when you do see him?

He'll talk to me about his life. We'll spend an hour or so.

Do you like him?

Sure.

Do you feel uncomfortable when you're with him?

Not necessarily. It's like anybody you don't know too well. I really don't know him that well.

Have you ever talked to him about why he walked out on you and your mother when you were still a small boy?

I would never mention a thing like that to him—what do you think I am, a traitor? [*Laughs*] I think it's more complicated than that. Besides, he didn't walk out. People separate all the time. That was part of it. There was a real economic crisis for them. They were very young when they got married.

Were you angry about your family situation?

Who isn't? I mean, you got 60 percent to 70 percent divorce today.

But it wasn't so high in the forties. Did many of your friends come from broken homes?

No, not too many. In one way I was fortunate. I had my maternal grandfather and grandmother, my mother, and my aunt. I've had the benefit of some very loving people, including my father's mother, who was just a great lady.

Did you get into many arguments with your mother?

I'm like anybody.

You don't really talk much about your relationship with your mother.

No, I don't.

I don't know very much about that relationship.

That's too bad, isn't it? Neither do I. I don't know too much about it either.

Was it very complex?

I wouldn't know unless I talked about it.

She passed away when you were twenty-two, and then your grandfather died soon after. How did it affect you?

It affects you for life. I was very close to both of them, and I loved them very much.

Do you still think about them?

Yes, still in my thoughts.

On the rare occasions you see your father, do you ever talk about your mother?

No. I never talk about that stuff. What is talking about it gonna do?

Well, it's where you come from. In analysis you usually wind up back in childhood.

Sure you talk about that stuff in analysis, or in a situation that is private, but this isn't that. I'm probably as complicated as the next fellow.

Did you ever perform for either of your parents when you were a kid?

I remember when I was five or six years old and I'd go see my dad—they were separated by then—he would take me to groups of people and tell me to do the guy from *The Lost Weekend*, looking for the bottle. And I would start looking through the shelves and stuff, showing how desperate this guy was looking for that bottle. But they all laughed at it. Then it would be, "Oh, Sonny, sing that song the way you sang it the other day," and I'd do it and get attention. So I'd get a sort of acceptance. People would like you for doing it.

Did you go to the movies when you were a kid? Were you influenced by any actors?

My mother took me to the movies when I was three and four years old, so

I saw all the actors growing up. But it really wasn't until I was already an actor and I saw Brando and Dean that I had a different response. I wasn't the only one; millions of people all over the world reacted to Brando doing something that was new, that was innovative.

You've had several relationships over the years, mostly with actresses, that haven't worked out. Do you think some of it stems from the relationships you had with your family?

What is wrong with you? What is this thing, relationships with actresses? Most of my relationships are with people. Men have had relationships with women, women have had relationships with men, it's part of life. Stan Laurel was married nine times. You gonna talk to him about his mother and father?

Well, you've never been married. You've lived with women; what's kept you from taking the next step?

Well, if there were steps that I could see, I would say I can go on to the next step. I don't look in those terms. At least I can say, for whatever it's worth, that I don't have a divorce situation on my hands. There's a certain kind of maturity to that.

Are you still hoping to find the perfect woman?

You know what's happening? Your beard is starting to shed, your eyeballs are darkening, and you're starting to look like Barbara Walters. [*Laughs*]

You're doing a good job of avoiding the questions.

Why do I feel like shining your shoes? You have any polish?

Can we talk about Kathleen?

Why do I have to talk about somebody who I do everything with? It's obvious how I feel about her.

To you, not to anyone else.

She's the woman I'm with all the time. I don't like talking about her. I don't want to make her public by publicizing her. That's not what we're about. What we have is good, why spoil it?

What is your opinion of her as an actress?

If you see her in *I Never Promised You a Rose Garden*, that is about the most evident, fabulous piece of acting I've ever seen. A talent that size should be used.

Okay, we're just about done for now. Would you say you're happier when you're acting than when you're in between parts?

There's no such thing as happiness, only concentration. When you're concentrated, you're happy. Also, when you're not thinking about yourself a lot, you're usually happy.

So what motivates you now? What keeps you going?

Well, I have to go to the bathroom right now. [*Big smile*] Next time we get together, I'll do some Shakespeare for you.

1990

THE RETURN OF MICHAEL CORLEONE

When Entertainment Weekly *was a young magazine looking to show they were in for the long haul, an editor contacted me about doing a cover story about Al because he was reviving his role as Michael Corleone in Coppola's* Godfather III. *It was the most anticipated film of the year. The first two had already become classics, and here was the long-awaited continuation of the Corleone saga.* Entertainment Weekly *wasn't alone in wanting Pacino—four other national magazine editors had gotten in touch with me about him. In the end I left it up to Al—was he interested in any of them? He wasn't, but he told me to go with the one that offered the biggest payday. And that's how* EW *got this story.*

They made me an offer I couldn't refuse.

"Sign it 'Big Boy,'" commanded a very particular ten-year-old who was standing by Al Pacino's table at the Old World restaurant in Westwood, Los Angeles; he wanted an autograph, and he wanted Pacino to sign as the character he played in *Dick Tracy.* So the actor grabs a napkin and complies. On another occasion, outside the chic Chaya Brasserie, a teenage girl shyly praised his work in *Raging Bull*; Pacino politely thanked her, not mentioning that the work in question was Robert De Niro's. At the Dorothy Chandler Pavilion, where Pacino went to hear the London Classical Players perform Beethoven's Fourth on period instruments, a young man approached him and said, "I bet my friend you're *not* Al Pacino." The actor shrugged and told him he'd just lost a bet.

AL PACINO WITH HIS PARENTS, SALVATORE AND ROSE, IN 1940.

AT AGE FOUR OR FIVE ON THE ROOF OF HIS BUILDING IN THE SOUTH BRONX.

PACINO AT AGE FIVE OR SIX.

A RARE PICTURE OF PACINO WITH HIS FATHER IN ABOUT 1944.

WITH LEE STRASBERG AT LEE'S 75TH BIRTHDAY PARTY.

AL WITH CHARLIE LAUGHTON.

LARRY GROBEL WITH AL AND LUCKY ON THE PADDLE TENNIS COURT IN 1987.

AL WITH JULIE, HIS OLDEST DAUGHTER, IN 2005.

AL AS BIG BOY, WITH MADONNA AND PAUL SORVINO ON THE SET OF
DICK TRACY IN 1989.

AL WITH UCLA STUDENTS AT GROBEL'S THE ART OF THE INTERVIEW SEMINAR IN 2001.

ON THE SET OF
THE MERCHANT OF VENICE
IN 2004.

WITH FORMER MANAGER AND PRODUCER MARTY BREGMAN IN 2006.

GROBEL AND PACINO IN BEVERLY HILLS, 2005.

Pacino is one of the most accomplished actors of his generation, but no one seems quite sure who he is. In an era when stars of his magnitude are recognized everywhere they go, Pacino is getting picked out for a cartoon-ish supporting role he played with makeup disfiguring half his face, for a part he did not play, and for not being himself. Unlike Nicholson or Hoffman he has no strong public persona apart from his characters. And even his roles, ranging from the mastery of *The Godfather* movies to the intensity of *Serpico* and *Dog Day Afternoon* to embarrassing missteps like *Revolution*, send an enigmatic message. Instead of plotting his career along traditional points of stardom, Pacino seems to choose his parts according to some inner compass, often playing quirky roles that do little to enhance his fame—but that engage his fascination with the *process* of acting.

In fact, Pacino sometimes seems happiest when his acting projects are most obscure. For much of the 1980s he was absent from the screen while he labored in small theater workshops and endlessly polished a self-produced, self-financed film that has been shown only at small private screenings. At times it seems that Pacino actively evades his public; the passionate actor is a reluctant star. Perhaps it's no coincidence that *The Local Stigmatic*, the movie he's been tinkering with for years, is about a man attacked by thugs simply because he is famous.

Still, the fame has been inescapable. Pacino's intense stare has burned its way into our cultural consciousness. When John Travolta's Tony Manero in *Saturday Night Fever* closes his door and looks at the poster on his wall, it is Pacino as Frank Serpico who looks back at Travolta grunting his macho war cry, "Al Pa*cino*!" When he turned fifty this year, Pacino bumped into Bruce Springsteen on the street, and Springsteen took off his satin jacket and gave it to him as a birthday present. Francis Coppola, who has directed the actor in all three *Godfather*s, attributes Pacino's impact on-screen to his ability to project "coldness when he wants to be cold, and heat when he wants to be hot."

At the center of the Pacino mystique stands Michael Corleone, the Mafia chieftain and tragic hero of the *Godfather* pictures. It has been Pacino's fortune—he might say his burden—to play the pivotal role in what many consider the greatest of modern movies. It's a role he owned from the time Coppola first considered the project. "When I read the book," the director said, "I visualized the character as having Pacino's face." The first two films have earned nine Oscars and about eight hundred million dollars. More important, they have become a grand metaphor for modern life, what critic Pauline Kael called "an epic vision of the corruption of America."

The first *Godfather* ended when Michael Corleone looked into his wife Kay's eyes and lied to her about not having been involved with the murder of his sister's husband. *Godfather II* ended in 1959 with Michael all alone, staring out at the lake where he'd had his brother Fredo killed. In *Godfather III* it's 1979 and Michael is hoping to divorce himself from mob affairs, but there's this one last temptation involving the Vatican and six hundred million dollars that pulls him back in.

A week before *The Godfather Part III* opened in eighteen hundred theaters, Pacino was standing just short of the summit of a remarkable career. The movie was plagued with problems, but if it were to deliver on the extravagant promise of the first two *Godfather*s, it would be a virtual coronation for Pacino. After so many shadowy years on the margins of Hollywood, he was clearly back in the forefront. He could even at long last have won the Oscar that had eluded him through four Best Actor nominations and one Best Supporting Actor nomination. At the time, he was about to start filming *Frankie and Johnny*, a love story with Michelle Pfeiffer. But Pacino takes an ironic pleasure in not acting like a star. Asked whether he looked forward to the opening of *Godfather III* and his future projects, the actor said evenly, "The last time I looked forward to anything was waiting for my Tom Mix spurs when I was a kid. I kept going to the mailbox, and they finally came—on the day my great-grandmother died. Since then I stopped looking forward to anything."

Sitting in his enormous suite in L.A.'s Four Seasons Hotel, Pacino pondered the origins of the third *Godfather* picture. He was dressed entirely in black—black silk pants, black silk shirt, black silk jacket—but his mood was upbeat. After months of work and worry he had just seen a rough version of the film on a VCR in his room, and seemed content with the results. "I didn't know if there would ever be a *Godfather III*," he said. "There was always a lot of talk, but Francis wasn't interested and I would never have done it without him. Francis has the feel for the material." After Coppola accepted Paramount's offer, which granted him complete creative control, Pacino signed on in the summer of 1989, but he still had his doubts. "I didn't know if I could be that guy again," he said. "Seventeen years have gone by; a lot has happened. Michael's not the most pleasant character."

The most fascinating aspect of the character in the earlier movies is how subtly he changes as he takes on the power of the don. Pacino was intrigued by the script for *Godfather III* because it portrays an older, remorseful, and still evolving Michael Corleone. "Francis gave him more colors as he got older and matured. Just to have come through and still be alive—a character like that would have to have reconciled himself to certain things."

In a Burbank studio Francis Coppola took a break from the marathon editing of *Godfather III* to recall how the fifty-five-million-dollar project got under way in January of 1989. Paramount wanted him to try to produce the movie in time for the 1990 holiday season, a tight deadline for a film that didn't even have a script at that point. Coppola enlisted Mario Puzo, author of the original novel and cowriter, with Coppola, of both earlier movies. "I worked out a concept," he said. "Then I met with Mario in Reno and talked it through." They put together an initial script in March and were still rewriting it when shooting began in November 1989. "You could tell just by reading the script that you are in *Godfather* territory," said Pacino. "*The Godfather* is Francis and Mario. When they get together, they immerse themselves in that world." The entire project moved at such a pace that it sometimes threatened to fly apart.

"Having your back to the wall can make you do some great things that you otherwise wouldn't have done," Coppola said, propping his feet on the studio sofa. The last few months have been frantic as he has rushed to finish the film, despite predictions that he would never meet his deadline. "I would have enjoyed working on the movie more, but at the same time I felt it had a life of its own," Coppola said. "It was coming alive, and it wanted to be born now and it *had* to be born now."

Coppola knows what it's like to have his back to the wall: After mortgaging his house to complete *Apocalypse Now* (1979), he lost his studio, Zoetrope, in the financial fiasco of 1982's *One From the Heart*, and further tarnished his reputation with the expensive disappointments *The Cotton Club* (1984) and *Tucker: The Man and His Dream* (1988). All of that became an indirect part of *Godfather III*'s evolution. As much as he resisted making the saga a trilogy, Coppola remained fascinated by the Corleone story; his own aesthetic drives and financial straits conspired to make finishing the *Godfather* cycle a kind of destiny.

Coppola is not noted for stress-free movie production, but the third *Godfather* was particularly harrowing. "This is a big one. This is like *King Lear*," Pacino said last spring while the movie was shooting in Rome, noting that he hadn't had a day off in ten weeks. Besides the grueling schedule and the multiple shoots in Rome, Sicily, New York, and Atlantic City, chaos dogged the project. On the day of her first scene, Winona Ryder (cast as Michael's daughter, Mary) dropped out, complaining she was exhausted from shooting three movies back to back. In a highly unpopular move, Coppola replaced her with his then eighteen-year-old daughter Sofia, whose only film experience was bit parts in her father's movies, most notably as Michael's infant godson during the baptism scene in the first *Godfather*. Many on the set and at Paramount protested the choice, but Pacino now defends Coppola. "He thought that would serve us in the film," Pacino said, "because his vision of the part was that kind of innocence. He knew what he wanted. Casting is what a director does, it's part of his expression. So you have to grant him that."

Another unpopular bit of casting was the replacement of Robert Duvall, the Corleones' consigliere in the earlier films, with a new character played by George Hamilton. Duvall asked Paramount for a reported $3.5 million to return, and after rounds of haggling refused to join the project. Pacino laments Duvall's absence. "The character he portrayed so subtly and vividly had such a place in those two pictures," he said. "I don't want to make Bobby into a villain here. He must have had his reasons. But, yes, Duvall was missed." Still, Pacino was impressed by Hamilton. "I never met a guy like him," said Pacino. "He's what I would call an authentic high roller. He's capable of doing much more than he's been given a chance to."

Another new member of the cast was Andy Garcia, playing the illegitimate son of Michael Corleone's dead brother Sonny, who becomes Michael's potential successor. Garcia, a star of *Black Rain* and *The*

Untouchables, was in awe of Pacino on and off the set. "I opened a lot of doors for him," Garcia remembers. "Even when the cameras weren't rolling, I was still opening doors." Gazing at Pacino, made up to look sixty, Garcia found himself thinking, "When I get older, *that's* what I'm going to look like."

Diane Keaton, who played Michael Corleone's wife, Kay, in the first two *Godfather*s, was also back. She and Pacino had an on-and-off romance through much of the eighties, and though the couple split soon after their work on the new film ended, Pacino remains an admirer. "Diane is one of our foremost actresses," he said. "To see her go from that girl in *Baby Boom* to *Godfather III* is a transformation that's exciting. In the first two films her character was youthful and always looked a bit out of it. But in *III* a new awareness has come to her. It allows Diane to use her talent more fully." Then he slipped effortlessly into discussing the characters Michael and Kay. "Michael loved her when he met her and he loved her throughout his life and he loves her to this day, even though their relationship was surrounded by a lie. He not only loves her, he admires her."

Many actors try to keep their private and professional lives separate. Pacino's and Keaton's have often been intertwined. "Our relationship at times has been complicated," he conceded, and he sees value in that. "It's generally more interesting to work with people you know—that's why a lot of families act together. It's like being a trapeze act: You depend on each other, and when you know each other's moods and rhythms, you are able to guide each other and get across." Rumors flew during the filming of *Godfather III* that there was tension between them, and Pacino didn't deny it but said that tension was not an acting ploy. "Everyone who has ever breathed has had these things happen, but it wasn't because we were preparing for our roles. That's a misconception. There are actors who consciously and unconsciously choose to set up these kinds of juxtapositions to serve their roles, but I am not one of those actors." He paused to think about that: Pacino is a great one for mulling things over endlessly. "Maybe I *was*," he added, "but I certainly don't feel I'm that way now."

Pacino likes to think and talk—exhaustively—about his roles before filming begins. He has a soul mate in Coppola. "When he theorizes," marvels

Pacino, "all you have to do is listen for ten minutes and you've been given a wealth of imaginative, stimulating insights and images. I've read where people compare him to the don, but he's more an *emperor*sario—maybe we've found a new word—than a don. He's intense, preoccupied, doesn't miss a trick. He's a maestro." Coppola values the same traits in Pacino: "I tend to have a running stream of dialogue with Al, telling him how I feel, what's gone on before, more or less random thoughts, knowing he will seize on something that's helpful and disregard what isn't. Al is one of the most intelligent actors I've worked with."

In the *Godfather* films Pacino sees a sweep that is nothing short of Shakespearean. "There is the king, who is the don [Marlon Brando], and there are his sons and his kingdom. The don's life is threatened; he knows he is going to die. Which son will defend him? He loses one, Sonny, and the other one, Fredo, is inadequate. And then there's the third one, who comes to his aid and takes over the kingdom, even though he never wanted it."

But for all that grandeur, Pacino thinks, the movies speak to viewers in a very intimate way. He compares the situation of the Corleone brothers to that of second-generation immigrants in general. "The first generation of Italian Americans in this country brought with them the old cultural ways. The second generation sacrificed themselves for the third, which was supposed to achieve the American dream of power, success, and money. It has to do with holding on to your family, the old values versus the new, the old country and the new. It's a family film, and it always has been. I think that explains its popularity."

At the Burbank studio where Coppola has been editing *Godfather III*, the director, producer Fred Roos, and Pacino are sitting in a screening room watching a scene from the almost-finished movie. On the screen Michael Corleone is alone, kneeling by the casket of an old don, a man who had been his protector and surrogate father in Italy. As he quietly speaks to the old man, Michael slowly loses the steely composure that has masked his emotions ever since he became a don himself. Finally he breaks down and weeps. "It has to do with the fractiousness of family today," Pacino says, "of the old values versus the new, of the acquisition of power, of redemption and betrayal." It's a crucial scene, the kind that wins Oscars, and even in this rough black-and-white working version, it's a powerful moment.

When the lights come up, the three men sit quietly. Then Pacino speaks. He's concerned that several lines of dialogue have been cut, and he thinks they should be restored, perhaps as a voice-over. Coppola is under intense pressure to get this movie locked; a delay of even a few days would mean missing the all-important Christmas Day release. But he listens to Pacino and promises to reconsider.

"That's the great thing about Francis," Pacino says on the way to the parking lot. "He listens." And he should. By now, hearing Pacino discuss Michael Corleone—a character he has known most of his career—is like getting advice from the don himself. To Pacino the casket scene reveals the crux of Michael's tragic nature. "Michael can't understand why this old man was so loved while he is feared," he explains. "Because Michael always wanted to do good with his life, but he never got that kind of response. He says, 'Why? Because I thought too much about things? Was it my heart? Or my mind? I wanted what you wanted.' It's so revealing," Pacino muses, "it touches a universal nerve."

"We tried in the third one to deal with the cathartic themes of finally dealing with your life and coming to terms with your sins," Coppola says. "I'm making it from the point of view of a man in his fifties; I'm getting the inkling that what I do now counts more for what comes after me than for me." For Pacino at fifty the part of an older, more rueful Michael Corleone may just be the role of his career. When he talks about Michael, it's hard not to see Pacino reflected in the words. "I've thought a lot about Michael as an enigma," Pacino says, "someone who makes you feel uneasy. He's someone who is searching. It's about destiny and someone who has resisted his destiny."

The *Los Angeles Times* calls *Godfather III* "the most anticipated film of the last decade," and Pacino's performance will be crucial to its reception. "It's a picture people seem to be rooting for," Pacino mildly observes, "even in the industry." If the picture succeeds, Pacino may receive a measure of respect and recognition to surpass even the triumphs of his early years. How does it all feel?

"It doesn't do anything to me," says Pacino. "I'm just an actor." After all this time he maintains that playing Michael Corleone isn't a challenge. "A challenge is a role you find difficult," he says. "Doing a great role is an opportunity. It's a gift to be able to play a part that can afford your acting talents to be freed."

LOOKING FOR AL

I was meeting Al for lunch at the Four Seasons Hotel in Beverly Hills. Outside the hotel an attractive black woman in an African-print dress swallowed hard and hesitantly approached him. "Excuse me," she said to the unshaven actor whose wrinkled clothes looked more Sears than the Armani they were, "but I'm in the middle of this fixation with you. I've been watching your films every weekend, and I just wanted to tell you how much I think of you."

Pacino smiled, thanked her shyly, and said he hoped she would see the film he'd recently produced, directed, and starred in. "It's called Looking for Richard," *he said. "It's a kind of docudrama about Shakespeare's* Richard III, *only it's more than that. I think you might enjoy it."*

The woman promised to look for it and graciously left without asking for his autograph.

Pacino: See what I mean. I told you if we got out of the house, we'd have encounters. People on the street come up to me, they talk to me.

[We walk through the lobby and out to the patio. A nervous waiter approaches. "Mr. Pacino, I hate to trouble you, but the last time you were here you forgot to pay your bill. I'm sure it was just an oversight."

"Why didn't you charge it to me?"

"You don't have an account here. I can just leave it, and you can take care of it with today's bill."]

You wanted to get out. You're out!

[*Looking at a man sitting alone, his head buried in a book*] That guy there, reading and eating, annoys the hell out of me. He's not tasting his food, I can tell you that right now.

I do that when I'm alone.

You read and eat? How can you read and eat? You don't enjoy your food. That's like reading and listening to music. You read and listen to music?

Yes.

You can listen to Beethoven and read a book?

Yes, and I sometimes write with Beethoven in the background, while eating a sandwich.

You're a drag, is all I can say. You're just a drag.

Why shouldn't I be stimulated while I'm thinking?

I say, "Who do you think you are?" That's what I say. Either you're listening to Beethoven, because that's what's happening, or you're reading a fucking book. You can't do both. [*He stares at the guy.*] Should I go over and tell him? Think it would matter?

Sometimes eating is just nourishment.

Then you should do it intravenously.

Now you're being silly.

What else can I be? I've been talking to you for two days. You haven't asked me one fucking intelligent question.

If O. J. Simpson were sitting where that guy is and came over to shake your hand, would you?

That's an interesting question. People think, "What would I do if I ran into O. J.?" At first you see someone whose face is familiar. Then you have to think about the context. You'd have to decide whether you think he's guilty or not, and should you be shaking his hand, and you drive yourself nuts. I would trust my reaction.

Do you think he got away with murder?

I wouldn't go on the record with that, one way or the other. I would stay away from that.

Would you have stayed away from him—or whoever was killing his ex-wife, Nicole—if you had been Ron Goldman and stumbled onto that scene?

You never know how you're going to react. Something strange happened to me recently in the city. I was coming from my apartment on the East Side late at night, and a woman across the street was being sort of accosted by a guy walking behind her. He wasn't doing anything physical, but she was nervous. Suddenly I'm in a drama, the knee-shaking kind. I had to do something. So I went out to the middle of the street and started walking in a way that made my presence known. I was monitoring my distance to her and the guy and thinking about what would happen if a weapon were drawn, and I thought, *I'm in the middle of this. This is nuts.* But I did it. She saw me and came into the street and started walking behind me, and I was thinking, *What the hell am I going to do if this explodes?* Then another guy came out, and everything was cool again. Manhattan.

The city you can never leave.

I ever tell you about the coat I bought when I was feeling cold? I was wandering around the city, it must have been winter, and I saw this tan overcoat in a window. I went in, got fitted, paid the guy. He wanted to do a little thing to the coat, so I left it at the store and was going to pick it up later. But I forgot the store where I bought it. Now somebody's got that coat, and I paid for it.

Somebody also has your BMW.

Oh, that was funny. I paid cash, thirty-five thousand, for this BMW, and while I was purchasing it I knew it was wrong. First of all it was white, and new, and I'm not really a good car person. I should have a Jeep or something. I drove it to my apartment and parked it in front, but I kept thinking, *It doesn't fit. It's making me uncomfortable. It looks too showy.* So I went upstairs and had a cup of coffee, came down, and the car was gone. I just started laughing. It was a vivid moment.

Do you lose a lot of stuff?

With me it's a trail of missing things. Lighters, cigarettes, umbrellas. I've long given up on umbrellas—that's why I wear hats.

At least those things aren't expensive, like cars.

It's all expensive. Everything costs a thousand dollars, no matter what it is.

Do you lose keys?

No, I have keys tied to me. I had a key implant.

Your wallet?

Never goes out of my pants. That's why I wear the same black pants for fourteen years.

Are there things you want? I mean the way the character in Saul Bellow's *Henderson the Rain King* had this nagging voice inside him saying, "I

want, I want, I want."

Yeah, I've heard that voice. It said, "I want, I want, I want—pizza."
[*Laughs*] I don't know . . . We know nothing. If somebody wants—I don't
know what the hell that is. Want what? It's all relative to me. So Saul
Bellow's guy goes into the jungle—I don't envy the guy. Where is he
now?

Still on the pages of Bellow's novel.

Did you ask Bellow if he ever went into the jungle?

Only in his mind—he wrote the book never having been to Africa.

He probably never goes out of his house. See what I mean?

Not really. Why don't you tell me what you mean?

Sometimes you ask a question that is so general, so unspecific, I think
you've become laid back or something. When did that happen? That's
California. You used to have those piercing eyes. Now you just say, "This
guy's dull. He's a dull actor; he thinks he's Don Rickles."

Hey, I have never thought that.

I wish I were. Sometimes I get this urge to be funny in public and
think that I can do what Robin Williams does. So I try it and it's a real
turkey.

**You were pretty funny dancing the tango with Barbara Walters on TV.
What was that about?**

That was about a guy who was hiding. I was terrified, and I managed to
reveal very little, which was not her fault because she was scared herself. I
was a tough interview. I'm thinking of going on *Larry King Live* for *Richard*,

but it scares me to death because what happens is you hurt yourself. You can't help it. You say things you don't mean.

Have you thought about what you'll be asked by the women who will inevitably call into King's show?

I don't care about the questions. It's how I answer them.

You're going to get the marriage questions. Why haven't you been, and will you ever?

I don't know why I haven't gotten married. It seems simple to me, but I guess it's more complicated than I admit to myself. There were a couple of times I maybe could have done it, and I sort of feel I should have, at least once. Maybe I don't care about marriage. Maybe I don't believe in it.

Do you or don't you?

On that subject I am unclear. My mother and father didn't make it together. There's a high divorce rate. Maybe people shouldn't think about that when they're married. You've got me talking about this stuff, and I don't think I have anything to add to the subject of why people marry or don't.

I think you touched on it with your mother and father.

Well, then, there are a lot of me's around, because a lot of people come from broken homes. My dad's been married five times. The only time I think about it is when somebody talks to me about it. But I know if I were in a situation with someone where I felt it worked for us, I would marry. I have no problem with marriage. I'm as ready to get married now as I ever was.

Yeah—you're not at all ready to get married, and you have plenty of problems with marriage.

Would you be asking me these questions if I had been married once?

No.

Why?

Because you would have gone through the experience.

You'd just say, "How come you're not married now?"

No, because you would have shown you could commit to someone.

This used to be fashionable five years ago. Now nobody talks about it. Look at "commit" in the dictionary. Marriage is not part of the definition. I'll tell you what, the library's downtown. Why don't you go there and call me in a week. I think I'm gonna commit you.

You know what the antonym to "commit" is?

What?

Al Pacino.

You're out to lunch. I've committed to people my whole life.

On your terms.

Believe me, it wasn't always my terms. I don't know what world you are in.

Not the same one you're in. You've been famous a long time. Ever wish you weren't?

I want to tell you about anonymity for an actor. Very important to me. That's why I'm reluctant about interviews. Once you know things about an actor, as you're watching his work, you start to read into it. I read a book on

Montgomery Clift and then saw him in *A Place in the Sun,* which was fascinating. But I was fascinated with the guy I read about, and I wasn't in the picture, in his performance as much. I wasn't listening to the violin being played, I was looking at the violinist. That's what concerns me and always has.

Did reading about Clift diminish him?

It's not a question of diminishing. It alters his work and what he as an artist is trying to portray. That's what I've been trying to preserve. To keep the characters as pure as possible. And that's why I always say my work speaks for me. But we are in a world of promotion today. So while you do that, you still try to maintain your—

Mystery?

Yeah. I don't try to be mysterious for the sake of being mysterious. I do it for the work. The overexposure of an actor is a strong idea with me. Even when I go see a play, there's a tendency for me not to go backstage. Simply because I want to keep the performance that I've seen. I don't want the illusion broken.

Are actors too overexposed?

No, I don't think so. Actors suffer a problem we all have: We have to learn to cope with fame and attention. There's a contradiction there. In a way you have to be an observer and have anonymity to approach the work freely. Sometimes the lure of fame is there with all the sirens calling you, and so you're torn. That's where I've seen actors go from actors to personalities. They become so flattered and turned on to that fame that they lose their purpose. They get caught up in their celebrity and stay there.

[*The ice cream we ordered arrives. Pacino's eyes widen.*]

Wait till you taste this; it's your youth.

How come you can talk to me?

Because somehow we found a mutuality. You were at a certain point in your life, as I was in mine, and the timing was there for it. I knew when I first met you—what, seventeen years ago?—that that wouldn't happen again.

Didn't it ever worry you, to befriend a journalist?

In the end it doesn't matter what you do but who you are. I don't know why we clicked when we did, but we did. I got to see you and your family and your house and to know you as a human being. We've gone through so much. I told you about my having a kid before almost anyone else. The one-on-one as a journalist is a whole other thing. You collect information in a certain way. You assume your own rules. Sometimes you just don't get it, but, then, you're coming from a different place. The big thing is that I trusted you, after I saw the first thing you wrote, because you were fair to me. Do you still think of me as your older brother?

Sometimes. When we wrestle. How would you describe yourself?

I'm easy. I know you don't think so. If something were bothering you, you'd tell me, wouldn't you? You'd trust me?

Sure.

Would you trust me with your life?

What does that mean?

That in the end, no matter what you think of me, and we've been through a lot, I think you would. That says something about a relationship. I'd trust you with a secret. I'd trust you to keep your word. And I think you'd trust me that way.

At what point would you not trust me?

In what way would you not trust me?

I asked you first.

No, you didn't. Listen to the tape, play it back. I asked *you* first. Trust me. [*Laughs*] Got you there.

All right, I'd trust you with my life. Would you trust me with yours?

Yeah.

How many people do you feel that way about?

A lot more than I thought. Five or six. And I had some very close people die on me.

[*There is a silence between us. I'm giving him time to think about his boyhood friend Cliffy; his brother Fredo in* The Godfather, *John Cazale, who died of cancer in 1978; his* American Buffalo *costar Jimmy Hayden; his mentor Lee Strasberg. Or perhaps he's thinking of his dogs, Lucky and Susie, whose deaths touched him deeply. He breaks the silence with a bit of irreverence.*]

You know what your problem is, Larry? Either you're getting old or you don't look at me fresh anymore. I'm like used goods to you.

I'm thinking.

No, you're not thinking. You're dozing.

So far, I'm laid back, glassy-eyed, and half senile. You're tougher on me than I am on you.

Because I love ya. In the end, when the cows come home to roost, that's all that counts.

Speaking of love . . .

Here we go. You're starting to drool. You're heading somewhere.

What is love to you?

"Perdition catch my soul, but I do love thee, and, when I love thee not, chaos is come again."

From?

Guess.

Richard III?

Othello. Sometimes it's hard to articulate it, and that's why Shakespeare's so great. You hear it and you go, "That's exactly how I feel." Think of it: You're in love, and all of a sudden life comes into focus. Before that person was in your life, it was chaos. And when that person is gone, chaos returns. With love there is a wholeness; you eliminate the chaos. It's the highest form of civilized life. That's Shakespeare. You understand? That's the beauty. That's how you relate to it.

You know what Anthony Hopkins said about doing Shakespeare? That he'd rather be in Malibu. To him it's a bloody nightmare. Dead stuff. You're doing what fifteen thousand actors have done before you. As far as he's concerned, Stratford-on-Avon should be knocked down and paved over.

He sounds like a reformed minister who's turned against the church . . . or God. I don't know if he really feels that way, frankly. Beethoven is old, Mozart is old; why play them?

Hopkins feels he doesn't belong in the English theater because it's the

same old thing, Chekhov and Shakespeare, like a Laundromat going around and around.

You've got some hard-on for Anthony? Leave the guy alone. Life's tough. I don't know why he's saying those things. Apparently, he doesn't want to do theater anymore. Let's give Anthony Hopkins some oranges from that tree there; let's send him some. We'll send him a picture of Chekhov with a big smile saying, "Anthony, I love you. Come back, Anthony."

[*We leave the hotel and drive to a coffee shop on Sunset Boulevard.*]

How come you keep coming back to Shakespeare, since your stage experience with *Richard III* didn't meet with critical success?

Shakespeare is the writer most likely to touch us, because he speaks to the emotions and feelings that are in all of us, and he speaks to them in the grandest way. We feel enormous things, and Shakespeare, in his genius and incredible sense of the human phenomena, was able to reach through to us and touch those feelings. He encompasses the size of stuff we feel. If he's talking about love, it is in such a way as you have felt it on your great love day. You can release it through Shakespeare because he gives you so much. To block yourself off from the deepest primal places that Shakespeare goes to because of some idea that he is highfalutin or above it all would be to deprive yourself of something. It's not everybody's taste, but there're a lot of people who don't like Beethoven, either.

There seems to be almost a Shakespearean revival in the movies, with Mel Gibson, Ian McKellen, Kenneth Branagh, Laurence Fishburne, and now yourself all filming the Bard. When did you know you wanted to make your directorial debut with such a risky project?

When I was going to colleges doing poetry readings around 1977. When I came to Shakespeare, people didn't want to hear it. I couldn't believe that in a reputable college they didn't know *Hamlet*. I would start to explain it but in a colloquial-style language I felt they would understand, and I thought they would start getting it. As I moved from that into the Shakespearean dialogue, it was easier for them to grasp because they had been tuned up and were ready to hear it; they had lost their prejudice. See, the ear automatically closes when it hears Shakespeare, and it doesn't open easily. You have to coax it. That was the seed of my movie, that's when my movie was born.

But why did you choose *Richard III*? It's such a complicated play.

Because it was the one I knew best, having done it so many times onstage.

[*At the coffee shop we order two strawberry-banana smoothies. Al pulls out a small Tootsie Roll from his pocket and puts it in his mouth.*]

Here, you can eat the wrapper. It's got a little flavor on it, that paper.

How did *Looking for Richard* come about? What you've done isn't exactly the play as Shakespeare wrote it. You're out there interviewing street bums and Oxford scholars, you're swinging on a swing wearing a baseball cap backward and reciting monologues, you're setting off fire alarms in Shakespeare's bedroom in Stratford, you're sitting around a table with Kevin Spacey and Penny Allen arguing how to play a scene, you're in costume seducing Winona Ryder, sending Alec Baldwin to the tower, screaming for your horse. People are going to have to be prepared for this—it's unlike anything they might expect.

Yes, but I think there is an audience for this movie. Everybody's always interpreting it in different ways. This is just another way. I didn't want to do the entire play; I wanted to do a taste. Maybe that's what it should be called: *A Taste of Richard*. The person who sees this picture and enjoys it the most is the person who has a respect for Shakespeare but is afraid of Shakespeare. Like Lee Strasberg used to say when they asked him to swim in the ocean: "I love the water, but I don't want to get involved." There's that kind of a thing with Shakespeare: "I like it, I know it's good, but please, Al, I don't want to go through all that." This picture takes all that away; it allows you in. It's not like we're doing it backward or something.

Why did you use your own money to finance it?

There's something liberating about that, because you don't have anyone to answer to. All you have is your canvas and your paints, and you start putting it up there and seeing where it goes. It's like writing something on spec, except the paper is very expensive and the pen costs a lot too. But I'm not doing anything that hasn't been done before. Orson Welles, John Cassavetes, they spent their lives doing that. They'd give up their houses to do a movie. When your passion is connected to it, you go for it.

I've seen eight different cuts of *Looking for Richard* over the years, and I still have a hard time pinning it down. Is it a documentary? A film about the making of a play? How do you define it?

That's what I say to myself: *What is it?* I'm worried about that. When you say Shakespeare, people aren't going to want to come. Then you say documentary, and they're really not going to want to come. The fear is that it's a documentary of Shakespeare, or it's a docudrama, and linking those two words is almost insurmountable. So you have to be careful how you pitch it, because it isn't that. It's entertainment. They want me to call it a personal film, a personal journey. Harvey Weinstein at Miramax thinks it's a non-fiction film. It's a jaunt, it's jubilant. I enjoy the humor of it; the things that happen spontaneously on the street are very funny. We can call it *Funnybones*.

And will you promote it as "Al Pacino as you've never seen him before"?

I've got a problem with that. That stuff has always been a pain in the ass, frankly. Who is Al Pacino? What does that mean? After this many years of being an actor, it's almost insulting to ask me about who I am. I hope every part I play is as-you've-never-seen-me from the last part I played.

But in this particular film there are many different you's: There's the on-camera director and producer, there's the contemporary actor struggling to get his part and the meaning of the play, there's the character of Richard III, and there's the guy I'm talking with right now. So it is like nothing the audience has seen before.

You want to say that, go for it. But it seems egocentric. Al Pacino is separate from the part I'm playing, from what I'm trying to say as an actor. Al Pacino is personal. As the actor and the filmmaker, you want Al Pacino to stay out of the way. But at the same time you need him because he's selling the picture, giving it a kind of identity. But you can't promote it like that—it sounds artificial, Barnumesque.

[*He tastes the smoothie the proprietor brought, and makes a face, not liking it.*]

There are moments in the film when you're walking the streets of New York, people are recognizing you, and then you start to become King Richard. It's a metamorphosis that takes place before our eyes. Where did that inspiration come from?

I got that from watching Picasso paint in a documentary. He had a glass he put in front of the camera, and it started off as a flower and then it turned into a woman's private parts and then it blossomed out into the rest of her—this flower became this woman. He finished the sketch in less than two minutes right in front of your eyes, then stood there with the sketch, and it was magical. It didn't matter that we had just seen him do this. It had its own life. I was inspired by that and wanted to see if that kind of thing could happen in acting—and *Richard* was the opportunity to do it. In regular movies you want the story to take us away and get us involved, but the nature of this film is showing process, and eventually you get into *Richard* and you forget about process. You're into the story, and you don't know how you got there. That's the trick.

This is the second film you've done at your own pace with your own money. The first, *The Local Stigmatic*, you've never released. Would it be fair to call these your private obsessions?

No. Obsession is a pejorative. I don't think one's work, one's passion, is obsession. I think one has a fixation on something. We spend a lifetime doing stuff that's out of our hands. I just made a movie, *Donnie Brasco*, and whatever I did is in that director's hands. A lot of people's work in our business has been dictated by the clock. Because the clock says you've got to bring in a film in this much time, we think, "Oh, if you've got the deadline, you'll do it." I think that's a crock. As long as the clock is ticking and you're trying to accommodate that, your technique and vision are going to just accommodate that. It's got to affect it. So, if you take the clock away and just deal with the event, with what you're doing, then that's what I'm doing. I just remove the clock. But I'll tell you this, *Looking for Richard* has cured me of documentary filmmaking. It's easier to do something already written than this freewheeling spinning and putting it together.

[*The proprietor comes and asks Pacino why he hasn't drunk the smoothie. "Tell me what's wrong with it, because my smoothies are famous," he demands.*

"How'd you hear about my not liking it? Was it on radio?" Pacino asks.

"On Hard Copy," *jokes the owner.*

"Don't worry about it. Maybe my taste is really caca."

The man leaves us. I drink my smoothie.]

How can you put something in your body that tastes like perfume? I think instead of drinking it you should pour it on yourself. Dab it behind your ears. Wonderful scent. Scent of a Smoothie.

I hope that Oscar hasn't gone to your head. Your puns were better when you were an eight-time nominee rather than a one-time winner.

You know, I was surprised how I felt after that. There was a kind of a glow that lasted a couple of weeks. I'd never had that feeling. It's kind of like winning an Olympic medal, because it is so identifiable. Only in the Olympics you win it because you're the best—with the Oscar that's not necessarily the case. It's just your turn.

You've been singled out for recognition at the Venice Film Festival, the

American Museum of the Moving Image, the Golden Globes. What has all this glory done for you?

I think it has helped my paddle-ball game. [*Lights a cigarette*] Every time I lose a point, I think of my awards, and I get back in the game.

I thought you quit smoking.

They're herbal. You don't die of cancer, you die of boredom. It smells like marijuana, so you come off kind of cool.

When's the last time you smoked a joint?

I smoked dope years ago. I wasn't big on it, but I liked it occasionally with wine.

Why not now?

I'm afraid of hallucinogens or mind-altering things. They make me feel muted. It's like living in a kind of gauze—it takes the power, the energy, the edge out of life.

Have you ever done acid?

I had acid laid on me when I was younger, in my thirties. It was terrifying. It was a Mickey Finn sort of thing. I knew there was something different happening to me, and it just escalated.

You mean it's not up there with seeing Madonna naked?

That's private information, Larry.

But you have seen her.

Yes, I have. She was doing a dance, and she was naked under her coat. In the course of the dance she became inspired and opened her coat, and there it was. She has an extraordinarily beautiful body, like cut out of ivory. One day when I'm old, and I'm wheeled out onto the porch wrapped in a blanket to get a little autumn sun on my face, if I have a beatific smile as I'm basking, I'll probably be thinking of that. [*He looks at his watch.*] If we were going to play paddle tennis, we'd better get moving.

Were you much of a womanizer when you were young?

Why would you say I'm a womanizer? I was brought up with women; I've lived with women all my life. I don't know anything else. They're my friends.

You lost the most important woman in your life when you were twenty-two. Do you think about her?

I think about my mother all the time. I heard this kid, Oscar De La Hoya, talking about his mother, who died before he had made it, and how the material things that he doesn't seem to have much feeling for, his mother would have gotten a lot out of. I feel the same way. I think my success would have saved my mother's life, because it was poverty that took her down. She died very young.

Your grandfather died right after your mother did. Were you there?

My grandfather came to this country motherless when he was four, and on his deathbed in the last moments of his life he was speaking in Sicilian to the mother he never knew. Life . . . What the heck, somebody is going to tell me the truth about something? Come on.

[*At the paddle-tennis court Al puts on new sneakers and tells an anecdote about hiding in his grandmother's closet, then jumping out when her leopard-skin coat seemed to move on its own.*]

Were those happy times for you, the innocence of childhood?

Every time I think of happy I think of h-a-p-p-y. It's a funny word. I think of slaphappy. What's "happy"? There are feelings of well-being and comfort and peace, love, of feeling assured.

And then there's the confusion of getting those Tom Mix spurs in the mail on the day your great-grandmother died.

Why all this pressure to be happy? What difference does that make? Things are the way they are. Things happen.

Maybe happiness is convincing a girl you're worthy of her.

If that's happiness, how's this for unhappy: I was once auditioning for a part in a play in acting school and had to sing a little. A girl I had a crush on was waiting outside the audition room, sitting on a staircase with a guy she liked. I didn't get the part, and afterward I came out, and she was there and she looked up at me as if to say, "That was not a very impressive audition." And with that look she said aloud, "I didn't know you could sing." I said, "Yeah, and I can fly, too." And with that I leaped over her down a whole flight of stairs. That *really* didn't impress her. And as I was in midair I thought, *This isn't working*. I knew that guys who would do that don't stand a chance with girls.

[*We begin to play ball.*]

Why do you keep looking at your watch after each point?

Leave me alone.

What is it about this game that keeps you coming back?

So I can beat you.

We'll stop playing once you win?

You only think I can't. I pretend to lose to you.

You're the great pretender. The very definition of an actor.

It's wild being an actor. You take your psyche and bounce it off walls.

Of all the characters you've played, which played most havoc with your psyche?

I felt the most disturbed when I played that race-car driver in *Bobby Deerfield*. It was a personal journey into someone who was isolated and depressed. And it was the first time I was sober. I'm not terribly fond of that performance, but I felt close to it at the time because I was moving away from a world I had known—I'd had a lot of successes in a row. I felt like I had been shot out of a cannon, and I was a little isolated.

You also felt isolated after the initial reviews of *Scarface* came in and they weren't the raves you and I both thought the picture would receive.

Scarface wasn't understood. It was about excess and avarice and everything being out of proportion. The character didn't try to explain himself. It was originally conceived so brilliantly by Paul Muni in the thirties, and that's who I emulated. Oliver Stone did a tremendous job bringing this character to life. It was a real piece of writing—when you hear lines quoted at you in the streets everywhere you go, and not the same lines either. I'm walking, and somebody says, "Hey, Tony? Can I go now?" These are the kinds of lines they quote. The picture had a fire to it. That was part of Brian's concept, to do everything in an extraordinary way— to have the violence blown up, the language blown up. The spirit of it was Brechtian, operatic. It didn't opt for sentiment but had an almost fablelike quality to it. It was probably the most popular picture I ever made, but the reaction to it was stranger than any of my other films. The picture was perceived by some as a failure, but it wasn't. It was a lot of movie. You go to a movie, you get a *lot* of movie with *Scarface*. That picture did something to me.

[*He hits a ball past me as I charge the net, but it goes wide.*]

Oh, Al!

[*After one set we stop. He mentions that he's been having trouble sleeping.*]

Do you ever dream of being King Richard III?

Yeah. With *Richard* I'd go to bed thinking about it and in the middle of the night get up.

What about playing real-life characters—do you like to meet the guys you play? Does it give you any insight?

When I met Frank Serpico, I saw in his eyes a maverick, eclectic person. I felt I would like to express what I saw in his face, but I was unable to do it. I avoided meeting the guy in *Dog Day Afternoon* because I had an idea of the kind of person I wanted to play. That was a mistake—it would have served me to meet him. It always does.

What about Michael Corleone? Did you ever meet his Mafia prototype?

No, but I was lucky there. Francis had created this character, and I clearly saw the way he wanted it.

Were you as clear about *Godfather III* as you were about the first two?

There had been a sixteen-year respite between the second and the third one, and it felt odd to pick up that character again. It was also a feeling of "I've been here before," so it was easier to play. But the third one didn't seem so focused as the other two; it seemed unfinished. We missed the Duvall character strongly.

How would the film have changed if Duvall had been in it?

Michael's relationship with Duvall's character, Tom Hagen, was the catalyst for his involvement in that whole thing with the church. Hagen was under a lot of pressure, and his life was being threatened and finally he was killed, and it was Michael's investigating his murder that brought him into the church. He wasn't coming there with hat in hand. A totally different idea. And to suddenly switch that around—as much of a genius as Francis is—that's a hard one.

Was Duvall's absence because he wasn't offered as much money as you?

That's what he says, but I don't know.

What else could it be?

Think about it. That's all I'll say. Just think about it.

Okay, I've thought about it. It has to be the money—that's what it always boils down to. Why else would you remove yourself from the third part of one of cinema's great trilogies?

Because we actors are nuts.

It wasn't nuts for Michael Mann to get you and De Niro together for *Heat*. That was a long time coming. Were you as conscious of the hype created by the two of you acting together for the first time and the inevitable comparisons over who's the better actor?

No, I wasn't aware that would happen. We weren't "Dueling Banjos" there. We were in it *together*, trying to bring off the moment. You feel good working with an actor like Bobby because you know he will be there with you. Having known Bobby as long as I have, it did make the situation easier.

De Niro seems very different from you, less relaxed, more edgy, though he looks at his watch almost as much as you do. Is he more wary of the media than you?

One time me and Bobby were at some event, and when we were leaving, he got me to go down a back way. I said, "No, Bobby, I think it's best we just go right out, have our pictures taken, so what? What's the big thing?" But we decided to avoid that. He said, "Don't worry about it. I know what I'm doing." That was a scene. We went down the wrong way. Bobby ended up getting caught between the revolving doors. [*Laughs at the memory*] I remember the vision; I was standing there looking at him, saying, "I guess we made a mistake." He's cool about that stuff now. Bobby doesn't care. When I was younger I did that more too; now, like Lee Strasberg told me long ago, you just got to accept it and adjust to it. I just keep wondering now every time people see me that they're going to say, "Still around? You're still around?"

Better than disappearing and having to start all over again.

I went to a one-year-old's birthday party the other day. I tell you, the kid was looking at the one candle on his cake, and he had a look on his face, he was so perplexed, he didn't get it. I said he looks exactly how I feel every time I have a birthday. One day when he gets older he's going to look back at the video of his first party, and he's going to say, "I had it right then. I knew what was going on." He was calling it as it is: "What is this about?"

It's about money, power, fame, and not falling from the high wire.

You think so, Larry?

I'm being cynical.

You're kidding. When I was a kid, I never had money. I was born and reared in poverty, and as I got older and was by myself, if I didn't eat, so what? I had a room with a bathroom in the hall. I lived like that, and it was part of life. Then when I was a superintendent, I was making fourteen dollars a week. Every time I'd get it, I'd spend it in three-and-a-half minutes—you'd have a couple of quarts of ale, and then nothing mattered. I remember sitting on the edge of the bed in this tiny room I lived in when I was a super, thinking, *What am I going to do? I have six and three-quarters days left before I get my fourteen dollars.* It was really boring to have to always be worried about where I was going to get my next meal. It was like a dull, persistent thud.

And now, with the money you make, the sound you hear must be like champagne corks popping.

It wasn't that long ago, the mid-eighties, where I didn't work for four years and ran out of dough.

That was after *Revolution* and before *Sea of Love*. Did your on-screen disappearance have anything to do with your dissatisfaction that *Revolution* was released before you thought it was ready?

The whole idea of presenting something as a piece of work that wasn't finished was odd to me. It had another six months of work. It was like selling somebody a car without a motor. Still, it affected me tremendously. I loved playing a guy who had to take care of himself and his family, living off the land, making his own fire, just surviving. It made me understand my roots and what it was like here two hundred years ago. When somebody talks about the Revolution now, I feel as though I've experienced it. But the audience saw something incomplete. You get upset when you move into your house and it doesn't have a kitchen. It made me feel at the time that I had no recourse. That the only thing I could do was to think about what I could do where I wouldn't have to have that feeling— and so I went off and did my own little film. I put a lot of money into doing *The Local Stigmatic*, and then I had a tax bite and owed the government, so I had to go make some movies. But I don't feel like I make money. I work, I make films, I do plays. I don't make money, that's not what I do.

So who's getting the millions for your services?

I like what Charles Bukowski said about money: Money's magic. It gets you things. You spend it, you use it to make movies, you give it to charity. You don't just take that money and make more money with it. I don't feel comfortable doing that. Maybe there's a reason for it, I don't know. It's just the way I've been.

So the stock market's not an option for you. Has your money ever made money for others?

Seventeen years ago, after seeing what they did to *Cruising*, I put a half-million dollars from the money they owed me into a trust fund. The interest still goes to everything from AIDS to the homeless to feeding children to supporting theaters. So there was some good that came out of that. [*Unlacing his sneakers*] We'll meet here in the morning, play another set. Maybe we can go to a baseball game one night.

I thought you didn't like to go where you might be spotted.

I love to go to the games, but I don't like when they put the camera on me. That's why I don't go to boxing matches. I don't want to feel like the announcer is going to come up to me afterward and ask what I thought of the fight.

Think you could hit a professional fastball?

Never. I'd like to go down to the batting cages and see where we are. My biggest problem as a baseball player was I couldn't hit a fastball. I could hit a curve, but not a fast curve, because I'd step in the bucket. I was with John Goodman in Toronto watching the Blue Jays play. This guy gets up; the pitcher throws the ball so fast, I don't see it. The batter swings—I hear it, but I don't see it. The third baseman catches it, I don't see it. He throws it to first, I never saw the ball. That's a beautiful thing. That's baseball.

[*His driver arrives to take him to Santa Monica to meet his friend Charlie, then to dinner with Harold and Susan Becker, Ellen Barkin, and some other people.*]

Why are you such a big shot?

Why? [*Barks out as his Big Boy Caprice character*] Because I was born that way. Big shots are born, they're not made.

If you could have selected your biographer, what writer would do you justice?

Dostoyevsky. Though he's not a lot of laughs.

Do you see yourself as a Dostoyevskian character?

No more. A couple of years ago, yeah. Now I'm more a Chekhovian character. I was brought up on many different writers, from Balzac to Shakespeare. I know I come from the streets and had no formal education, but I read this stuff, and it's the Russians that I really felt. Reading saved my life.

How smart do you think you are?

What's smart? Am I smart like Stephen Hawking or Joseph Campbell? No. Like Walter Cronkite? Yes. [*Laughs*] If I didn't do what I do, I'd probably be delivering packages to CAA.

When's the last time you were conned?

I was Jimmy Caan'd once. And it's happening now, isn't it? C'mon, snap that machine off so we can arm wrestle.

THE CENSURE OF THE WHICH

It's a beautiful sunny day in Los Angeles, one of those days when the smog seems to have disappeared behind some distant mountains and there's a fresh, foreign fragrance in the air. Al is fumbling for the seat belt in my 1975 Fiat Spider, finally giving up trying to find it. "I've got to learn how to get around out here," he says. "Maybe you could draw me a map. Something very simple, you know, so I can have an idea where things are." He looks up at the sky and says, "I like convertibles. If I get a car out here, it should be a convertible." Then he asks about a mutual friend, and I begin to answer as I head toward the Santa Monica Freeway. Al's looking up at the sky and out at the buildings, and I can see he's thinking, but not about what I'm saying.

You know, I don't mean to interrupt, but when Jack Warner and Sam Goldwyn and those guys were in control of the movies, it was a different place out here. It's changed now. You can feel it.

It changed in the fifties, when the studio system broke up. Those guys cared about making movies. Now it's accountants and lawyers who only care about a bottom line.

They were European. . . . [*Reflects* . . .] There are no monuments here, nothing built to recognize D. W. Griffith, Greta Garbo, to the people who made Hollywood. There's no recognition of what they did. It's like they never existed.

You just feel displaced out here. You're used to walking the streets of Manhattan late at night having some fellow New Yorker shout out your name.

I've been thinking of getting out of New York. Last week I was out walking, and some guy picked up a garbage can full of garbage and just threw it into the street. He didn't care. It's all that crack that's destroying people's minds. It's becoming very dangerous.

Still, it's a good place to learn how to understand the devil's mentality.

Yeah, it looks like I'm in a hit.

The Devil's Advocate **opened big. Congratulations. Where did you go for inspiration?**

There wasn't any particular person I could go to. What was challenging was deciding the kind of devil he would be. We all have an idea about pure evil, but how do you make him into a character?

Watch old movies?

I looked at a lot of them. There was *The Witches of Eastwick*, *Angel Heart*, *Angel on My Shoulder*. But the one that gave me wings was Walter Huston's performance in *The Devil and Daniel Webster*. He was brilliant. He didn't have to do anything, yet you felt his power. That helped me.

Did you look to literature as well?

I looked at Dante's *Inferno* and Milton's *Paradise Lost*. The devil, after all, is a classical character.

But your devil is a pretty funny guy.

He's got that pure evil philosophy, but I tried to find stuff that was funny as well. I wanted to run the gamut, from sincere to flamboyant to enraged. It was fun.

There's a scene where you lip-sync Sinatra's "It Happened in Monterey." Was that in the script?

That was something I did in rehearsal, and the director liked it.

How often do you get to improvise in a movie?

With *Sea of Love*, Ellen Barkin and I spent a couple of days just transcribing improvisations. *Dog Day Afternoon*—the entire phone call was an improvisation that was written by Sidney Lumet, myself, and Chris Sarandon; we spent days improvising, and it was transcribed, and that was turned into a scene. That doesn't happen often. We did it with *The Godfather*, but Francis wrote it in a formal language; it was a different style. I tried out stuff with Michelle Pfeiffer on *Frankie and Johnny*. It's like in paddle tennis: You hit the ball over the net, it's not like you hit it always in the same spot. In certain movies that's what it is: The ball goes over one way, then another, but you're still in the same court, you're playing the same game. Michelle prefers not to improvise, but to set the thing. So then you're working with someone who has another style of working, so you have to find a way to accommodate that. With *Donnie Brasco* there was no improvisation. In *The Local Stigmatic* it's not done. *Scent of a Woman* was pretty much as written, except for that "Hoo-ah." I got that through improvisation off the set, my own private rehearsal.

Dancing the tango obviously couldn't be improvised—how long did it take to learn that?

To have learned to tango would have taken me years, but we just limited it to the steps in the scene and learned that. Robert Duvall does it all the time. I was just servicing the film. The freedom comes once you've learned the steps, then you're free to enjoy the music. That's the whole idea of technique. If you've got music in you and you sit down at the piano but you don't got the fingers to play it, what good is it? Feeling all that music? You need a craft. You need craft for inspiration. And that's true with acting. A ballet dancer spends all that time working on her movements, hours of labor, so when she jetés across the stage, she's not thinking of anything else but the power of the music around her and the story she's telling physically. You're trying to get yourself in a state where you're no longer thinking about what you're doing, but you've prepared yourself. And that's what improvisation really is.

Why don't you put some sunblock on? It's pretty hot, and we're going to be on the court soon.

I don't like to block the sun. I'll get some stuff to keep me from burning, but not block. Be careful driving. I was in an accident last year. Gotta be careful.

I remember that, when your driver went into an intersection and you got hit from behind. You've got a lot of car stories—remember when you were driving yourself back to Sneden's Landing and your car went dead during a snowstorm? You wound up watching TV in a stranger's house, waiting for someone to get you.

Yeah, lucky for me they let me in. And the woman was from the Bronx, had six kids. She sat down next to me and said, "Who would ever believe that I'd be watching Gary Cooper in *The Fountainhead* sitting next to you in my own living room?"

Ever go back to thank them?

I sent them a basket of fruit and flowers the next day.

[*We get to the private court. Al's boyhood friend, Robert Miano, who played Sonny Red in* Donnie Brasco, *is already there. "He goes way back," Al says. "He knows me when."*]

Miano: Hey, Al. I was trying to remember that play you were in, in junior high. What was the name of it?

Home Sweet Homeward

Miano: Let me ask you a question before we start playing. I recently shot a jail scene for a low-budget film with Lou Ferrigno and Lyle Alzado. I think I might have done something to upset the scene. The big guys were about to get some guns, and I picked up this tiny American flag on a table and began to wave it. I hadn't done that in rehearsal and was wondering if I should have done it during the take.

That was your instinct, to wave the flag, so that's telling you something. It's okay to go with your instinct, as long as it isn't hurting the scene. Remember Hamlet's advice to the players: "Be not too tame . . . , but let your own discretion be your tutor: suit the action to the word, the word to the action . . . Now, this overdone or come tardy off, though it make the unskillful laugh, cannot but make the judicious grieve; the censure of the which one must, in your allowance, o'erweigh a whole theatre of others."

Miano: I'm not sure what you're getting at.

"The censure of the which." You must censor yourself for the sake of the play, if what you're doing doesn't suit the action of the play, because "the play's the thing." "And let those that play your clowns speak no more than is set down for them."

Miano: So it was all right for me to wave the flag?

Not necessarily. What Shakespeare is saying is sometimes you shouldn't do any more than what is written for you to do. If you go beyond that, "That's villainous, and shows a most pitiful ambition in the fool that uses it."

Miano: Then I shouldn't have waved the flag. I was being villainous.

Not if the scene worked. Then it was okay. I remember going to see this actress in a play. She was a good actress, but she kept swinging her leg in a certain way during one scene, and I said to the person I was with, "I'm watching her, I'm no longer watching the play." It's a fine line. But if we think too much about it, then "conscience does make cowards of us all; and thus the native hue of resolution is sickled o'er with the pale cast of thought." Don't you just love that? "The *pale cast* of thought." Not just thought, but the *pale cast*. That's Shakespeare. You can just see the kind of thought he's talking about. And if you think too much about what you're doing, you can lose the hue of resolution. So if the director didn't ask for another take and didn't say anything to you, it was probably all right for you to wave the flag. The camera was probably on the guys with the guns, anyway.

All right, guys, we going to play or turn this into an interview?

[*We play ball for the next two hours. Al is as quick and graceful as a gazelle on the court. He easily switches from his right to his left hand when the ball is hit to his left side. Other than a wicked opening serve, his game is one of finesse and angles. During a break the reminiscing begins.*]

Miano: You remember how poor we were starting out?

Who can forget? I was living in a kind of avant-garde community. I'd go to some local party and I'd see a refrigerator, open it, and maybe there was one meatball in there. If there was, I'd just snatch it up. That's how I lived. It wasn't fun.

Miano: Do you remember how we'd earn money?

In Greenwich Village we would pass a hat around after we would do plays. Or a girl went around with a straw basket and asked people to drop their contributions inside. That's how we lived. I was really an actor from the streets, a gypsy, homeless and penniless. My education comes from the sixties. I lived in dives and dumps, in rooming houses and shitty hotels. To me, anything that had running water and a bathroom in the room was paradise.

What were you seeing on stage in the sixties that excited you?

Things I saw from the Living Theatre, like *The Brig* and *The Connection*. They were just the greatest things I'd ever seen, and have ever seen. Then they went on tour and came back and did *Frankenstein* and *Paradise Now*. It was when I saw *Paradise Now* that I learned something about what they did. There was an explosion of emotion from the audience. The actors were taking off their clothes and at the same time doing this play. It was frightening; you didn't want to be there. I felt, *Something's going to happen to me here; this is going to turn into a riot.* So I went outside and had a smoke, and my girlfriend wanted to stay. I was afraid if I did they were going to ask me to take my clothes off. It had to do with the relationship between being outside, where I was standing, and then going back into the theater, because going back in was like going into an enormous heart. It was beating, pulsating, full of life and excitement and energy. The people in the audience who had been yelling and cursing at the actors were now on the stage performing. I saw Julian Beck on one side and Judith Malina on the other corralling this fucking thing, moving it one way, and all the time they were in control. It was like this enormous dynamite keg that they were maneuvering, and I knew that it came from a lifetime of devotion to this kind of thing. It registered. I never forgot it. It's motivated me throughout my life. It's the thing that I aspire to, like Brecht and Joseph Papp in the early seventies.

[*Back in my car I ask him if the Living Theatre had as much impact on him as a young man as the circus did when he was a boy.*]

I always had this idea of joining the circus and traveling as a kid. I'd have been a clown. I'm afraid of elephants. Part of the fantasy includes the anonymity attached to it—the nights filled with wine and peace and kids, the extended family that travels and performs. It's always been a daydream of mine. And I've lived such a life in the theater. I like to take my kid to the circus because the performers have that look—like they're not in the world. I once talked to this high-wire guy who walked across the World Trade Center towers and Boulder Dam. He was up there walking the wire at St. John the Divine, way up in the belfry. They have this place where there're pigeons, and he couldn't go up there because you could get this disease from pigeon excrement. I said to him, "Anybody actually get sick and die?" And he said, "All the time." I saw his face and it looked like he meant it. There's this element of that in the circus, they're giving that much. They give 100 percent. And when you do that enough in life, it changes you. It makes you different.

You love that image of life on the wire, don't you?

If you're a tightrope walker, that's what you do. You can't paint a line on the floor and keep doing that. Pretty soon you've got to go up there one hundred feet. And maybe sometimes you have to take the net away. You know why? Because something in you changes when you do it. Your chemicals change; something happens to your adrenaline. I also think you've got to be a little mad to do it. As I get older, it's harder to do, to sustain it eight times a week. And yet when I do go onstage, that's where I feel I belong.

You can't get that with a movie?

Never. And I love movies. I loved them even more when I had this guy once explain to me what film really is. You never know where you're going to learn something.

Who was the guy?

Robert Dillon, who wrote *Revolution*. He started talking to me about film and filmmaking in such a pragmatic, realistic way, with both irreverence and reverence, that he made it come to life for me; he made it tangible. And once he did that, I found myself ready to go out and make my own film.

So that's the inspiration for making *The Local Stigmatic* as a movie?

That's it. Even though I didn't direct it, I found myself holding the film in my hands and seeing the magic of what it's like when you put paints on a canvas. It made me feel that I could make movies.

Too bad it's such an expensive hobby.

It is expensive, and I often hear the echo of Orson Welles ringing in my ears, because it's debilitating to go and look for money to make movies, to go out with hat in hand, begging, borrowing. But as luck would have it, I take some of the money I earn from the other pictures I'm in, and do my own films. No big thing. I'm buying paints, that's all I'm doing. Expensive paints.

And it keeps you from getting bored.

I'm never bored. Like Einstein. A guy was once late going to meet him and apologized for keeping him waiting. "You must have been so bored," he said. And Einstein answered, "I wasn't bored, I was thinking." I get restless, but that's not bored.

You seemed restless at the court today, talking to your friend about whether or not he should have waved a flag.

That wasn't restless; *that* was boring.

I loved what you said . . . that the cameras were probably on the guys with the guns.

You liked that, huh?

Pretty funny.

Would you get me home already? I'm getting hungry. There might be a meatball in the refrigerator.

THE NIGHT PACINO CAME TO CLASS

I was sitting under a patio umbrella playing chess with Al at the Mulholland Tennis Club, telling him that the chairman of the English department at UCLA had asked me to teach a seminar on interviewing.

"How can you refuse? You've got to do it," Pacino said, moving his knight aggressively. He had become a much better chess player over the years because he played a lot, especially on the set of movies. And since he had been in a moviemaking mode over the last few years—having done S1m0ne, Insomnia, People I Know, *and* Chinese Coffee—*he'd become proficient at castling, trading queens, and zeroing in on knocking off an opponent's king.*

*A week later I told him I had accepted UCLA's offer, and that I had come up with an idea. "There's an organization called The Friends of English. They do fundraisers and give scholarships to English graduate students. Why not come and show selections from your personal films—*Looking for Richard, The Local Stigmatic, *and* Chinese Coffee—*and talk about the process of turning plays into films? You can come an hour early, and my students can interview you."*

"Let me think about it," Pacino said.

Came October and Al agreed to do an Evening with Al Pacino at the Fowler Museum auditorium on campus. We picked a date when I was teaching, and sure enough, while I was in the classroom, he stuck his head in and asked, "Am I in the right place?"

"You sure are," I said, and smiled, as eyes nearly popped out of a dozen students' heads.

Two weeks after his visit they gave me their papers where they described his visit. Many wrote about how nervous they were and how they warmed up as they got to talk to him. They remarked how Al seemed "a bit unsettled," playing with his silver and black ring. His eyes seemed to go in and out of focus; his bruised fingernails matched his all-black ensemble. "He looks like he belongs in some small, smoke-filled Italian restaurant in a tough neighborhood, the kind of place where the regulars leave through the back door. But his shoes tell a different story. Poking out from the bottom of his slacks are a worn pair of black sneakers. Michael Corleone in sneakers? Fugghetaboutit!"

After these visual assessments they settled into asking questions. As one student wrote: "The evening had a schizophrenic sensibility. The class may be The Art of the Interview, but for Pacino to be the subject of the first assignment was akin to assigning a fledgling alleyway caricaturist to paint the Sistine Chapel."

The questions beginning with the letter Q were asked by students.

Q: Why did you agree to come here?

Larry's such a persuasive animal. I'll tell you the truth, the reason I did it. Sometimes you go through life saying, "No, no . . . yes . . . no . . . yes." This was a yes. You don't know why, really. I rarely do it. But Larry and I are close friends, and he asked me.

Q: In *Looking for Richard* you asked, "What's this thing that gets between us and Shakespeare?" What do you think that thing is?

It's prejudice. It's what we heard about it. It's all myth. We get a kind of atrophy of the ear as soon as we hear Shakespeare. We don't want to know. It's a knee-jerk reaction to it, that's the thing.

Q: After filming *Looking for Richard* did you see any change from the first time you did *Richard III*? Did you grow in your understanding?

Richard is different for me onstage. It's also different if I'm playing it in the context of a play, or a movie. Just *Richard*. But I was being kind of a moderator for *Looking for Richard*, so my *Richard* was colored by my own moderation of it. It didn't quite have the kind of thing I would do if I had a director and I was doing *Richard* alone. I would have approached it much more seriously. I was doing it more tongue in cheek for the film. Occasionally I got into it. But I was always using it as kind of an example, so my interpretation would change. If I did *Richard* now, it would be different.

Q: Why did you choose *Richard III*?

Because I did it when I was young twice. I knew more about it. I know *Hamlet* very well, but I have not done *Hamlet*. I know *Othello* well. The tragedies I know fairly well, but I haven't done them. *Richard* is not necessarily my favorite play.

Q: Do you consider Shakespeare therapy?

I consider this therapy. It's all therapy. If you're trying things that are new, you're stepping out a little bit. There's a kind of therapy in that.

Q: In the film *Glengarry Glenn Ross* how much was David Mamet involved?

David wasn't that involved with it. He wrote it, and mainly as a play. It was Jamie Foley who directed it, and in movies it's the director who gives you the leeway. Mamet writes in a very restricted way—you've got to do Mamet's words, because if you don't, you lose the syntax somehow. He's brilliant at that. It's very helpful. At the same time, if you use the words, you can't just get locked in to only the words; you have to fill it with your own imagination. That takes time.

Q: With *The Godfather* trilogy out on DVD, will you watch it?

No. I don't think so. You know when I watch *The Godfather*? When you're flipping through the channels and *Godfather I* comes on. It's so constructed a movie, in such a way, it's one of those lucky, magical things that happened. Just as a story it's so interesting. It holds your attention.

Q: Do you feel that way about [*Godfather*] *I* more than *II*?

One more than two. Although two said a lot more. It was more risky, but the first one is great storytelling.

Q: What about *Godfather III*?

A major mistake was made in *Godfather III*, I think. That was to try and redeem Michael Corleone. Because I don't think the audience wants to see Michael Corleone as someone who is wanting or needing of redemption. It got a bit esoteric. It would have been better if it was done in a more subtle way. I appreciated Francis striving for that, but it isn't where that character's power is as a hero.

Q: What was it like working with Francis Coppola?

He's got that kind of a largeness. That's why he can do some of the things he does, because he really can listen. He's one of the most intelligent people I've ever met. His intelligence is a kind of sensor for him.

Q: Do you get excited when you're switching through the channels and you see yourself in those films?

Excited? I got a lot of problems, but that's not one of them. [*Laughter*] I'm grateful for that.

Q: When you're choosing projects now, do you look mostly at scripts or the director?

It's the script first. And then, of course, a good script with the wrong director? Forget it.

Q: What other passions do you have besides acting?

I have passion about everything, really. I like that you used the word "passion"—because sometimes wise guys like Larry say "obsession." But it's passion.

Q: What's the difference between the two?

If I have to tell you, man . . . [*Laughter*] Obsession is another kind of thing. I don't see life to it. It doesn't have a drive. It isn't all-inclusive, it's relegated to just a person.

Q: What motivated you to be an actor?

What motivated me as a youngster was the fact that I was able to find through acting—in certain kinds of plays, certain material—a way of expressing myself. That simple. I was able to say how I felt about something through speaking.

Q: With the U.S. at war in Afghanistan, do you think movies are frivolous?

Well, everything is, sort of, with the way things are now. Everything does seem frivolous. You have to adjust. One has to think about throughout history what was done during wartime. We continue as best we can. There's a story about when they were bombing in England and they were doing the plays. They'd go downstairs, and the bombs would stop, and they'd come up and do the plays again. Things are frivolous if they're frivolous. At any time.
     What is this class, anyway?

This is a class where these students are learning to ask questions, without having to come up with answers! Most classes, you need to have answers. Not this one.

That's what we say in acting all the time, when we're working on a play, we say, "Ask the question." You don't have to answer it, just ask it.

[*The hour is up. There are three hundred people, including Benicio del Toro and David Spade, sitting in an auditorium in the next building waiting for their turns* to ask Pacino questions. Al had worried about the timing of doing this, with our country dropping bombs in Afghanistan, with people worried about anthrax in their mail. He asked me to preface my introductory remarks by expressing his concern about the possible inappropriateness of spending an evening talking about theater and Shakespeare and whatever else might come up. But once he gets onstage, he is home. As a student later wrote:

"Al wasted no time in taking center stage. At first he fidgeted with whatever was at hand, including a water-bottle cap and a small charm, and later played with his lapel microphone rather than wearing it. He seemed oblivious to the finer technological points of public speaking. He constantly sat at the edge of his seat, ready to jump up and perform; ready to demonstrate at any moment exactly how deep his passion was. He was animated; he was excited."]

Q: Harold Bloom once called *Richard III* a comic villain. Do you agree?

I see everything as comic. You have to.

Q: What about Michael Corleone? Did you see him as comic?

Michael Corleone? Not funny.

[*Under the heat from the stage lights, Pacino bends to take a fan offered to him by a Japanese woman. He opens it and fans himself.*]

Now that's theater! That's funny!

[*"He spoke with a touch of sarcasm," my students observed, "made eye contact, and flashed his mischievous smile when no words were necessary. Whatever hint of apprehension he seemed to show in the beginning of the night vanished as he roamed the stage, taking up all available space, prowling and gesticulating animatedly. I could literally feel the intensity with which the audience's attention was riveted on him. They felt comfortable interrupting, laughing, and asking questions in an extremely informal manner, even prompting a young female and two male students to propose to him after he discussed wanting to get married some day."*]

Q: What is it about the theater that centers you more than making films?

You walk on a wire if you're a tightrope walker. You go way up there, and if you fall, that's theater! In movies there's a wire, but it's on the ground. That's the difference. Your body changes when you're up there on the stage. Your chemicals change to cope with that. The lifestyle of the movies is a different experience. Not that it's less of an art or a craft. It's apples and oranges. When theater or whatever we do is strong enough, it can alter or change the course, or your way of thinking and seeing things. You start by tasting the words. You try to make them your own. You serve them, and they in turn serve you.

Q: How did you come to appreciate language the way you do?

I've always been drawn to the beauty of language. If I could write, I wouldn't do any of the other arts. I once wrote a letter, which I never mailed, to a woman I was really in love with. I had a hard time with it; the only way I got through it was to write this letter to her. I'd sit there writing, and I'd look up and five hours had gone by in, like, five minutes. I thought, *What a wonderful way to live*. That's how I feel about my movies, the little ones I do. Just to be able to be in there and getting lost, and time just disappears. It's wonderful to get involved.

Q: What about the audition process? You don't go through that anymore, but when you did, was it tough?

I used to like to go to auditions, just for the chance to do it in front of somebody. They'd have material for me and say, "Do this piece." And I'd say, "Listen, I have a monologue I've been working on." And I'd do *Hamlet* for the guy, and they'd look at me like I was crazy, and I'd never get the part. But so what? I got a chance to do the audition.

[*Describing a Jonathan Pryce rendition of* Hamlet, *he tells us how Pryce interprets Hamlet's encounter with the ghost as a "regurgitation of his own father!" And as soon as he says it, it's happening to Pacino. His body is wracked with gagging*

spasms, his face is contorted, his throat heaving, and when he finally releases it all in a final retching expulsion, you half expect to see the dead king of Denmark.
"He sees this thing, can feel this thing, and hears it . . . and then his body just starts to shake and then [Shaking] 'MAAAAAARK MEEEE.' Whoa! Hold me down! How does he do that?"

Pacino's performance in just those few moments is so captivating, so real, so scary, it elicits several nervous titters from the audience.

"So I said . . . fuck this!"

The audience erupts in laughter. These are not the words of a sixty-one-year-old without a definite passion for what he does.]

Q: Why haven't you released *The Local Stigmatic*?

I don't know—I kind of like that I haven't. It's like my own private film that I can show whenever I want, and no one else owns it. Steven Spielberg says, Don't make your own pictures with your own money—and he's right. But I'm going to continue to do it anyway. Because I'm a sucker for a good script. But let me ask you all something, we've been here nearly four hours, aren't you tired of me yet?

AUDIENCE MEMBER: We're not tired, and we're not hungry!

[*"This night had taken on a life of its own," a student summarized. "No longer was it 300 strangers in a room, but it had become one body, one group enjoying the offerings of one man. 'I don't feel I am a teacher,' Pacino said at one point. I disagree. I believe that he is a teacher of the best kind, the one who teaches without an agenda, the kind who lets the knowledge guide the endeavor, always willing to see where a new thought can lead.*

"After the night ended I kept picturing the warm smile that came to Mr. Pacino's face when he mentioned his three children. At no other point in the evening did Mr. Pacino smile the way he did at that moment. This smile spoke from his soul, removed him from his stardom, and made him one of us."]

Two days later I had lunch with Al at Chianti on Melrose. He had two dog-eared copies of Angels in America, *which Mike Nichols was going to direct for HBO.*

Meryl Streep had already committed, and they wanted Al to play Roy Cohn. He also had two scripts with him: The Recruit, *a CIA thriller that was being rewritten because of what happened to the Twin Towers in New York, and* Gigli, *which Ben Affleck was going to do with Jennifer Lopez. They wanted him for a small scene in that one. "That was a good night," I said to him.*

He looked at me not knowing what I was referring to. "At UCLA. I've been getting a lot of calls about it."

"Yeah, that was a nice evening," he said with a sense of nostalgia in his voice. It was already very much in his past. He had other things on his mind.

Thanks to my students who contributed to this: Mike Maloney, Nathan Ihara, Rhea Cortado, Tenny Hovsepians, Mary Yoon, Chris Moriates, Antero Garcia, Mary Williams, Matthew Ball, Maryellen Whitlow, Ryan Joe, Lynn Kwan, Jenny Kim, Boaz Ronkin, Kelsey McConnell.

AL'S CALLING

Al had been working hard: five films in the can, a cameo for Martin Brest, and playing Roy Cohn opposite Meryl Streep in Angels in America. *In 2001 Beverly D'Angelo made him the proud father of twins, a boy and a girl. He also has a twelve-year-old daughter, Julie, whom he sees frequently. In March his house in Sneden's Landing caught fire, sending him, D'Angelo, and the babies to live in an apartment in Manhattan.*

Hello, Larry?

Hey, Al. I just saw *Insomnia*.

No.

Yeah. Did you know I was seeing it?

How would I know? You're there and I'm here.

What are the odds of you calling just when I got back to the house after seeing it?

Isn't that something?

You in the car?

Yeah. I'm heading to my office . . . at about eleven miles per hour. It's really hectic. Cities are not cities anymore. Your memory of a city is: You're in traffic. You go to London, you're in traffic. Paris, you're in traffic. Rome, New York, it's traffic. It's like being in somebody's mouth who's had extensive bridgework. But it's dusk, the lights are starting to come on, I'm listening to Mozart, reaching for the martini that isn't there.

The picture surprised me, Al. It's better than the screenplay.

Yeah. You know, Chris Nolan and I worked a lot on it after you read it.

It ties together a lot better now. The ambiguities I thought were missing are back in a different way. I've now seen your quintet—and they're really different. This is going to be a good year for you.

I'm gonna quit show business. But I'm not gonna announce it.

Perfect timing.

You laugh.

No, why not go out with a bang? *Insomnia* **in May,** *S1m0ne* **in August,** *The Recruit* **in the winter, and** *People I Know* **and** *Chinese Coffee* **whenever the fuck they decide to release them. You can quit and nobody would know for two years.**

How can I quit? I'm doing *Angels in America* now.

That was a short retirement. About two minutes.

You're funny, Larry. You should be a comedian.

What would you do if you weren't acting?

I can't think of life without this, doing what I love to do. Probably just be around my kids, playing with them. I enjoy that.

So where are you now?

I'm on Columbus Avenue. It's a great day. . . . You should really come to New York already. I don't know what you're doing in L.A.; there's no work there. Since the fire in my house, Beverly and I have rented an apartment, and now when we wake up we're in the city. I've been living in the country for twenty years, and I ask myself now what was I doing there all that time? When I'm in the city, I'm alive! I watch, I see people, there's a museum on every street. . . .

I've got friends who tell me that New York has really changed since 9/11.

You get that feeling about everything: 9/11, the economy. When those towers went down, I was in L.A. I felt a longing to go back to my home—a real need—but I couldn't get back: Planes weren't flying. It shook my whole being. I didn't know how it would be when I got back. But you know what it feels like here now? The late seventies. Before the eighties came and really changed things, when they got rid of the automats and the cafeterias and places where artists and people could live cheaply. But the people . . . You can still go up to somebody and ask, "How many New Yorkers does it take to screw in a lightbulb?"

I thought this was a Polish joke. How many?

One, you asshole! . . . [*Pauses*] I hear you laughing. That's New York too; you'll always have that. You know what New York is for me, it's an anodyne. And how many places are that?

Are you in that much pain that you need relief?

I'm in pain just talking to you.

You're a regular mini-Trump with your loft, your office, and now the apartment.

Mini mini mini mini.

I still don't know why you've never gotten a place in L.A., so you could enjoy both coasts.

As the great Satchmo used to say, "When you leave New York, you ain't goin' nowhere." I like Los Angeles, most of my friends are there, but it's that creature of habit thing. When you have a memory on every single street, when you can relate to a place that feels like home, when you feel a kind of comfort just in being there, how can you knock that?

Did you see that play the other night with Mike Nichols?

Yeah. Really, really good. *Topdog/Underdog*. It won the Pulitzer. I thought I was in the presence of the next *Waiting for Godot*. It had that kind of power. The first act did. The second act went in a slightly different direction. It's definitely a new voice, a new set of characters. We haven't seen these people on the Broadway stage before. You gotta see it when you come here.

Did Nichols like it too?

He loved it. Jeff Wright's in it; I'm working with him in *Angels*.

Where are you with understanding Roy Cohn?

He's a classic character, complicated and beautifully etched by Tony Kushner. This is not the Roy Cohn story. It's based on some things that happened to him, like he did get AIDS, he was this lawyer that they were after. This is months before he died.

Does he feel betrayed by people?

Yeah.

So should I expect this to happen between us? You'll start becoming distant?

That's not going to happen.

It might. It usually does when you start getting into certain characters.

You're crazy, Larry. I play characters.

When you were doing *Devil's Advocate*, you were really becoming a devil. When you did *Carlito's Way*, you began to distrust friends. So I just want to know what to be prepared for with you over the next few months.

You're being too subjective.

You don't think you do this?

Hey, I just played four characters over the last year—was I four different people? Of course! We're all different people; that's why we go to the movies.

Well, at least you weren't a bastard. But neither were any of those characters you played. I mean, your cop in *Insomnia* is perhaps semi-corrupt . . .

You really think he wanted to kill his partner?

There are moments before it happens when he's eyeing him, when he gets disgusted with him and leaves the restaurant without eating. He's obviously not comfortable with his partner. He tells him he's going to ruin his career if he talks to the commission investigating them. He sees that his partner may screw him. So does he want to kill him? He wants him not to talk.

He has a lot of sleepless nights.

And Robin Williams's character doesn't help that.

No, he's a bit of a worm.

Robin told me he saw his role like Iago, working on your conscience. Were you aware of that?

No, that's a good choice. I wasn't Othello.

If you had to compare your character to a Shakespearean one, who would that be?

In *Insomnia*? Hamlet, of course. [*Laughs*]

Do you relate at all to this cop you played?

You relate to everybody when you're an actor. You're always identifying.

I was trying to think if this morally ambiguous guy was anything like any of your other characters.

I've played so many different roles, there are probably one or two back there it resembles. Hopefully it doesn't. But I doubt it.

Robin wondered with all the running around you were doing from Alaska to L.A. to see the babies, and not getting much sleep, how much was real life and how much was method acting?

It's always real life. Method acting, that's a label.

Did you miss Robin the comic when you worked with him on this?

No, never, because he was always funny when we went out. Robin is serious and funny; he's both. Sometimes he'll get on a cylinder and go for a while. But he's a very thoughtful person.

He told me about the interesting dinners you had on different boats up in Seward, Alaska.

Yeah. One woman had a wolf as her pet. And the other wolves would come around and talk to it. Can you believe that? That's how far out we were. And grizzlies were everywhere.

What's interesting about that film being shot in Alaska when it never gets dark is that it's actually got a film noir feeling to it—the alleys, the fog, the inside of rooms with light filtering through.

I know what you're saying. Chris Nolan doesn't like to film at night, so that might be a happy coincidence. The choice of putting that movie in that setting in the summer was very interesting, because we haven't seen that kind of thing. It becomes part of the story. It exists because of the light.

How talented is Nolan?

If I were to predict, I'd say he'd eventually be in the category with the Michael Mann's and Soderbergh's of the world. He is to the manner born. It's wonderful to come in contact with someone doing what he's meant to do. He's in the game. It comes out of him with ease and naturalism. I saw him every day up there doing it.

How'd you decide to work with Nolan, since he'd only made one previous picture?

I knew he was a new director, so they said to me, See *Memento*. After seeing it, I realized he was a major filmmaker, so I was only too happy to be a part of it. We worked on the script. It was a struggle for me to finally say yes to that. But it was him, and what I felt he could do.

He told me he was very nervous when he first met you. He said the same thing Hilary Swank said about working with you: They couldn't believe they were going to work with Al-*fucking*-Pacino. A lot of people in the industry refer to you that way. I hear it all the time. Al-*fucking*-Pacino.

Well, you know, I never had a middle name. It's about time. . . . I think what it is, is that most of these people, they grow up seeing your movies. So there's a certain response to that. They develop a relationship with you based on that. What happens is, as you start to work together, that relationship recedes. Then you go out for Twinkies.

Nolan's really blown away by your performance. He thinks you're going to win awards. I don't want to inflate your ego where you'll outgrow your hat size, but he compared you to Michael Jordan. You want to hear what he said about you?

I probably better not.

He said you're a better actor than most people think, and that most people think you're the best.

I don't know what to say to that. Acting is still a mystery to me. You never understand it. You can rehearse, you can figure out how to deal with the boredom, the waiting around—but the actual acting, I still don't get it.

Nolan thought you found your character in *Insomnia* when you interrogated the murdered girl's boyfriend.

That's very astute of him.

Want to talk about that?

No.

He also thought the key scene in the film is when you're with your partner after he's shot, when your face runs through the gamut of emotions.

Where you going with this?

I was just wondering if this was the trickiest problem you had to tackle with the script.

We liked to say, "What if this really happened?" And take it from there. And that's what Chris and I did. It's always different than you would imagine. We tried to cover those pitfalls, to withstand the pressure of scrutiny. Most of the time you're doing movies, there are illogical holes in them. It's subliminal illogicality. Audiences want to believe, they want to go with it, you have to cover that—it's always the case with good writers, that subliminal logic. It takes the film to another level when that's done.

"Subliminal illogicality," I like that. Hilary said her favorite scene with you was at the end. She thought it kept getting deeper, working with you one-on-one.

The thing with Hilary is, she's right there. She's got a three-dimensional presence, she really exists, and that presence very much comes to life when it's working. She's wonderful to play off.

By the way, how was your dinner with Hilary the other night?

I like Hilary and her husband, Chad. You like to keep in touch with people you work with, when you enjoy their company, because movies are such a temporary time. I try to carry on relationships with people after the movie's over. I usually do that with directors.

I asked Nolan if he saw the original *Insomnia*, and he said he loved that film. And what he loves about his remake is that it takes the same events and transforms the meaning because of your performance. You never saw the original, did you?

No, I didn't want to be influenced by it.

Do you have any curiosity about seeing it now?

No. I prefer to see a movie I didn't do. There're a lot of movies going on now, an influx of independent films. I love what Coppola said, that somewhere in the Midwest there's a six-year-old girl with a camcorder who will alter the state of film. It will happen. I just watched a fantastic documentary about getting that Nazi guy, Barbie. Did you ever see it? My God. What's so amazing about it is it's so complicated. . . . You know that's what's probably going on now with terrorism, this underground network. The murkiness of it all. And those characters—who are those people? The stuff down in Bolivia and all over the world, the contacts, the money going back and forth. Say what you want to say about Oliver Stone's *JFK*, he got a lot of that feeling, that texture.

Are you looking at any new scripts?

I've been staying away from scripts, not saying yes to movies, because I've done so much and I'm tired. I don't feel like taking on a big project right now. I'm about to really climb a large mountain with *Angels in America*. I want to get through that, and then see where the future is.

What do you weigh now?

I don't weigh myself. It's a deceptive thing, to weigh yourself. It's how you look. Sometimes you feel fat, there's water retention or whatever. Weighing yourself is not an accurate account of what's going on with your body. What's your weight?

I'm close to one ninety.

Oh, boy! That's encouraging.

My sister says that the only time I will lose weight is when I have a bet with you about it.

Well, you've never won that bet yet.

So it looks like Mike Tyson will finally fight Lennox Lewis.

Yeah. He's a great fighter, and he should be doing what he does. I think it'll be a great fight.

Would you want to go?

I don't go to fights. I saw De La Hoya fight because he invited me. I was put in a seat behind a pole; I kept looking to see it on the monitors. It was weird. It's easier to see on television. Except when you're there you really see the craft of a fight, which you don't see on television. You see the dance. Everybody thinks they're fighting, but they're doing something else. They're thinking, they're measuring each other, countering. You can see it in the ring, it's beautiful to see live. I know it's brutal, and I don't want to like it the way I do, but it's a great sport.

What else would you rather watch from a distance than up close?

Basket weaving.

Did they ever discover what caused the fire in your house?

No . . . that was so sad. You can't go in there. The house is inoperable. A lot of rooms were severely damaged. It may be a year before we can go back in. What a night that was. Four o'clock in the morning and there are rooms on fire, and we had to get out of there—we were driving into the city with the babies, looking for a place to get more diapers and milk. It was a record fifteen degrees out, coldest day on record for March. I'm telling you. We had to find a place to live; we were suddenly homeless.

How are the kids?

They're great. Julie's become such an athlete, I love watching her play. And the babies—I just love being with them. You want to hear something funny? For the last few months I take them on my back and run toward the mirror, and they laugh seeing themselves running toward themselves. So I got my hair cut real short for *Angels*, and now I'm running toward the mirror with Anton and I realize he looks just like me. It took me fourteen months to see this. We've got the same head. The haircut made me see it.

Did they think you were different when you had your hair cut?

I had it cut in front of them. I went to a lot of elaborate trouble, but it was unnecessary. These kids get it all. You see, I'm underestimating them already. What a thing, Larry, at my age, having these two babies. What a thing. Positively millennial!

Anything else besides the babies keeping you happy?

I like what Shakespeare says in *Hamlet*, "I'm happy in that I'm not over-happy, on fortune's cap I'm not the very button."

A woman's voice: AL PACINO! I don't like you anymore.

Who's that?

I don't know. Some woman is shouting at me. I'm at a light. [*To woman*] Hi, how are you?

Woman on street: You're not good to your fans. I told you once you were my favorite actor, and you just touched me on the shoulder and left.

I'm sorry. Maybe I was in a rush.

Woman on street: You look tired. Want me to give you a couple of bagels?

Gee, that's nice of you, but that's okay. I'm not hungry. But you're right, I am tired. Okay, the light's changed. I've got to go now. See you.

Did she have the bagels, or was she offering to buy some for you?

I don't know. Funny, huh? *You look tired, want some bagels?* I spend most of my time talking to people on the street. There's your answer to why I can't leave this place. It's the only place to live.

2004

THE OPERATIVE WORD, DEAR SHYLOCK, IS SOBER

These days, spotting Pacino in public isn't as unusual as it once was, not since the birth of his twins, Anton and Olivia. Now he can be seen in Central Park or in a Beverly Hills park with them, watching the two three-year-olds as they slide or play in a sandbox, balancing on a seesaw with them, sharing fruits, juices, and cut carrots. When people approach to tell him how much they love his work, he thanks them and says, "These are my children." He carries one on his shoulders and pulls the other in a wagon.

Pacino is adjusting to being bicoastal, following the twins between summers in New York and preschool years in Los Angeles. He wrestles with movie offers that would take him to Spain (to play Salvador Dalí), have him remain in New York (to play Philip Roth's seductive professor, David Kepesh, in an adaptation of The Dying Animal*), or take him to Vancouver to work in a small film (*Two for the Money*) with Rene Russo and Matthew McConaughey. His decisions are now based on how much time he might be away from his kids.*

He's been linked to big-budget films about Napoléon and Italian car-designer Enrico Ferrari, but those are still undecided at the moment. He's contemplating making films of either Eugene O'Neill's Hughie *or Oscar Wilde's* Salome*, which he's done successfully on stage. His last pictures were hit (*The Recruit, Insomnia*) and miss (*S1m0ne, People I Know*), but the work he did as Roy Cohn in HBO's* Angels in America *earned him a Best Actor's Golden Globe and Emmy.*

"Acting," he feels, "is using what you can. I always used to say, 'What you can't lose, use.' Because whatever somebody gives you, you can reject it if it doesn't work

for you. With Roy Cohn in Angels in America *it was desperation. What worked for me metaphorically was, here's someone alone and defiant. It was his fierceness, his reaction, in this lonely place that he was at. He took comfort in this ferocious place all by himself. He took refuge in being alone. Mike Nichols was helpful to me because he was sort of a censor and a guide. When Mike Nichols is your guide, you're in really good shape, because he is so sensitive and smart."*

Pacino's next film, playing Shylock in a film adaptation of Shakespeare's The Merchant of Venice, *is a return to what he loves best: talking Shakespeare. The film is directed by Michael Radford (who directed* Il Postino) *and costars Jeremy Irons, Joseph Fiennes, and Lynn Collins. Pacino knew Shylock would present problems to modern-day audiences. But never one to shy away from a challenge, he found in the character a strength and depth that scholars have often missed, and thus he brings a new and touching interpretation to what until now was a stereotype of greed and villainy.*

Well, it looks like you're back doing what you love, wrestling with the Bard. Shylock is one of Shakespeare's more controversial characters—is that what drew you to playing him?

To me it's a man against the system. And I like those parts. It's sort of in the tradition of *Dog Day Afternoon* and *Serpico*. A man wronged. And then going too far.

Mel Gibson's *The Passion of the Christ* seemed to have milked the anti-Semitism controversy about as far as it could go and still return a huge windfall. Will your interpretation of Shylock stir those same anti-Semitic flames?

I don't see it as controversial. The film directs itself toward an understanding of a character that's given great passion. My hope is that that's how the movie is perceived. Great characters are great characters. They are profoundly human characters, and hopefully I engender a certain humanity in the role. If you make the character a human being whom people can identify with and see the frailties and qualities of the character, that's what people relate to.

For *Looking for Richard* you went to see scholars to talk about the play. Did you talk to scholars on how to play Shylock?

I wish. Have you seen any scholars who can also act lately? I hope the Shylock I've interpreted is sympathetic without pandering to it. I said that the only way I would do this movie is by giving Shylock dimension, and depicting his position in the community.

One famous scholar, Harold Bloom, claims in his book *Shakespeare: The Invention of the Human* that "One would have to be blind, deaf, and dumb not to recognize that Shakespeare's grand, equivocal comedy *The Merchant of Venice* is nevertheless a profoundly anti-Semitic work."

I know it has anti-Semitism in it, but I was hoping that the movie version would change that, since you would be able to understand more visually and in movie storytelling where Shylock was coming from.

Bloom believes Shylock is a comic villain.

I don't see Shylock as comic or a villain. My interpretation of Shylock is someone who has been abused, victimized, and through his rage gets hoisted by his own petard. When you put it in our world today, in the realistic medium of film, to me it looks like Shylock is a profoundly depressed man who lost his wife and is living under the oppression of the Christians in Venice. He's living in a ghetto. He's deprived of a lot of the social enmities afforded to so many other people. That's the position of the Jews in that time. Hopefully the version we've put out in the film expresses this and explains it, which only a film can do when you adapt it. You get a sense also of the profound rage that is his experience; it's Shylock's accumulative depression over the loss of his wife, who died the year before, the racial abuse, and the fact that, according to him, they steal his daughter. His daughter leaves him to marry a Christian. This allows him the feeling that it's within his right to get revenge. He's not a happy man, but he has a lot of dignity and a lot of heart and a lot of courage. Probably one of the great speeches ever: "Am I a Jew? Has not a Jew eyes?

Has not a Jew hands? Organs? Dimensions? When you prick us, do we not bleed? If we're like you in everything else, why should we be different in revenge?" It's the most antiracist speech I've ever heard. Shakespeare wrote that. Shakespeare could not help himself from being human; it was his genius.

So why do you suppose Bloom insists that "Shylock would be very bad news indeed if he were not funny?" Especially since you chose not to interpret him as funny or as bad news.

It would be great if Harold Bloom played Shylock. Let him do it, and then talk. I'm not a scholar; I don't know what he knows. But I certainly know that in acting throughout the ages, parts have been interpreted. What made Edmund Kean a phenomenon was his interpretation of Shylock. And he was anything but funny. He was ferocious. It's like saying, is *Scarface* anti-Cuban?

Laurence Olivier, Dustin Hoffman, and George C. Scott have all played Shylock, yet Bloom believes that "there does not appear to have been an overwhelming performance in our own time." Think he'll change his mind after seeing yours?

I don't think mine is an overwhelming performance either. But it is an interpretation. This movie has a very easy way of seeing Shakespeare—with actors like Jeremy Irons, Joseph Fiennes, and a young girl named Lynn Collins. The director directed them toward an un-Shakespearean style of performing, so it looks and feels very natural. You're not turned off immediately by the lines. I made a movie, *Looking for Richard*, and I was surprised how much I retained a Shakespearean blabber. The director of *Merchant of Venice* said "Take the Shakespeare out of it, Al," and I was grateful for that—it was helpful. With Shakespeare a little knowledge goes a long way. Too much knowledge screws you up. Which is the opposite of "A little knowledge is a dangerous thing." If I would have listened to Harold Bloom, I wouldn't know what to do. I wouldn't know which way to enter.

The word "Shylock" is almost synonymous with "greedy Jew." What do you think motivates Shylock to behave the way he does?

When they take his daughter from him. Not that they kidnap her; she went of her own volition. But it's like that. It motivates Shylock so much. He's a tragic figure.

Tragic is anything but the way Mr. Bloom sees it. He said, "If I were a director, I would instruct my Shylock to act like a hallucinatory bogeyman, a walking nightmare flamboyant with a big false nose and a bright red wig."

I can understand that interpretation on the stage, but when you deal with film language and realism and intimacy, you have to approach it in a naturalistic way. For example, in the very opening of the movie there's a scroll which talks about the condition of the Jews at that time. We see in the opening Antonio spit on Shylock when Shylock asks him for help when they're throwing Jews off the bridge. This has great visual impact. And it later justifies the scene when Antonio comes to him later and asks Shylock for money. "What should I say to you?" Shylock responds. "Should I not say, Has the dog money because you call me dog? Does a cur have money because you call me cur? Or should I bend low and in a slavish voice say, Do whatever you want to me and I'll give you money." Then Antonio gets mad and storms, and Shylock says, "Look, I'll do whatever you want me to do." He doesn't know that Antonio won't be able to pay him, so who's the one who's giving something away? Shylock is. He doesn't know that Antonio's boats are going to fall through. He didn't do that to Antonio. But by the time that happens and Antonio's money is cashiered, they have stolen Shylock's daughter. And it's then that he says, "You do this to me, and now you say I cannot exact my pound of flesh? You screw me, I can't screw you? Screw you."

Shylock's demanding his pound of flesh, essentially being willing to take Antonio's life, is of course what makes Shylock one of Shakespeare's most memorable characters. It also is what has stained

the image of the Jew for four centuries. How he behaves in the court scene, when he insists on the flesh, rather than three times the money he is owed, has to be one of the great challenges for an actor. How did you come to play it as you do?

In the court scene, when Shylock is fighting for his pound of flesh, the director, Michael Radford, kept telling me that Shylock's defiant. And I kept thinking, *How the hell do you be defiant? Act it?* It wasn't making sense to me. I wasn't living it; it wasn't coming to me. I didn't know what defiant meant. So I wasn't doing what the director was telling me to do. He's shaking his head. It's not working. Finally, it came to me: Shylock was sober. There was a sobriety in him when he said, "I want my pound of flesh." It wasn't done with malice or anything like that. It just was clear. Sober. The operative word was sober. It worked for me. I was able to understand that on a visceral level. I like that—when a director gives me something. Rarely do you find it.

Like Hannibal Lecter, who appeared on-screen for only seventeen minutes in *The Silence of the Lambs*, Shylock speaks only 360 lines, yet his presence is felt throughout.

This play is beautifully acted by Jeremy Irons, which takes a lot of the onus off Shylock, because it becomes a story about Antonio's need to sacrifice himself for his sort of gay influence in terms of his love for another man, Bassanio. He also feels as though he's lost touch with what he wants and needs in the world. He would just as soon go off into another sphere, and in a way it's welcoming what Shylock does. Then it turns scary when the actual taking of the flesh is going to happen. And one has to see how it plays itself. Because we don't know whether Shylock would actually cut the pound of flesh from him.

Do you think he would have done it had he not been challenged?

I think he has driven himself into such pitch that even he doesn't know if he will or not. He's working himself up to it. But to have executed that, he would have been driven insane. It's a very somber affair. It's like what they said about *Dog Day*: It's this man's moment to have his say in court. And Shylock tells them all, "You dispute me here, but listen to your own logic." He throws it in their faces in some of his speeches.

They want to pay him three times the amount owed him if he relents about taking his pound of flesh, but he still says no. So he's holding on. The final insult is that they are so cavalier with the contract that he made just because he's a Jew; they assume that he will kowtow to their outrageous demands not to honor a contract. He's ganged up upon. It's his way of saying, "Stop spitting at us!" It's almost like Michael Corleone letting his brother go. Part of his identity was tied up in that.

Shylock is a man first, and a Jew second. Witness him as a human being first before you make an assessment about Semitism. Because every other Jew in the play is sympathetic; they go to support him in the court, so he doesn't feel he's alone—but they're against this act he is about to commit.

In the end, when he is forced to choose between converting to Christianity or being put to death, Shylock chooses to live, and says, "I am content." How ironic is that remark?

What happens is he has to deal with the fact that he went too far. That his rage at the injustice put upon him was because of that. Now the punishment is partly self-inflicted. His anger is: Why did I go so far? But it's justified in light of his life. Shylock is one man, who happens to be Jewish—that's his religion. There are other Jews in it who don't do what he does.

His saying "I am content" is the lament of a survivor. He concedes reluctantly. He sees the writing on the wall and knows that he can't get away, they've got him. And a survivor knows how to react in that situation. He's been down that road before. He knows these fuckers are going to try and put it to him. He's very gifted at what he does, and he knows he can still work.

Sounds like you're describing yourself.

I don't know; I feel I've been in a void lately. You wait for something to come that's going to ignite and trigger the imagination, that's going to allow you to connect in some way. It's no longer about the score, it's about, How do I bring my life together with a role to make it become expressive and moving? It's a quest. You're always going after that. That's what *Looking for Richard* was for me. The reason that was inspired was because there was a real need for me to deal with my relationship to Shakespeare vis a vis my movie status, my star status. How does one get the opportunity to play *Richard* and express it without it sounding like, "He did a soap opera for ten years and now he's going to go out and play *Hamlet*." You know that joke, where John Wayne plays Hamlet. And after it's over, he goes up to the footlights because everybody is booing him, and he looks at the audience and says, "What do you want? I didn't write this shit." If it's for you, it's for you; if it's not, it's not. No big thing. John Wayne was great at what he did. Why should we look down on him for not doing *Hamlet*? It's absurd. You couldn't ask Humphrey Bogart to go play Hotspur. It's like asking why Beethoven didn't write "Like a Rolling Stone."

With *Richard* you figured out a way to do it. . . .

I had a real desire to do it. As crazy as it may seem. Because I wanted to impart some of the difficulty and mystery we have with Shakespeare. But it was also a way of interpreting *Richard III*. I knew I could do a couple of those scenes in a way, but I needed a concept in order to do them and bring forth that character, and consequently the play; and I thought that was the way to do it. There was a bit of anarchy in the thing. I like that. In the end I wanted to ask questions and not necessarily answer them. I wanted people to feel Shakespeare, and not know why. That picture gives me a lot of pleasure.

As did *Scarface*, which has resurfaced, after twenty years, as one of the biggest-selling DVDs ever put out. That picture is a favorite of yours—

And yet it was pretty much put down when it came out. But I knew that Oliver Stone was writing about stuff that was touching on things that were going on in the world; he was in touch with that energy and that rage and that underbelly. And I found that when I hooked into that, there was a kind of expression coming out. It felt the closest I've ever been in a movie to really speaking out. I thought I was reaching an audience. And I was. It was palpable to me. Some rappers actually did a video about *Scarface*, as a revelation, as a morality tale. What they say about it on the DVD is quite interesting.

What did you learn about yourself by playing Tony Montana?

A dog once attacked me while I was playing Tony Montana, and I tapped it on the snout. I couldn't believe I did that. I love dogs too—but it jumped at me. Normally I would have run for the hills, but I was fearless, and I like that whole idea of being fearless in that character. That is one of the great things about acting—to suddenly be able to tell someone who has a chainsaw at your face to go shove it up his ass. Not many people around would tell someone to fuck themselves when they're about to cut your head off. So, in a strange way, I admired these traits. I like the fact that, to me, Tony Montana was two-dimensional. I didn't want to make him a three-dimensional character. What you see is what you get. I like that about him. The fact that he didn't contemplate too much. That's why he was so totally thrown when he killed his friend. He couldn't handle it, so it froze him; that's why he dug into the cocaine.

Another "scarred" face you got to wail on was Big Boy Caprice in *Dick Tracy*. How did you come up with that look?

I was looking for a head. . . . I always thought it would be great to be able to sculpt the head of that character. Look at what Charlie Chaplin did with a hat, a mustache, and a walk. Pow! That's three dimensional; that's the body, the whole thing. I was into that; I had done that with *Scarface*, trying to sculpt the character. But with Big Boy I could actually put a mask on it; I could put something on that was sort of a culmination of this kind of a life. Why did they call him Big Boy? Maybe Big Boy was fat; but no, too obvious. We kept trying different facial things. The first one was so good and funny. Warren Beatty said, "No," but I loved it. I had a head the size of a third-world country. Finally that face came out. I found that character to be a lot of fun to do.

That film was so artfully done. Warren Beatty did such a great job of putting it together. The story was a little loose, but it was a wonderful artistic film, even though it's like that picture doesn't even exist.

Can't say that about the *Godfather* trilogy and the Biggest Boy of all, Michael Corleone—a character you almost didn't play.

For the first few weeks they were thinking of firing me. And I couldn't understand why they didn't. I didn't know what to do, frankly. I was a kid and it was my second movie. I didn't know what was going on. I had no idea *The Godfather* was going to be what it turned out to be. I just thought, *Francis wants me. I don't know why he wants me, but he wants* me. He saw *me* in that part and nobody else. I wanted *all* the other parts—I thought they were all better than mine. The only reason I stayed in the movie is because they saw that Sollozzo scene in the rushes, where Michael shoots the guy, and they thought, "Wait a minute—this ain't bad." So I stayed in the picture. [*Pause*] I found that out later.

Was that a character you could easily return to twenty years later?

Doing Michael Corleone when I did him in part three was a strange visitation. But that movie, for me, never quite found itself, because of one main reason: Robert Duvall did not want to play it. Francis Coppola wrote a screenplay that was really there. Robert Duvall not playing the part of Tom Hagen changed the movie. Francis then rewrote the script, and cast his daughter as Michael's daughter. I think that's when everything sort of changed. If I were to do it over again, I would do it differently.

What would you do differently?

For one thing I wouldn't have that hair. It was, again, a concept by a director. I resisted it. Diane Keaton, who was my girlfriend at the time, said, "Al, don't do it. Don't do it." It was a mistake. It was the antithesis of what that character was and of how I saw him. Worst of all, how I really saw him. I think it offset everything. Funny how that can do it to an actor. Certain things can just change the way you look at something.

What about the end of *Godfather III*, when your daughter dies, and your cry is silent? Did you scream and did Francis cut the sound, or was it silent from the start?

I didn't know it was going to be silent. That's just great editing. I exhausted such passion from that moment that I was in the pain; I thought it was a great idea. You never know what the voice would sound like. The voice was coming from the bottom. I never heard the real scream. But in movies you can do things like that. What I liked about taking the sound away, it was less interpretive; it had more life to it. Had I done it as an idea—to do a silent scream like one of those Goya or Munch paintings—it wouldn't have worked as well. But I didn't do that, so it had an even more profound power.

Great editing was also what worked for your first film, *The Panic in Needle Park*. . . .

The director, Jerry Schatzberg, got Adam Hollander to shoot it. He had a vision. One thing: He thought of the camera as a voyeur. That was his image, and he just stayed consistent with that. And for some reason this story blossomed. I had no idea the kind of movie it was. It was based on a true story. It was a love story as well as a dark story. I grew up in a world that had people like that in it. My best friends died of overdoses. But who had any idea? For me, the excitement of being in a movie superceded everything. There it was, what I grew up with, what I was inspired by all my life: films. And now I was in one. It was too exciting for words. It was overwhelming.

Then, following the first *Godfather*, came *Dog Day Afternoon*, also based on a true story. *Dog Day* was the first gay character you played. How did you come to understand him?

By trying to make him as human and complicated as I could.

That was some run you had to begin your film career.

When I made those films—*Panic*, the *Godfathers*, *Serpico*, *Dog Day*—I wasn't allowed to make a normal picture. Every picture I made had to have this thing in it. There was a kind of unconscious pressure I felt. I got caught up in the fame machine. It's like a tidal wave that just takes you.

And then came something different, *Bobby Deerfield*. . . .

At the height of my career then, I was exactly where I am right now: where I didn't know what to do next. I couldn't relate to anything. Paul Newman said if you want to work in a movie that you like, you do one every five years. Sydney Pollack was a wonderful director who was doing *Bobby Deerfield*, a romantic film about a racing car driver who's very tied up and tight, who meets someone his opposite and opens him up. I felt I could identify with it, because I felt very lost in my life. Bobby Deerfield was a character who was lost. I just don't think I had the acting technique to handle that part. I found myself too subjective. It's a movie that doesn't quite work. Paul Newman or Robert Redford, both of whom were considered for the role, would have been brilliant in the part. Yet I felt connected to the role. And in a few moments I thought I expressed something, like the Mae West, scene, where he's trying an imitation of Mae West, but he's lost the ability to do it, it doesn't come back to him. But there was a sentiment in the movie that just turned everybody off, that was her dying. It didn't quite work. And yet, it was Henry Fonda's favorite film.

Newman was in the generation of actors before you; he was Brando's contemporary. Though his fame grew large, he was overshadowed early by Brando. So perhaps you're right, it might have been a good role for him.

Yes, Brando overshadowed everybody. But he also inspired. Think of what he did in *On the Waterfront*. When I was a kid and saw it, I didn't move from my seat. I had to watch the second film over again just to see *Waterfront* again. It was inspiring. I was in the presence of something I had not seen before. It was original. But seeing it in retrospect, his work in *Streetcar* is far better. It's more kinetic and more visceral. He did it on the stage. But what it isn't, that *Waterfront* is, is an understanding of life and the actual paving of a new world. He opened the door to what we are today in acting, and made us all see what it is. The possibilities. His influence still has presence. Nobody has come along to change it. We have traditional actors, which I like to think I'm a part of. I approach things in a certain way. I have my own stamp on things like all people who pursue something have; I have a style. But Brando set the stage for all of us today.

As a kid were you ever compared to Brando?

Acting came to me through a different thing. It was a way to get attention; it was a way to connect to things. It was a facility I had, and I enjoyed it greatly. So when I saw Brando on the screen, I was a kid who was acting already for years in school plays. The first time I did something on the stage, somebody came over and said to me, "You're a Marlon Brando." And I said, "Who is Marlon Brando?" I was thirteen and I hadn't seen him yet. Brando was the new voice. Afterward, I found myself mimicking him a bit until I found my own voice. And now I'm Robin Williams. [*Laughs*]

And how did you compare Brando's voice with James Dean at the time?

James Dean was an acting sonnet. Marlon was a planet unto himself. But he needed to explore his gift, and to fail with it. Success had an adverse effect on him. I've always felt that Marlon, genius that he is, was uncomfortable later on being an actor.

Who are some of the actors you've felt something special about?

I saw John Goodman in *Babe* recently—he's one of our greatest actors. This is what I see in him. I like Tom Hanks. I'm a big fan. He's in a movie, I'll go see it. Same with John Goodman. He and De Niro are great actors. Bobby's comic performances are just pure genius. To make comedy at this point in your career, to understand yourself well enough to put yourself in those roles: *Analyze This*; then to become the CIA guy [in *Meet the Parents*)—this is great invention. It really impressed me. Brando did it with *The Freshman*, which was almost surreal.

I loved Ben Kingsley's performance in *House of Sand and Fog*. The last quarter of it. He's very much "the actor" most of the time. When you see Kingsley go through his steps—from the moment of death to his recovery and subsequent agitation of whether his son lived or died—his body language is a remarkable feat of acting. I have not seen its like in a while. It touches you. And what's greater than that? When an actor moves you, reaches you? I love Ralph Fiennes, too. And I think Philip Seymour Hoffman's got the potential to be a great actor. There's a lot of actors I enjoy. How could you not enjoy being with Meryl Streep? With Michelle Pfeiffer? With Sean Penn? Johnny Depp? There's nobody in the world funnier than Johnny Depp; nobody has ever made me laugh that much. Colin Farrell came close. And I really liked working with Paul Guilfoyle when we did *The Local Stigmatic*. We rehearsed three months together and shot in nine or ten days.

You made this enigmatic *Stigmatic*, which you have never released, during the mideighties, when you dropped out of the movie scene. What caused your disappearance at that time?

I was a bit disillusioned by the way a movie I made called *Revolution* was treated. The right narrative, and more cutting—viewing the movie more as a silent film—would have helped. Like *The Red Badge of Courage*. The lesson I got from it was that it was important to pursue something to its end. Either it fails or succeeds, but you don't quit on it; that doesn't make sense. *Revolution* was one of those things that happen in a career, where you learn so much from it because it was such a disorienting experience. After that kind of work and energy and the talent put into it. I expected that they would have worked on that film, but they just let it go. They put half a film out. I was appalled and shocked by that. I didn't know what to do. It was that single film that took the rug out from under me; I lost interest for a while. I went back to the drawing board, and experienced my life in another way. So

I returned to some of the things that got me here in the first place. I did a movie of *The Local Stigmatic*, my own little picture, and it got me in touch with things I remembered as a young actor working: trying to really pick through things and find an expression of some sort. I was doing it in my own private world where I was able to not have anybody looking over my shoulder, not having to please anybody by it. I had been in movies for so many years, and I had never really understood what it was to put a film together—the magic of that. I was very inspired by it. I spent a few years doing that. Then I turned around and I was broke—that was a rude awakening, and I had to go back to work.

Looking back at what you did with *The Local Stigmatic*—any regrets?

The Local Stigmatic is the most potent, powerful thing I've done in my life. That is something that I'm so glad I did. I didn't even understand at the time why I needed to do it, but I knew there was something pressing to do it. It doesn't belong to any quarter; it has its own identity.

The two Cockney characters are really lowlifes who follow people, beat them up. They seem more out of it than in it.

These guys are nomads. They're not conscious of their feelings. They're nuts. They get off on acts of violence that they do together against a society that is violating the so-called Silent Majority. There's an unspoken language that they have with each other. They do not participate in worldly things. They see a movie, they come out, and they don't even talk about it. It has no effect on them. They use it as something to energize themselves, to get themselves excited. They follow people to do that. This is about people who have not made the grade. They are game playing all the time. They play at being gay, and they play at being heterosexual and macho. They are asexual.

You first did it onstage back in 1969. How was it received?

When that play came out, it was so visceral. Jon Voight was around, and he gave us a thousand dollars to run for a week, and it closed in one night.

It was the only play that I was really booed at. That made me really know that I was onto something good.

And when people who see the film version come away confused, does it make you smile?

I showed it to my daughter Julie, and when it was over, she looked at me and said, "I don't get it." And I said, "Nobody gets it." That's the beauty of it. And if you get it, it speaks to you. It's not about being entertained, which most movies are. It's a matter of taste, like food.

You're planning on finally releasing it, along with *Richard* and *Chinese Coffee*, on a DVD. Why the change of heart? Is the world ready for the avant-garde Pacino?

Enough time has gone by. It really made such a profound change in my life, doing those kinds of pictures. *Stigmatic* was at the Whitney Museum, and it is still in the Museum of Modern Art. It was voted in Canada one of the top one hundred films of all time. It's time for me to show what I did, and how I felt about things.

You directed two of them: *Chinese Coffee* and *Looking for Richard*. Will we ever see you directing a big-budget film?

I don't see myself as a real director. I see myself as an actor—who directed this thing. A real director is someone who sees the world like that, who says, "Hey I just saw something. I just read something. I gotta direct that." I don't. I see something and I say, "Wow, I gotta act that." Big difference. Sometimes I feel that maybe when I die and go to heaven, I'll direct.

Heathcote Williams, who wrote *Stigmatic*, said that "Fame is the perversion of the natural instinct for validation and attention."

That's from *The Local Stigmatic*. *Fame* is the perversion of the *natural* human instinct for validation and attention. It's part of what motivates *Stigmatic*.

Is that how you feel about fame?

There's a line in *Stigmatic*: "Fame is the first disgrace." And the guy says, "Why?" And he says, "Because *God* knows who you are." Basically, fame was the motivation why *The Local Stigmatic* was made, because everybody wants to be famous essentially. But fame is different now than it was twenty years ago. I don't know what the hell it is now. It doesn't mean anything.

Is fatherhood anything like being a director, or is that more the role your children play with you? You've turned sixty, and you're running after three-year-olds. How has it changed your life?

How about, it's my whole reason for living. I have three children; it couldn't be better. It makes me happier than *anything* ever has. I never take the time to look at anything. I'm in my head. I'm thinking about all the things I have to do. But children make you look at things. And you start seeing things you never saw before. I'm walking around, and I don't see a fucking thing. I'm just thinking about all kinds of things, and not seeing what's right there in front of me.

"YOU CAN'T DO GONE WITH THE WIND WITH A NEW YORK ACCENT"

Al is on a lounge chair in his underwear, bronzing himself by the pool in the back-yard of his rented house in the flats of Beverly Hills. He doesn't use any sunblock, just protects his eyes with a pair of sunglasses; a vanilla Pepsi and a screenplay about Napoléon on the table next to him. His cell phone rings continually, and he conducts his business . . . with his agent, a London stage producer, two movie directors, a few different women, and his fifteen-year-old daughter in New York. For a die-hard New Yorker, he is the spitting image of a Hollywood movie star.

He could be the poster man for "sixty-five is the new forty-five." He's still got that animal magnetism, that electric smile, that highly cultivated sense of self. He's slowed down on the paddle tennis court, but not on the action. He enjoys playing poker and chess, and keeps his mind in tune by reading plays. He has no trouble quoting Shakespeare, and can almost keep up with his twin four-year-olds for hours at a time. His latest film is Two for the Money, *and his next will be a thriller called* 88 Minutes. *In between these two will be a play,* Orphans, *and after, another play,* Salome, *which he has done a few times already. But the project that's dearest to him is the release of the Al Pacino DVD collection.*

I put on my sunglasses, cover my head with a hat, and try my best to avoid those strong sun rays that Pacino absorbs like a sponge. It's worth the sweat when you get a chance to sit by the pool and talk to Al Pacino about all the things that he's done to bring him to where he is.

You've finally let go of these independent films of yours and released

them into the world. It's only been twenty years. . . . What took you so long? And why put them out in a box set rather than individually?

My accountant suggested it. I didn't think they should be viewed as movies. They're not. They're plays that have been filmed with a movie style.

What makes the release of these DVDs so special?

Part of it is because of the kinds of films they are. And two of them—*The Local Stigmatic* and *Chinese Coffee*—have never been seen. Primarily, though, it's been an effort of mine to try and turn material that could be viewed as obscure and difficult into viable and active play-films. I use the word "play-films" because it's that hybrid of a play presentation on film. If I ever direct again, it will be an effort to take a theatrical piece, a play written by a play-wright, and adapt it to the medium of film. It's a desire I have. Maybe because I've thought of myself over the years as someone connected to the live theater more than to film. My expression and relationship to work is vis a vis the theater, the performing arts. The movie interpretations came second. The early part of my life made the most impression on me and is the one I'm most connected to and most comfortable with.

How do you distinguish these plays from movies?

They're renditions of plays. I would like to do more in the future. The problem is to be able to communicate that. To say I am not adapting a play into a movie. I am doing the play *as* a movie. It's tricky. The difference is, you try to keep the spirit of the play, the sense of it as a play, but at the same time you're adjusting to the medium of film. For instance, if you have a play that was done on a stage that had a proscenium audience, and then you did it in a theater that had the audience all around, you would adjust the play to accommodate the geography of the audience. In a sense, what these plays are doing is accommodating the medium of film, but at the same time keeping its rhythm and vitality as a play. You're trying to keep that idea of theater in the movie. What happens sometimes is the camera moves in a certain way, the close-ups can go on for a long time, the use of music. . . . You can go through a period of minutes in a movie without any dialogue, where you don't hear a word spoken. This is not done here; the word and the image are equal in both *Stigmatic* and *Coffee*.

What also distinguishes a play from a film is that a play is done from beginning to end, and a film often is not. With these two did you try to film it as a play in developing the scenes and characters?

Usually in movies you can't do continuity. I tried. But what's important to do in movies that are dialogue driven, and in this case actual plays, is to rehearse them. In the rehearsal stages you have continuity. So you have a sense of where you're at when you're filming, because you rehearsed it long enough. But this hybrid of film and theater is what sparked my interest and made me want to do it. And to make a record of these plays and these characterizations.

Are you concerned at all that the fact that some of these works have never been released in theaters can be interpreted as failures? Otherwise, why weren't they released?

The truth is, they could have been released. There were distributors who wanted to release them. But we—me and Fox Searchlight Pictures—came to the conclusion it was better for the films for them to be released on DVD. There was much discussion about it. I just didn't want to go through the whole film-opening thing. It didn't feel like it would be served. I didn't think it was fair to the play that Ira Lewis wrote, to bring it out as a film and have it marketed that way. It's like a paperback, not a hardback. Who knows? Maybe in time they will be released as films, too. I always prefer them on the big screen. I prefer all movies on a big screen. But our world has changed. DVDs have become more acceptable now as a form where pieces can be seen. When we consider the film, we have to consider what we've got and not pretend it's something else. We're not pretending that these are movies that are going to compete with other movies. I just made a movie, *Two for the Money*, that's for the main market. Even films like *In the*

Bedroom or *Sideways*—independent, small movies—are cultivated. In the back of everybody's mind there is the hope that they will strike lightning in a bottle. And sometimes it happens to these pictures because they are topical and people can relate to them. Their value is more widespread. These pictures that I've made are not for that kind of consumption; they're not made with that in mind. They were made because the ideas of the writers and what they were saying was something that I related to. So in a way they're personal art films. By their very nature they're not trying to compete.

Would people who enjoyed *In the Bedroom* and *Sideways* also be an audience for your independent films?

Absolutely. I don't want to sound like an elitist. I've seen how things are promoted and brought along, and we're dealing with an exotic situation here with these films. They're plays that weren't particularly successful; they have themes and ideas that appeared off-off-Broadway, which is different from those on or just off Broadway; there's a reason for this. It's where they belong. In film there's the idea that each one might have the potential for some award or other; because it's such an expensive medium, we're not geared for movies that are just there as small works of art, or as sketches. I don't know if these pieces are that accessible, or if people are interested in seeing them; however, that doesn't mean there isn't value in them. I think they're just as valuable as commercial movies that people go to see. I think people's lives would be affected by seeing these films. People would think about what they've seen and have feelings and opinions about them. They have a value. I wouldn't put them out if I didn't think they did. It's not like these are home movies of me sitting around playing by the pool.

Well, *Looking for Richard* is you and your fellow actors sitting around talking about Shakespeare.

Looking for Richard had a real pointed purpose that took me four years to make. It was relatively very successful.

Were you surprised that you won the Directors Guild Award?

Totally surprised. And it also won an Editor's Award. And it was on many top ten lists that year—also a surprise. I'd be just as surprised if these two other pictures, the *Stigmatic* and *Chinese Coffee*, get well received.

Are you surprised to hear that someone like Anthony Hopkins, who claims to have a disdain for Shakespeare, is a fan of *Looking for Richard*?

Aside from making me feel great, it makes me sad he has disdain. I'm sure he meant something else.

Do you feel what you were trying to do with *Richard* was to bring Shakespeare to the masses?

I was trying to open a door to something. But more than anything else, I was trying to get people to relate to *Richard III*, to feel it, to get a sense of it. That's really what I wanted to do, more than educate the masses. Shakespeare doesn't need me for that. That was the only way I knew of doing it.

Getting back to the other two play-films, neither *The Local Stigmatic* nor *Chinese Coffee* would have had any kind of recognition had you not done this. How did you know?

One never knows. People sometimes pull plays out of the vault and do them and reinvent them. But I don't think that would have happened with these.

If Heathcote Williams was to be pulled out of the vault, it most likely would have been his play *AC/DC*.

Yeah, that was a successful play. But I like to use examples of plays that failed, like Eugene O'Neill's *The Iceman Cometh*. That failed in 1945 and was revived by Jose Quintero in 1957 in the Circle in the Square downtown and was reborn and became a classic. Which shows you how interpretation plays into these things. In this case the director found the play, with Jason Robards Jr.

Did the director find the play in *Stigmatic* and *Chinese Coffee*?

You can't compare them, since they were both really at their heart one-act plays. Whereas O'Neill's *Iceman* was a masterpiece at five acts. *Chinese Coffee* and *Stigmatic* are both unfinished plays. They have in them what I believe is inspired writing. But they're not complete plays.

How did you know to champion these plays, which you did for years? They didn't smell of money or commercial success; they were both somewhat obscure, small, kind of elite. You had an inner drive to make these plays work. What was that drive?

You get a feeling for something. I felt it at the time. If I was handed these plays now, I don't know if I'd feel the same way. But I knew there was something in them when I read them. I believed in them. They weren't immediately accessible to the crowd at large. They had in it certain things that I saw. In the DVD I compared *Stigmatic* to *The Indian Wants the Bronx*, which was a huge success—one of the biggest successes I personally ever had. Nobody knows of that play; it isn't done often anymore. And then *Stigmatic* was a failure. And I believe *Stigmatic* was just as strong, if not more so. Because of its theme, it's almost as though the play was hidden, because of the obviousness of the characters being people coming from a certain breed, a certain society—some of the value and nuance of the writing escapes because of that. People don't attach themselves to it. They see the raw emotion of these guys and the situation and compare it to something like *The Indian Wants the Bronx*. I will say this, however: When you read the *Stigmatic*, you're genuinely confused by it. After two or three readings you start to see what he's getting at, and it's a revelation. It's the difference between Heathcote Williams and other writers. Heathcote was writing about something that was deeply personal and much more far-reaching than the other plays of that period. In terms of that, he was at a disadvantage. He was unfairly grouped into the angry playwrights of the time. But if you look closely, it's like looking at an impressionist painting and saying, "Well, Degas, Renoir . . ." But they're distinct, they're different. They may come out of the same period, but they're not dismissed because of that.

I realized this as I got further involved with *Stigmatic*. When I first read it, I thought it was a hodgepodge. I didn't understand it. And yet, after three readings I thought there was something that had lasting value. It could easily slip by. This is not a boast on my part—that I know more about things—but I had the privilege of reading it three times straight before I realized something was there.

But how did you know after the first reading, when you were confused, to keep on reading it?

Being an actor and being engaged in plays my entire life, you hear things. As if it was a piece of music. Your ears have been tuned over the years, and you have a sense of what rings and what is harmonious and what works. It's like if you're a poet and you understand a certain kind of poetry, because that's what your life has been spent doing. I heard that with *Stigmatic*, that other thing he was going for. I identified with the writer.

When did you meet with Williams?

After I had done the picture.

You never met with him before?

No, never. I didn't have to, because I felt I understood what he was saying.

But the play closed in one day when you first did it onstage. Was it the reviews that closed it? Or was it that just nobody went to see it?

It's complicated. You and I saw *Scarface* before it came out, and we thought it would have a different kind of life. How did we know that? It was vilified, for the most part, when it came out—but here it is almost twenty-five years later and it's still surviving with tremendous gusto. Why? Why did we know that at that time? It was because we related to it; we heard it, in a certain way. Why do people have a certain taste for things? Why is it now that broccoli can help prevent cancer? Or blueberries as an antioxidant? And maybe in ten years we'll find out cigarettes are good for you. Who the hell knows? I just heard coffee was good for you. I was sure, ten years ago, that coffee was killing me. You don't know. That's why you have to stay with a thing if you feel it. I felt the *Stigmatic* so strongly. It was pretty hard to let go of it.

Some people don't particularly enjoy language; they don't have an appreciation for it. And some people do. It's like poetry. Sometimes when you hear good writing, it intoxicates you, it makes you feel good. When the writer is connected to the writing, it can be magnificent.

Besides Shakespeare, how often in things you've done have you feasted on words?

I wouldn't call *Chinese Coffee* poetic dialogue—I'd call it amusing dialogue. Clever. There's some wonderful dialogue on some TV series. You'll hear an exchange and go, "That's good writing: It's funny, it's amusing, it makes you think." I thought some of *City Hall* had good words in it. Of course, *Scarface*. *Glengarry Glen Ross*. *Frankie and Johnny*—I thought that one was overlooked as a movie that had some wonderful things in it. That came out when Clarence Thomas and Anita Hill was an issue regarding his Supreme Court nomination. That was the weekend we opened the film, when men and women were at a standoff with each other because of Thomas. The timing of the opening had a lot to do with it being ignored. It didn't take off. But it's a nice film with some wonderful exchanges. *Heat* was a good film; it didn't have that. Even *The Insider*, which was a good film, didn't have that kind of dialogue in it. *Dick Tracy* did in a certain way. *Scent of a Woman*—Bo Goldman wrote that as well as *City Hall*—had certain exchanges that had a good rhythmic pop to them.

I see it in a lot of films that I'm not in. You recognize it. It's fun. The movie writer is not encouraged to do that; he's encouraged to make the movie vivid and be sparse on the dialogue. Paddy Chayevsky was notorious for his dialogue on some of those Lumet pictures. Although the dialogue was good in *Dog Day Afternoon*, it isn't the dialogue but the situation and the emotions and the kinds of characters they are that drives the picture. It's not so much what they're saying.

Could you have done *The Local Stigmatic* in a different way? Making the character different than a Cockney wise guy.

Not by me. People tried to change me in it a couple of times, but I saw it the way I did it. I translated it that way. When different people translate Pushkin or Pasternak, one can work better than another. It's all about how you see it, how you hear it.

Could you imagine doing the *Stigmatic* without the accent?

No, because that's what it is. Can you imagine doing Mozart's piano concerto without the piano?

That's a stretch. What if you transported the play to New York? Made it horse racing instead of dog racing.

But part of the beauty of the play is the way the dialogue rides. It's written in a certain iambic, which gives it an identity and allows the piece to transcend. You can't do *Gone with the Wind* with a New York accent. Vivien Leigh had to be Scarlett O'Hara from the South.

You don't like it when someone analyzes the two characters in *Stigmatic* as gay. Why does it so bother you?

One of the things I disagree with you about is that you think the two characters in *Stigmatic* are homosexuals, because they're not. The author of the play never thought that they were gay. And I never thought that.

But the author doesn't always know!

You're missing the mark completely.

Look, I think *The Local Stigmatic* is up there with the best of your work. It's going to last for as long as anyone remembers you.

That's why I'm surprised. Because I know you know better than that.

You think that it has to be your interpretation or none. And I'm saying that what's so wonderful about it is that it's *open* to interpretation.

But can you concede that these guys *play* at being heterosexual and they play at being gay? This is nihilistic stuff, Larry. It's about another thing. You obscure the metaphor if you try to pigeonhole it in your effort to understand it. If they were gay, the theme would be different. It wouldn't be what it is, and you would totally miss the point.

The obscurity of the play starts with the title, which I understand the playwright wanted to change.

He wanted to call it *Fans*. I say that in the epilogue. Because that was a more commercial and understandable title. But *The Local Stigmatic* is going to live on. *Fans* is a little obvious. It's cute; it's trying to be ironic. In the past I said it was evil. I don't need to do that.

   This is a delicious piece which is, like you said, open to many inter-pretations. It's riveting because something is going on. You watch it because of that. I've been in audiences—they are not bored. Even ones that don't get it and don't like it are not bored.

Even though you never released *Chinese Coffee*, you did show it at vari-ous festivals, and it got decent results, including a standing ovation from the audience at the Tribeca Film Festival in New York.

If I knew that I could corral the audience and have the proper marketing to get the right audience—who would enjoy the picture—to see it, then I'd have considered it. But I've had these experiences and they've taught me certain things. You can't often get the audience you want to come out and go see this kind of film.

Is it like a *People I Know* situation, where it got no marketing and wound up being opened on the Concorde jet between London and New York?

Sort of. If I knew that it was going to play at a museum, or at a cinema that was restricted to these kind of movies and let them run for four weeks, so the people who went knew what they were going to see, yes I would have released it. I wish we had more cinemas like that throughout the country. Like the old Bleecker Street Cinema, where I'd see a movie that I wouldn't usually see in the main market. But they can't afford to do that anymore, so what's the point? That's why I figured the next best thing is to put it on a DVD. And that is the most articulate I've been on this subject. . . . I hope you got it on tape. Because that's really the reason why I didn't release it as a movie.

The play *Chinese Coffee* got some negative criticism. When reviewed with *Salome*, you got good reviews, but the plays didn't fare as well.

Well, I don't know. You'd have to tell me what they said. It's an exploration of a kind of friendship; it's very fragile, this thing called friendship. I tried in performance and in my direction to go there, and I do try in the commentary of *Chinese Coffee* on the DVD to cover what I believe the play is doing to me.

Not only are you releasing these three films, but you've included a fourth DVD, which you call "Babbleonia." It's you talking about acting. How'd you get the idea for it?

What I like about "Babbleonia" is not so much what I say but the feeling you get when you look at somebody who has obviously been doing something for so long, like if somebody made refrigerators his whole life and then talked about that. It could, in some ways, bring a little insight into that area. It could be helpful to actors.

Why did you call it "Babbleonia"?

Because I didn't know what I was going to say, and I just babbled on. I just free-associated. I was at the Actors Studio. I think it explains what the Studio was and is to me. Because there's such a misunderstanding of what the Studio is, and I don't think that aspect of it has been clearly presented to the public. It's a very unusual place.

Why is the Studio misunderstood, and what is it you feel you're clearing up?

There was a period when it was misunderstood about the way it was with techniques. . . . Once you go and witness it, you get a sense of what it is. It's varied. It's not just one thing; it's different to a lot of different people who attend. It serves the actor. Like anything that endures this long, it's not controversial anymore. It just is what it is. The Actors Studio show [*Inside the Actors Studio* with James Lipton] is a kind of flag for the Studio. It puts its name out there. But it doesn't express what the Studio does. It talks to celebrities, which is fine because it's giving the Studio a great deal of revenue, and it's entertaining.

How do you hope the critics will handle the DVD set?

I think the reviewers will have to be patient, in terms of listening to the whole thing—the commentary before and after and over the movie. All in all, there'll be something for them to write about, however negative or positive.

It's also kind of mythical—like did these films really exist? You've been talking about *The Local Stigmatic* in interviews for years. . . .

Yes.

Would you say the *Stigmatic* is a good date film?

[*Laughs*] If you happen to be a resident in a mental institution and you get breaks periodically. It's only fifty-two minutes. Maybe if you take your nurse or psychiatrist.

And what about adding *Chinese Coffee* as a double feature?

Well, if you weren't a resident of an institution, you'd be joining one shortly after seeing both of those together. Listen to me boasting. . . .

That's not boasting. . . .

Sounds like boasting to me, Larry. I just hope people get through it without falling asleep or turning it off. Basically what it is, is pieces of material that I enjoyed, that I liked when I read them. There's something about getting a reaction to something that stimulates you. You want to share it with someone. That was basically the principle of it. When I saw *Chinese Coffee* as a play, I told my friend Charlie to come see it. And then I carried it over to the real world. So when you ask me why did I finally release these pieces, that's why. Who am I to hold on to this stuff? When a lot of stuff I've done is already out there, open for scrutiny, and they're not nearly in the same class as some of these things. So I thought, *What the hell, I might as well release them. What can happen? If people like it and it becomes a collector's item, or if they don't and it doesn't, I made the effort.*

Do you think you're starting to change your own personality, your own sense of things, now that you're letting go of things you held so tightly?

I'll tell you the truth: I don't know what the hell I was doing not letting them out, frankly. Why didn't I? I don't know why.

Still, in many articles over the last fifteen or so years, the reporters are always writing that before they could meet you, they had to see a private screening of *The Local Stigmatic*. So, you used it as a kind of calling card: No matter what commercial film you were supposed to promote, this is who you are.

I thought if I showed them a couple of things that I did, they would have a sense of me. It's worked several times. I've done a couple of interviews where after the interviewer saw it, they talked to me about different things. I know that they wouldn't have done that had they not seen it.

When you read reviews, do you shy away from the bad ones and embrace the good ones?

The positive ones can be as harmful as the negative ones. When I was a young actor, I hoped to go unnoticed. I only hoped that they would say I was adequate, which I thought was better than being told I was lousy. That's where I was coming from. I have two stories about reviews. One was when I was in a play called *Awake and Sing!* at the Charles Playhouse in Boston. There was an actor named John Sykes backstage while the show was going on. He was reading something and banging his fist, saying, "Wow! Fantastic!" When you're backstage, you're listening for your cues from a speaker installed in the dressing room from the stage. I came around the corner, and I said, "What's going on, John?" And he said, "Oh, nothing." He got a little nervous. He then said, "Just a great notice." I said, "Oh, yeah?" And I started reading it, and it *was* a fantastic, glowing notice. Until the last paragraph where it said, "With the one exception of Al Pacino in the role of . . . If you could tolerate him . . ." As I was reading it, I heard my cue from the speaker to go onstage. [*Laughs*] What the hell do you call a thing like that?

So how did you feel when that happened?

I'll tell you what I did. I was twenty-five. And I started laughing. I thought, *This is too funny*. I'd love to be at that stage again, where I could laugh at the magnificent timing of it all.

Did you feel that the reviewer was wrong about you?

I didn't know whether he was right or wrong; I just felt it wasn't quite the truth. I wasn't particularly good in it, but that's neither here nor there. I was trying.

What's the second story?

I did a play that was my first breakthrough in New York—*The Indian Wants the Bronx*—in Provincetown. I knew there was a character I was flying with. This young local critic saw the play and said in her review, "Remember the name Al Pacino, because it's a name that we will one day know very well." I didn't believe it, but it made me feel good. That very part, that very play, six months later in New York, the critic came and saw it and didn't think my character was good. Now all I can say is this: The critic from the *New York Times* and this little girl from Provincetown, who was right? Doesn't that say a lot?

Was it Clive Barnes from the *Times*?

No, he didn't come to it then, but he came to it later and he made me a star. What he said about me. I won the OBIE Award that year. But what I'm saying is, that is what we're subject to. The critic is very responsible. Because that play, which also won an OBIE, as did John Cazale in it, was denounced by the *Times'* first critic. And usually when the *Times* doesn't like something, you're finished. But Israel Horovitz, the playwright, pursued Clive Barnes, because he believed in what we were doing so, so much. It's so vulnerable, so susceptible to that kind of stuff. It's tricky business, talking about critics and reviews.

Have you ever thought of calling in a critic for advice on a project before its release?

I did. I've talked to critics one-on-one. I did it with *Stigmatic*. I had a lot of encouragement. Andrew Sarris was one; he went back to see it a few times. He encouraged me to put it out, and was a bit miffed when I didn't. Roger Ebert pushed *People I Know* in his festival of films that didn't make it. He actually screened it. So you can get critics who are supportive. I wish I would have done it sooner in my life. Sometimes they, too, like anybody else, need some information. What a critic can do better than anything is, not state the obvious but rather take what they believe in and promote it. That's the best thing a critic can do: support something they believe in.

With *Merchant of Venice* the critics couldn't help get it seen.

In retrospect it's understandable. But with DVDs these films are around. It's Shakespeare. Classic. It ran a long time in New York. It made money. For some reason the powers that be didn't promote it. The people whose job it was to do that didn't do it. They didn't think creatively about it, and I don't know why. I don't know how much it would have mattered if they did.

When you read reviews, do they ever alter your perception of the films you've done?

I usually agree with what critics say about movies. Not about mine, of course. I'm too subjective. But in retrospect, when I look back at their criticism of my movies, I would agree most of the time.

Scarface **took a pounding when it came out.**

Well, who could figure that one out? *Scarface* was more an underground movie. They didn't get the joke, because a lot of them were coming from another place. *Godfather II* did not get good reviews in the *New York Times*. Vincent Canby did not like it. I remember that. That sort of shocked me. That was one of the few times I felt, *Well, there're personal opinions.* I rarely get reviewed now without people talking about things I've done in the past. I liken doing a movie to pulling a pin out of a grenade, waiting for the fucking thing to explode. You don't want to be around. When people start talking about you, in all kinds of ways—whether it's a girlfriend you're going with or an incident or a movie—it's unnerving. Especially later on in life. I was flipping channels on TV, and someone was talking about me. I just couldn't believe it. How could somebody be talking about me and my not being there? Stating something that was totally untrue. I don't get indignant about it, it just terrifies me. It's uncontrollable, like a loose cannon, where people just say anything. In our world today there's just this open season. People will say to me, "Don't pay attention to that." And I don't. But I try to understand it. Is it an innate shyness on my part? Or as an actor not wanting to be known or seen? It's an infringement on one's privacy.

How satisfying was *Two for the Money* and working with Matthew and Rene Russo?

I enjoyed greatly working with them both. Matthew is a great guy. He really gets in there with you. He's extremely supportive, and he's wonderful in the role. And Rene Russo is everybody's dream to look at, to be with, to watch act—she's just a great gal. With all due respect to all the other women I've worked with, Rene ranks up there with the top three.

For the DVD boxed set will you be out there on TV promoting it?

I'm not ready for *Oprah*. I'm stunned that I ever did *Larry King*. Because what do I have to talk about for an hour? I'll go on *Charlie Rose* and just stare, let him do the talking. I'm not big on the visual, on being on television. I don't think I function very well on camera like that. Maybe I just haven't done it enough. I grew up where actors didn't do that sort of thing, and today they do. I'm a little behind adjusting to it. But here we are talking about these things, and I've become a promoter. Next thing, we'll be promoting the heavyweight championship between me and Dustin Hoffman. Did you know Alexander Cohen, that great impresario, had an idea many years ago to go to Madison Square Garden in a boxing ring and have me and Dustin put on the gloves? I wonder if he ever mentioned that to Dustin. Because he mentioned it to me. All I said was, "Can we do it without gloves?" People have these ideas. I swear to you, that was his idea.

Of the four discs in the boxed set, which do you think might be the most lasting?

You mean when you and I are long gone? Impossible to say. Things change. If I were to take a wild guess right now, it looks to me like *Looking for Richard* will last, because of the way it was done, the time spent on it, the subject matter, the interest, the element of it being a docudrama, the fact that it's teaching, it's exploration. . . . Although I'm partial to *The Local Stigmatic* because it has this thing in it. These are personal pictures. Not

Richard, but the other three; they're like sketches. To me *Richard* is a painting, and the others are sketches.

And what would be the *Godfather*s?

They would be major paintings. But they've got nothing to do with me. I was just in them. These are closer to me, they reflect an aspect of the way I see things.

If you could select five of your works to put in a time capsule, which would they be?

To show who I was? I would have to go back and painfully look at every one of the films I've made and discuss it with some people and come up with some conclusions. Just off the top I'd say *Godfather I* and *II*, *Scarface*, *Serpico*, *Looking for Richard* . . . and maybe stop there.

Interesting. You'd choose *Serpico* over *Dog Day Afternoon*?

Yeah.

I'd choose *Dog Day* first.

Well, *Dog Day* was at the early stages of television entertaining itself. It was the early stage of the car chase. It was the first time when the pizza boy delivers the pizza and turns around and says, "I'm a star!" That was the first time that kind of recognition vis a vis TV and the real world was shown. In a way it was reality TV.

So, taking the *Godfather*s together as one, you've got one more. . . .

I guess *Dick Tracy*, Big Boy, a comedy.

Big Boy over *Local Stigmatic*. . . . Again, interesting choice.

Maybe you're right, I'd go with *Stigmatic*.

What about the plays you've done?

The Basic Training of Pavlo Hummel. I liked that one. I should read you passages from that—it's a powerful piece of work.

When we first met, you said that *Cruising* was the most controversial movie of your career. That still hold true?

Yeah.

Was it also your biggest failure?

No. *Revolution* was the biggest failure I've ever had.

More than *Cruising*?

Uh . . . yeah. Yeah. I would say. It got me to quit films for four years. It was a failure for a lot of reasons. *Cruising* just wasn't a very good picture, but *Revolution* has in it stuff that's very good, so that's the failure. If a movie doesn't make it, because clearly it's not very good, that's one thing. But if it has in it potential, that's a failure.

You often don't like to watch dailies—

No, I don't.

But when you went to see the dailies for *Dog Day Afternoon*, you changed what you were doing and you had them reshoot what had been shot. That's early in your career. Why didn't that teach you the importance of seeing the dailies?

When you're working with Sidney Lumet, you can go to the dailies, because he's a great director. You know you can talk to him in this way. Also, at the time, I was organized differently. I was engaged 100 percent. I can't say that I am the same now. I mean, when I made *Looking for Richard*, I had to look at the dailies. But I was directing it. When you don't have control, when you're out there doing the pains of moviemaking, you're not interested in going at night to see yourself on-screen failing miserably, then having to go home and go to bed. You just say to yourself . . . Hopefully you felt good about a scene, or just a little bit inadequate and hope the director will give you another chance the next day, or he'll say to you, "We'll take care of it in the editing room," which they usually do. Mostly I don't look at dailies because, who wants trouble when you're making a movie? Who wants to start to brood about something? It's tough enough making these things without having to think about it. People have jobs; editors have jobs. They'll make the scene work. If the director felt he got enough, he got enough. It's all about control.

For what other films have you seen the dailies and reworked the character?

I know I looked at the *Godfather* films. I looked at the early rushes when they were going to fire me and Francis told me to look at them, because I wasn't doing the job, so to speak. But when I saw the rushes, I thought I was doing the job; I was happy with the direction I was taking the character. I had an idea of where I was going with it. I didn't say anything or disagree with the powers that be, but I didn't know what else I could do. And they were going to fire me.

It's funny about *The Godfather*, it's not obscure. . . . It's still in the culture somehow.

It's ranked higher than *Citizen Kane* now as the greatest film of all time.

Really? I didn't know that. Holy smokes.

Robert Evans claimed that Coppola missed a lot of scenes in *Godfather*, which Evans filled in. He said when Coppola showed him the film, it was not releasable. "He had taken out all the texture. The picture was supposed to open that Christmas, and I went to the Paramount hierarchy and said, we cannot open it then. I almost lost my job over it. They pushed it

back, and they added fifty minutes to the picture." Concerning *Godfather II*, Evans told me that at the preview, two months before it was to open, half the theater walked out. "[Francis] left out the entire Havana sequence, the Meyer-Lansky-Hyman Roth scene, and had more of Sicily with subtitles. It was a bore! We went back and made over a hundred changes. We put back Havana, which was the best part of the movie. He doesn't know how to structure a movie."

I wouldn't know about that. Either he's not telling the truth or he's telling the truth. That's self-aggrandizing.

Evans said that he didn't want you, but it was Brando who convinced him. Brando had called him and said that you were a brooder, "And if he's my son, that's what you need, because I'm a brooder." It was Brando's insight, Evans said, that made him understand why you would work. Did you know this?

No. I would have enjoyed knowing that. I don't even know how Brando could have known I'd be a brooder. It probably wasn't until after we started. Because how else would he have known who I was?

Evans dislikes Coppola because of what happened with *Cotton Club*.

Does he say that?

Yes, he's put his letters to Francis in print.

Those kind of vendettas that happen, in books and stuff like that, I don't know how anybody can really feel good when they've done that to somebody else. Because in the end it goes away and people forget about it. Feuds don't last, do they? You can say that to somebody in private, but to put it out in public—because it's always subjective: You're the one who got screwed. Well, according to you. In all due respect to Bob Evans, because he's a great producer, and I respect him: Francis Coppola is a writer. He's written other scripts. He won an Oscar for *Patton*. The chances are he wrote the *Godfather*. Maybe Bob Evans did what a lot of great producers do, and that is guide writers. Give them ideas. Look at Robert Towne: He wrote the scene with me and Brando in the garden. Francis openly said, "We need a scene here." In movies that happens sometimes. Waldo Salt wrote *Serpico*. But when we needed a couple of scenes with the girl, we got in Norman Wexler. That happens when somebody has a good feel for certain things. They don't do it as much anymore, but certain writers have specialties. If you get the right guy to write the scene, it's tremendous for the movie. But nobody wants to pay for that anymore. They weigh the balance and the powers that be often say, No, it's not worth it.

Are you aware of how you're referenced in *The Sopranos*? They actually use your name, not Michael's.

No. I think it's a great show, but I haven't seen enough of it to hear my name mentioned. With television, I don't watch it, I channel surf. If I hit it, which I have, I'll watch it, because it's so good. Like Jon Stewart; I'd like to see it, but I don't know where it is. I don't know what time it plays. Even Charlie Rose, whom I love, but I never find it. With TiVo I could probably get all of it, but I'm afraid of TiVo. It scares me. I don't know how to do it. But I'll ask my four-year-old boy to fix me up with TiVo. I think he can do it. He'll call it TiBo.

Did you learn anything when you worked with Brando?

I was inspired by him. What do you mean by "learn"?

Just from his behavior, his way of doing things, how he worked . . .

I learned that if you eat that pistachio ice cream that you love, you're going to get big. Every time I get that quart of ice cream, I think of that.

You're being glib, but I've always wondered why you didn't hang out with him.

It's never been my thing to seek out people. I don't do that. I don't know why. Maybe because I'm shy.

Michelle Pfeiffer said that when you were making *Scarface*, you and she went to dinner and neither of you had anything to say to each other because you were both so shy.

Maybe because we didn't have anything to say to each other. [*Laughs*] She was great. She was young, sweet. I liked her a lot. I didn't want to infringe on whatever it was she was doing in the film. I didn't want to get into talking about acting or about the characters, because that was what Brian De Palma was doing with her and I didn't want to interfere with that. I didn't think it would be good for the picture. Whereas me and Steven Bauer were inseparable for six months.

One would have expected to see more of Bauer—

It's not just your talent, Larry. You have to be able to handle your life, and what happens to you. It's a roller-coaster ride in anybody's book.

How do you handle it?

You're lucky or you're not lucky. I can't think of a way to handle it. It's fate, destiny, choice. And mostly luck.

When you were making *Frankie and Johnny*, Garry Marshall played a practical joke on you, didn't he?

He had those *Star Trek* guys come in.

William Shatner, DeForest Kelley, Leonard Nimoy, were all there when you opened the door to your apartment on the set?

Yeah. Everyone was laughing. And I pretended to laugh, since they went to the trouble of doing it. Why should I be somber? But I didn't know who they were. . . . I knew William Shatner, because I saw him on TV when I was a kid, but I didn't know *Star Trek*, since I never saw it.

So you didn't get the joke?

I didn't get a lot of Garry Marshall's jokes, but I pretended I did.

He made that film right after *Pretty Woman*, right?

Yes. He's a good director. And he made a good movie. I thought he did a great job. He had wanted me to do *Pretty Woman*. He's also a great guy, by the way. He's one of the best people you can meet in this business. He's a mensch.

Was he happy you didn't agree to do *Pretty Woman*, seeing how success-ful it was with Richard Gere?

Yeah. I probably would have brought the movie down.

I don't even know anymore when you're serious and when you're pulling my leg.

As it should be.

Still, you don't believe that you'd have brought *Pretty Woman* down, do you?

I do. When I saw the movie, which I thought was terrific, I couldn't see myself in that part. Richard Gere really did it well. I didn't feel I could have done that. Isn't that funny? I felt the same way about other movies which were offered to me, like *All That Jazz*. When I saw Roy Scheider do it, I thought, *Did they get the right guy or what?* He was great.

You turned down *Die Hard*. Could you have done that?

Die Hard I think I could have done. Except for those great jumps that were made. They would have had to use my stand-in.

There weren't enough jumps made to launch *People I Know*. Have you figured out what happened with that one?

That's a movie people are telling me they're seeing on TV. It's funny, because Harvey Weinstein always wanted it to go straight to TV—and he was right. Directorially, what was good about the movie also didn't work about the movie. What was good was the simplicity in which it unfolded. But what was missing for some people was the energy, or the style. Dan [Algrant] and I often talked about it. He's a real talented guy. Their first idea was to do it on video and then blow it up to thirty-five millimeter, which I thought was the way to go. But for some reason they didn't think I would comply with that, so they didn't do it. There was something in the energy of the movie, and also it was an exotic subject. I wish I could be more articulate about it. But sometimes if a movie doesn't fall into a particular category, it seems like, "Been here, done that." I felt that Robbie Baitz is definitely a voice as a playwright, and he's a writer of significant and catchy urbane dialogue. Maybe the movie just needed more writing work. We did it fast because I had a small window of opportunity. I saw a great character there, but the movie suffered because of a lack of time to do it. We needed time before we went out and shot it. We needed to find that other ingredient to take it over the top, as they say. It never quite got over the top. But I did enjoy it. When I first saw it, I was happy with it. As time went on, they started to strip it and make it more commercial, but I liked it anyway.

How did it happen that the movie wound up opening on an airplane between London and New York?

I don't know. The behind-the-scenes stuff that goes on with people who finance these things, they have their agenda. You've got to expect people who put lots of money into something wanting to find a way to get it back.

Did they think they were getting a different kind of Al Pacino movie?

Here's the thing that happened: Somebody showed the studio that backed it a five-minute trailer, and they thought they were getting another kind of movie. There's no doubt about that. That was a mistake which somebody did. But you cannot buy a picture on a trailer. You've got to read the script. See the kind of movie it is.

How disappointed were you about *S1m0ne*?

I liked the idea of it. I liked the script. Again, another example of a movie unenergized. The ball didn't go through the cannon. Yet it was good.

The director, Andrew Niccol, was also the writer, and he had previously written *The Truman Show*. Was it a mistake for him to direct?

He wanted to direct it. I don't think anybody else could have directed it as well, because he had a vision for it. And that's how he saw it. Now, it's not fair to say nobody could have directed it as well—perhaps somebody else would have taken it differently, and maybe it needed somebody who didn't write it. I don't know. That's possible.

And what's your feeling about *The Recruit*?

It was a movie that I personally couldn't follow. But I thought Roger Donaldson did a bang-up job with it. A lot of people enjoyed the movie. They took a ride with it. It was not the style movie that I'm usually in, but I like to be in one like that, that's a little more successful than what it's trying to do.

Let's talk about *Gigli*. It came, it got killed, it disappeared. J.Lo and Ben Affleck just didn't have the magic. Did you appear in a cameo part as a favor to Marty Brest, who directed you in *Scent of a Woman*?

No, not exactly. I do know Marty, and he was close to me. It wasn't a favor. Though I wouldn't have done it if it wasn't for having a history with Marty. But I felt he wrote some nice stuff in that movie, and I thought I'd try to do something with this character. I just trusted him to make a good movie, which he does. He missed with it. Sometimes you miss at the wrong time. [*Laughs*] You can miss at the right time, and you're lucky. But this was the wrong time, primarily because it had the two kids in it who were, at the time, having this romance. With Jennifer and Ben it seemed as though that was a scandal; it had all the stuff in it. That relationship just caught the imagination of the public. If it wasn't for that, it wouldn't have had that kind of infamy attached. I would have to see the picture again to give an assessment of it.

What did you think of what you did in it?

I didn't think I particularly caught any flavor at all. I didn't catch the kind of flavor I wanted. He was a crazy, disjointed character. They wanted to increase the part and have me go back for more takes, but I thought best let sleeping dogs lie. I didn't think it would contribute any more to the picture in any way. I feel badly for Marty Brest, because that takes its toll on a director, and he has made some really good and entertaining movies. He's a thoughtful, sensitive person. I don't know what happened. I wasn't on the inside of that one. He'll do something good again.

If you could eliminate any of the films you've made, which would they be?

With all the work that goes into a picture, there are certain values to it. Maybe this is me rationalizing lousy movies I've made, but it gives a lot of people employment: There's an effort being made, there is a struggle, an inordinate amount of work is put into it, and that's what makes life go on. You have to accept it, the good with the bad. It's all part of who you are, part of your struggle. Why would you want to get rid of it? It would bother me greatly if I could get rid of some of the lousy pictures. There were movies I didn't want to make that turned out badly, and there were movies that I really didn't want to make that turned out great. So what can you say? I was lucky to have the opportunity.

What was the difference between Jamie Foley's work as a director in *Glengarry Glen Ross* and *Two Bits*?

I don't know what touched him in *Glengarry*—it was a superbly done movie, as was *At Close Range* and a couple of other movies Jamie made. But *Two Bits* missed its target. I don't know quite what it was. You just don't know. I was happy with my performance in it. I enjoyed playing that character.

Were you playing your grandfather?

Absolutely, it was the image of my grandfather. That wasn't who my grandfather was, he wasn't that way completely, but if I were to paint him, that's how I would paint him. As that character. That's who raised me.

Your grandfather was your surrogate father, since your father left when you were a toddler. Was your father an insurance broker?

He was. Then he owned a bar. My whole young life he got into the insurance business and became top in his field. He was head of the union. Had a lot of friends. Then he went into the restaurant business, which he really loved, because he could entertain. My father was an actor—that's what he always wanted to do. He was in community shows way back. He loved going on TV, and he even acted in a few movies in his later life.

Tell me the story of how you once got into trouble for setting a garbage can on fire in your apartment . . . only you didn't do it.

My cousin Mark, who was five, did it. He lit the goddamn garbage. I was about eleven. I went to school, came home, and got smacked—because Mark said I did it. I ran into the bathroom, locked it, and started screaming, "What did I do? What did I do?" "Don't lie to me," they yelled back. They were really in a rage. It was a nightmare. I didn't even know what happened. But I was convincing. Mark didn't say a word; he just hid under the bed, which is what he usually did.

Did you ever go to summer camp?

Yes, CYO [Catholic Youth Organization]. I cried every day. I didn't go with a friend; I didn't know anybody. We played ball. I didn't do well. I was so damn lonely and homesick. I was crying every night. I hated it. I stayed for a week or two and never did it again. Missed my mother beyond words. I remember her leaving me off at the bus, and she was crying as I was waving. I couldn't believe I could miss anybody so much. I must have loved my mother something senseless when I was eleven.

Was that around the time you got your first girlfriend?

Yeah, but not at the camp. I didn't know what to do.

Moving from your youth to where you are today—you're planning on taking *Salome* on tour. What is it about playing King Herod that you want to keep doing it?

I can't explain it in terms of character. I can only say there are certain roles that instinctively you connect to, like a note of music or a painting that you see. You have a sort of symbiosis with it. You feel you understand it on a certain level. There are various levels of understanding. Some things you understand but don't feel you want to express. Other things, you strive to go further and further into a role and you can't go far enough. You can't! It isn't over when it's over. It's not like a painting, where you can say, that is now a painting. With stage acting it's ever changing and evolving. That's the beauty of doing things over and over again.

Does it ever feel like a job to you?

If my life were a job, I'd quit. Ever feel that way?

Not as often as you.

I have my moments.

Let's talk for this moment about politics. During the Watergate scandal, did you think there really was a Deep Throat?

I did. I was just glad to find out it wasn't me. More attention! I would have felt really good about it if it was me. Then there'd be a reason to go on these talk shows and do these interviews. Now I can't find a reason.

Deep Throat turned out to be the FBI's number two man, Mark Felt. Do you see anything of Frank Serpico in his character and what he did?

I don't know. What he was doing affected many more people in a more profound way than *Serpico*, which was a few cops on the take. *The Insider*—the guy going against the tobacco industry—anyone who goes against the great power is taking a risk, and if you've played people like that, you see what it takes to go against that power, to confront that power. It's awesome.

You've been in the presence of powerful people. Who were you more impressed with, Bill or Hillary Clinton?

Both. A lot of politicians are impressive when you meet them. Why? Because they're smart. And they do something. The reality and the image is different. So much of the image, we're projecting us on it. When you see them in person, it's them. Ever meet somebody you had an image of, and you meet them and it's a different kind of thing?

Yeah, you.

We're always projecting our own views and interpretations onto other people. That's why Warren Beatty, who's on the left, talks about some of these people you would never think he would like so much, people on the right. But he admires them and enjoys their company, because he knows them for who they are and what they have to offer.

He spoke out attacking California's governor, Arnold Schwarzenegger, and there's speculation that he might run against him. Think he would?

Warren's so mercurial. He's too much of an artist, I think, to go into politics.

Have you ever met Ted Turner?

Yeah. I thought if I get too close he'll take a bite of my nose. He's innately aggressive—that's how he operates. He's a person who engages. I can't say I met him in a situation I enjoyed, like a quiet place for dinner, like I met his ex-wife, Jane—whom I love, by the way. I really enjoyed talking to her. Smart, classy, attractive, wonderful person.

Where did you meet Ted?

At Larry King's wedding. Then later on at a dinner, I sat next to Jane and enjoyed that.

You and De Niro were recently named as the two greatest actors over fifty. How long do you think that will last?

I'm just hoping that when we reach 102, he and I will be the best actors over 102.

Premiere named the Fifty Greatest Movie Stars of All Time, and you were on that list as well. Does this stuff embarrass you or pump you up?

It flatters me, if the truth be known.

They say you are one of the great actors of your—or any—generation, but that you are "too often perceived as one of Hollywood's great overactors, a shameless ham prone to devouring the scenery." They point to Tony Montana, Big Boy Caprice, and John Milton [Satan] to illustrate such devouring. Care to make a case for playing those characters over-the-top?

You're expressing something, going for something, and you're either getting it or you're missing it. That's part of what a director should do: help guide you with those things.

So if you're over the top, a director should let you know that?

That's what helped me with Shylock in *Merchant of Venice*. Michael Radford did.

Are directors at times unable to tell you that? Do they feel intimidated?

There's an old saying: Ham is okay as long as it's not Spam. You can tolerate it more in certain characters than in others. Sometimes it's a quality that you'd be surprised how many people enjoy. But it's also a quality that can become tiresome and overbearing in certain roles. If I were to do them over again, I know that I would take some of that stuff down. But when it's really happening, when it's energized and motivated by something real, it has size, it's not over the top. The way a tenor will hit a note because the note is there to hit. And sometimes it doesn't. It's the call of the actor and of the director to moderate that. The whole view of *Scarface* was orchestrated that way with Brian and me. That was the direction we were going in. The motivation was there. What is it: The word to the action, the action to the word? Suit the action to the word and the word to the action. I thought that combust was there. I don't cringe at it. But there are some other roles I've done where I cringe. I thought I went too far.

Did that happen in *City Hall*?

Yeah. *City Hall* had one of the best scenes I ever did, and one of the most strident. There were other takes I had done that were less strident. And yet there's a lot of people who like that first take. Not to toot my horn, and I don't mean to, but I have to say that I have seen great actors go too far on occasion. I understand taking liberties. There's a certain style. Especially when you're not censoring yourself. Because then you're cutting off your instincts. Part of your MO is to go to places and work out of the unconscious. You're prone to make outrageous mistakes. If you watch children—the best acting teachers in the world—you see how they do things. If you're in a position where that stuff is what counts, it's not so much that you're chewing the scenery as much as you're expressing some particular phenomena. I see people do the most outrageous things in life, too. But in the art of acting, in the art of presentation, there are certain liberties that you're allowed, because it's a form of expression. Look at how Jackson Pollock sprayed paint all over the canvas. You're forgiven for that, because the art protects you. Sometimes you overstate, you go past the boundaries, so you have to be careful. But you can't put the lid on that, you can't limit that, because then you're censoring yourself before you start. Because you never know, you could have that moment. If I were worried about overstating, what would I have done in *Godfather III* when my daughter was shot? Where do you go with that stuff?

When did you first get to know your *City Hall* and *Sea of Love* director, Harold Becker?

I met Harold because we were going to do this movie that I always wanted to do, called *Johnny Handsome*.

Which Mickey Rourke wound up doing.

Yeah. Harold and I were trying to find the third act, and we couldn't. The first half of that movie is great. That was my favorite role ever in movies. I loved the whole idea of someone who's been grotesque-looking and has made a life having to cope with that kind of deformity, to then have it lifted from him, and to have to cope with the world now. It's like a 500-pound person losing 350 pounds. What happened was, in prison they were experimenting on people, and slowly they reduce his features so that he looked normal. That's why they called him Johnny Handsome, because he doesn't look at all like he was. And he goes out, and instead of having a new life he goes back to his old roots and seeks revenge. But he's really intelligent. The whole idea of someone having to deal with life, having been a criminal, the brains behind these robberies in Pittsburgh. He couldn't even speak right. I *loved* the role. Loved it. But once again, one of those roles that just go down the drain if they couldn't fix the last act. Mickey Rourke did a great job on it, but that didn't matter; the movie didn't have the finish.

You and Becker have remained friends. Do you often make friends with people in the business?

I become friends with a lot of people I work with: directors, writers, interviewers . . .

Anybody who will take you seriously. . . .

Yeah. There it is. A handful. It's funny when your own teenage daughter looks at you and says to herself, but you can see it in her eyes, "Is my dad really that dumb? Oh well, that's okay."

When _City Hall_ came along, did you like it right away?

No, not particularly. Bo Goldman writes a good script, and I thought there were elements in it. And I loved Harold, and it was his kind of picture. It went a little off, but I'd have to see it again to tell you what I really feel about it. I sort of liked it when I saw it back then. You never know with your own work, it's like looking at your own kids. But it did feel like he did some good stuff. There was something missing somewhere. I loved Johnny Cusack—he was wonderful in it. I think there was the question of the casting of the girl and Johnny together. In New York they liked it, but something bothered the rest of the world about that picture.

The generation before yours produced three original actors others emulated: Marlon Brando, Montgomery Clift, and James Dean. Your generation's three would be you, Robert De Niro, and Jack Nicholson. What three would you say belong in the generation that has followed yours?

You've got three: Sean Penn, Johnny Depp, and Russell Crowe. They should be in _The Brothers Karamazov_ together.

What about Tom Cruise?

Tom Cruise is a movie star, which is a whole other category. He has tremendous charisma and he's also a good actor.

Did you catch him jumping on the seat on *Oprah*, expressing his joyous love for Katie Holmes? Seemed he got a bit carried away there.

He was having an episode. We all have them from time to time; it's just that we usually don't do them in front of cameras. Celebrities get that opportunity.

Looking down your list of films—

I know, I haven't made a good film since *Dog Day*. . . . Somebody at a press conference once asked me, "Do you think you'll ever be as good as you were in *Dog Day*?" And I said, flatly, "No." That answered that.

No, I was just looking at a list of all the younger actors you've worked with, like John Cusack, Keanu Reeves, Russell Crowe, Michelle Pfeiffer, Johnny Depp, Chris O'Donnell, Sean Penn, Colin Farrell, Matthew McConaughey. Do you ever ask for any of these people?

No. They usually come on after me. Except for Keanu; I'm not sure about that one.

The way you wanted to act with Brando when you were young, all of these actors seem to want to work with you.

Is that what you deduced? What's your point?

Have you ever been disappointed with any of them?

Never. I sometimes was disappointed—and I'm not going to go into who— afterward, the way they went on. After the movie was over . . . I just had different ideas of what they were going to do. They're so much fun to be with and work with and to get to know, these guys. Some of them inspire me on several levels. Their talent, their personalities, the way their minds work, their commitment, their devotion—it's interesting to be around. They're sensitive and intelligent; therefore you get something from them that you take with you. I enjoy them so very much.

Are they often nervous around you?

Usually they get unnervous after five minutes, because they see what's up. They see that we are now dealing with something together. You can be nervous about the situation, but the celebrity factor goes. Most people who are nervous want to please, and they're hoping that they don't get inhibited. When I was with Marlon, I was hoping that it wouldn't cut off my instincts, because I was so impressed with him. So you censor yourself a little bit. That's an aspect of nervousness. People want to be themselves, they want to be free, they want to feel that they can say or do anything, and sometimes they may be inhibited because they want approval from somebody they respect, and that can cut off their spontaneity.

Being aware of that, what do you do to ease that situation with younger actors?

I sing "Yankee Doodle Dandy." It works every time.

You and James Cagney.

After five minutes of being around me, the air clears and they know who I am. They know what's going on. I get along very much with Sean Penn and Johnny Depp, because it's a vice-versa thing. We enjoy each other's company because of the wavelength we're on. I like the way their minds work. Not to mention what great actors they are.

Were you surprised that Penn wanted to get out of acting some years ago?

Sometimes you go through these phases. He has a real gift for directing, too, and writing. He's consummate in his gifts. Part of it is his need to be in control of things. When you're an actor, you don't always have that control. You've got to be able to let that control go as an actor. I think he's come to terms with that. He's a great actor in movies. Look at Bobby De Niro—he waited a long time to direct, and he made a wonderful movie with *A Bronx Tale*. Now he's going to direct another one, a spy movie with Leonardo DiCaprio. The point is, he's quite capable of directing.

Why aren't you?

I'm not. I don't know why. Why am I not a colorist? There's a misconception of directors. Directors are people who can bring you into a story in a certain way and tell a story directorially. Warren Beatty can do it. He's a sensational actor, but he's also a great director. Redford can do it. He speaks in a language only a director can speak. I don't see the world that way. I wouldn't know how to do it, nor would I care to. To me, only on occasion, like with *Looking for Richard*, which was an extension of my vision of something that I wanted to say. I knew I could direct that. Sometimes I'm very inarticulate unless I'm emotional. I can't express myself unless I'm emotional. I can't speak in a cold, clear, meticulous way and just lay it out. I'm not good at that. That's not the case with acting, because I've been doing it my whole life. I don't have to feel it to act. Acting comes more naturally to me. Or used to. I don't know . . . now bullshitting comes more natural to me.

So what will be your next small film? *Orphans? Salome? Hughie?*

I just go with the glow. There are so many other things in my life now that I have to address, it's hard for me to ruminate like I did on *Richard*. I spent years thinking about that one. I've got my eye on *Salome*. I've got some ideas about it, but I need to conceptualize it more to turn it into a movie.

Ever write anything?

When I had my babies, I wrote a poem, which is something I used to do when I was younger. It actually, to me, made some kind of sense. And my maid threw it out. She didn't know. I was inspired so I was writing on scraps of paper, left it in my apartment, and she threw it out. So there goes the one poem that would have changed the world! [*Laughs*]

Maybe it will pop up on eBay, and she'll buy her house with the profits.

Well, that would be all right.

The American Cinematheque honored you with a Lifetime Achievement Award in October 2005. Are you getting to that time in your life where such honors make you feel like you belong in a museum?

[*Laughs*] I love it. Do I feel I belong in a museum? I feel I *am* a museum.

How did you feel when Ira Lewis wrote a play about you? Did you ever see it?

No. As I get older, I don't care about those things, because I know the image is always going to be there. You would probably enjoy seeing something like that, since you know me so well. You'd see the ridiculousness of it. Forget the bull's-eye, they missed the entire target! People have their perspective. But hey, if I can inspire a good performance or a good character, I'm all for it. After I'm gone, they're going to be writing—hopefully—things about me for a little while. And then I'll be gone, just like the rest of us. Kaput. Completely. Videos will take over. And I'll be forgotten. As all my contemporaries will. As all of us will. It's not a thought you want to dwell on. But for now, as my kids grow up, one hopes for a legacy that they can deal with. That's why I'm doing this collection of my independent movies, so they can know who their dad is.

It's tough being the child of a movie star.

Now there's something I wouldn't know. [*Smiles*] I imagine it would be, Larry. If you really want to know, go ask Anton. He's playing with his trains in the other room. Hopefully by the time they're at an age when it really matters, they will be prepared to deal with it. My oldest daughter, so far, knock wood, seems to be doing very well with it.

How many friendships have you had that have come and gone?

Too many.

And why do you suspect it happens?

Disillusionment. There's a certain tenacity keeping up with a friendship. We get caught in our own lives. It's certainly geographic. And career. But I'm not lacking in friends; I've got some good ones. I love what Robert Mitchum said about celebrities: They don't have friends, they have disciples.

I didn't care for Mitchum when I met him.

That's because he wasn't nice to you.

I'm glad you're not like him.

If I was, I wouldn't be talking to you.

And I wouldn't be asking you to reflect about your life all the time.

How did I get here? Impossible background. Impossible life. How did I get this far? It's a bottomless pit, but relatively . . . Hey! Thank God I've got my health, friends, wonderful kids. I'm well off. I can do my work. . . . What can I say? How'd this happen?

Maybe it's your Friday ritual.

Maybe that's it. I don't eat meat on Friday.

EPILOGUE

TO BEE OR NOT TO BE

In the summer of 2005 I was sitting by the pool with Pacino at his rented house in Beverly Hills. He was having a moment of anxiety, he said, because he had just brought his kids back to their mother, and the way she reacted to something he had done had made him wonder if he'd done something wrong. His four-year-old daughter had seen a bee on the grass, obviously hurt and perhaps dying. She pointed it out to her daddy, who said, "The bee is not feeling well. Why don't we put it in a better place, and maybe it will feel better?" So he carefully lifted it onto a piece of paper, and they placed it in the flower bed. Later, when he was dropping them off, he said to his daughter, "Why don't you tell Mommy about the bee?" And Mommy said, "No bees! She was once stung by a bee. I don't want to hear anything about bees. You shouldn't let her near one." And that was that. Al wanted to explain that the bee was not a danger, that in fact they were saving the bee, that's the way he would like to teach his children. But their mother was coming from another place: Bees can sting, bees can hurt you, stay away from bees.

It was a classic Mommy-Daddy dilemma. One parent tries to teach one way, the other parent goes in a different direction. Neither is right or wrong. But Al was worried about how his kids would interpret it. Would they think that Daddy was wrong to have told them to be kind to bees? Or would they be confused when they saw a bee: Stay away vs. it's okay. This parenting thing wasn't easy. No matter what you did with your children, it could be misinterpreted, and would that affect them later in life? Would it be your fault if they ever got stung again by a bee?

"You know what?" I said. "Why don't you ask the kids next time you see them if they remember what happened with the bee, and with what Mommy said about it, and see what they learned from it? Use it as a teaching lesson. Hurt bees can be helped. Healthy bees should be stayed away from."

"Yeah, maybe. Or maybe I won't say anything and just let it pass."

"You could do that, too."

"You never know what's right," he said. "But that's my way. I put the bee in the flower bed."

"That's what makes you who you are," I said, making light of it. It was a warm day, the sun was turning him bronze, and when he said, "You're such a jerk," I laughed and started telling him about this book. "It is a kind of document, isn't it?" he said. "You know, I don't think I'll do many more print interviews. Might as well just go on TV."

"Well then," I kidded, "that makes this even more precious, doesn't it?"

He gave me one of his sideways glances that said all he wanted to say about that comment, and I changed to a more solemn subject, the passing of Marlon Brando. I wondered if he had cried when he heard the news.

"I did," he said. "I felt as though I lost a close relative. Which is interesting, because I really didn't know him hardly at all. I thought, *How are we going to go on without Marlon?* I actually thought that: *What are we going to do without Marlon?* He was a pillar; he represented somebody who stood by whatever it was and never wavered. He was what he was, that's why he was such an icon. Not just for his great acting, but because he was able to be who he was in this environment."

"Did you go to his funeral?"

"No, I didn't know where it was. I wasn't close to Marlon, but I adored him. Some people I know pretty well, like Sean Penn, Johnny Depp, and Warren Beatty, they were very close to him. Very close. He was an integral part of their lives. They were as close as you can be to someone. As close as I am with you. I talked to Marlon on the phone when he called me about being in his documentary. I said I'd do whatever he wanted. It was great hearing from him, just fun to talk to him. I was looking forward to talking to him again. He was always in my thoughts."

His feelings about Brando never changed over the years, and I asked him if some of the things he said to me a quarter of a century ago were still how he felt about things today. And was this a good or a bad thing, we wondered?

I brought up *Godfather III*—I was supposed to have visited him on the set in Italy, when his grandmother died and he had to fly to New York for the funeral. In our earlier interviews he had talked about losing Robert Duvall and Winona Ryder as the reasons why that picture didn't meet its potential, but this time he said something new.

"You know what the problem with that film was? The real problem? Nobody wanted to see Michael have retribution and feel guilty. That's not who he was. The thing about the other scripts was that in his mind he was avenging his family and saving them. Michael never thought of himself as a gangster, ever. Never. Not as a child, not while he was one, and not afterward: That was not the image he had of himself. So anyone who says to me that I played a gangster, I say, 'Not Michael.' He didn't come up that way. He's not a part of the *GoodFellas* thing. That's just not what Michael was. I've played gangsters . . . but not Michael. Michael had this code—he lived by something that made audiences respond. But once he went away from that and started crying over coffins and making confessions and feeling remorse, it wasn't right. I applaud Francis for trying to get to that, but Michael was so frozen in that image . . . Like he says to the priest, This is pointless to do this. But there was in him a deep feeling of having betrayed his mother by killing his brother. That was a mistake. And we are ruled by these mistakes in life, as time goes on. These crucial, brutal mistakes that we make in life. His choices—he was wrong. Like the way in *Scarface* when Tony kills Manny, that was wrong. And he pays for it. And in his way, Michael paid for it."

"What should Michael have done, in retrospect, with Fredo?" I asked. I loved talking to Al about *The Godfather*.

"Ban him, exile him in some way," he said. "He was harmless. That part of Michael was off. Just as he denies the mother of his children. How could you do a thing like that? You hurt the children. That's what made it powerful. But where do you go from there?"

"A lot of critics thought Diane's role as Kay was a weak, thankless part."

"She tried to do the best she could in *III*. There was a tragedy that Francis could have explored: What happened to her? The result of her loving this man. *Godfather III* should have been more about Kay. And Hagen. Michael could still have had that breakdown with the priest, that would have been fine, but that's it. All this contemplation and dealing with the epic *King Lear* connection: Maybe in retrospect the movie should have been about Kay. Giving her a tragedy and investigating that. Remember, the last time we saw her, at the end of *II*, he was closing the door in her face and keeping her children."

The mention of *Lear* led me to ask him if he was getting toward an age when he might consider doing *King Lear*. *Godfather III*, as he had just pointed out, was *Lear*-like, with Michael the patriarch calling his family together, concerned about his children and the fate of his empire. He said he'd have to have an understanding of that old fool, who divided his kingdom among his greedy daughters and left out the one who loved him most.

"I'd have to try *Lear* out," he said. "I'd have to try it on like you try on anything, to see how comfortable in the role I was. The questions I have to ask are, Why do his two daughters not love him, and why does the one love him? What has he done to her and not to them? That is the kind of work one does when one does *Lear*. On the first reading you see what you get metaphorically, what the ideas are . . . and then the next step is turning the play into something that you understand and you can interpret. I'd be interested in the relationships between the people, certainly the children, and the back life of Lear, his wife that was, how they came upon this moment. What was his engagement? What does he look like? Where would it be? How could it be done so that it meant something? That kind of nuance would be very important, it would be a start. If I were doing *Lear*, I'd have to come up with some character that Lear could pass through. Who could that be? What would give me distance in order to play it?"

I suggested it be modernized. "Suppose Lear was Kirk Kirkorian," I said. "He's in his late eighties, he just won some tennis tournament for the elderly, he bought almost a billion dollars worth of GM stock when it was tanking, he had all those Las Vegas deals. You could play Lear as this guy, flying in a helicopter onto the top of the MGM Grand, surveying his kingdom."

"That's a very good idea, but I wouldn't want to do it."

"Doesn't have to be him. Could be Donald Trump."

"That's a possibility. I have an idea about him."

"Or George Steinbrenner. Or maybe Howard Hughes."

"You're very creative with your choices about Lear. I think you should play him."

"You can almost visualize it," I said, wanting to keep him going, "a modern-day Lear flying in on his jet or helicopter to his Las Vegas hotel, looking over his various real estate, dealing with the two daughters who don't love him, and with the one who does."

"Pardon me for rhyming, but when you ask me about *Lear*, all I can say is, I'll do *Lear* in about a year. Or, It would take a year to play the part of King Lear. Maybe I could do it, but only if I could take it into orbit, to take it to a place where it transcends the character it is."

The thought of playing *Lear* got Al thinking about Shakespeare again, and he started reciting lines from *Hamlet* and *Othello*. "You never played either of those. How do you remember the lines?" I asked.

"I just love the language."

"What about the way *Romeo and Juliet* was updated with DiCaprio?"

"I liked what they did. I thought it was inspired, but I didn't think the young people in it—albeit they were wonderful—had a good sense of the language. But then, that's a tough play." And then he started reciting the verses about how fair Juliet was, and how he wished he was a glove to rest upon fair Juliet's cheek. "See how she leans her cheek upon her hand, oh that I were a glove upon that hand that I might touch that cheek."

There we were, again, doing what we both enjoyed doing, what we have been doing ever since I first met him. Me tossing out ideas, Al running with them. And always, coming back to Shakespeare.

When I think about it, I find myself smiling. Here I am writing about us sitting by the pool talking about a writer who died 500 years ago instead of about the latest freeway killings in L.A. or the latest celebrity trial. We do, of course, talk about those things, but they seem to pale in comparison. Why do I want to write down what Al Pacino had to say about Robert Blake or Michael Jackson or why Winky Wright outboxed and outfoxed Felix Trinidad when I could be quoting him on love or treachery, as he recites lines he has committed to memory? If this is what is in his head, isn't it more interesting? I can talk to any guy on the street, and he'll have an opinion about Michael Jackson, but will he be able to give me two lines from *Hamlet*?

The businesspeople around Al would prefer that he turn his attention more to the scripts that have him playing a good or bad cop, have him ducking bullets, flashing his killer smile at some female costar, raising his voice in a soliloquy of violence or righteousness, doing his movie Pacino thing. Al knows this; the scripts in his various rooms illustrate this. Al looks at how Dustin Hoffman has dusted off his career doing smaller and lesser parts than the ones that made Hoffman Hoffman; how De Niro has so cleverly reinvented himself. These are actors who have accepted the realities of the business, who have committed to renewed careers. They want to work and they will continue to work, and if the two of them can wind up in a mediocre film like *Meet the Fockers*, which turns out to be the biggest cash comedy cow of all time, then how can you fault them? And yet, Pacino is different. He still can't wrap himself around the idea of doing something strictly for the money. He can't bring himself to stand still for a high-paying nonverbal commercial that would air only in Japan. He can't take the millions and run when the script doesn't capture his imagination. He's a throwback to a time when artists did what pleased them, what inspired them, and if anyone liked what they did, fine with them. But if they didn't, it shouldn't matter. Of course, in the movie business, when there are so many millions at stake, it does matter. It will always matter. But Pacino is an actor first, a stage actor, then a movie actor who happens to also be a movie star. He'll take *Merchant of Venice* over *Merchant of Death* every time. He'll personally finance and then promote the DVD of his three independent films, but he will tell his publicist he'd rather not have to do similar promotion on projects that aren't as dear to his heart. He'll tell his agent he wants to take *Salome* on the road and then do the play

Orphans at a ninety-nine-seat theater in West Hollywood, when his agent is telling him to do movies that will allow him to continue to rent houses at twenty grand a month. Because it's not about money. It's never been about money, with Pacino. It's about how he feels inside his body and his head. It's about his art. And in an age of commerce, Al Pacino just may be the last artist standing.

THE FILMS

Me, Natalie (1969)

The Panic in Needle Park (1971)

The Godfather (1972)

Scarecrow (1973)

Serpico (1973)

The Godfather Part II (1974)

Dog Day Afternoon (1975)

Bobby Deerfield (1977)

. . . And Justice for All (1979)

Cruising (1980)

Author! Author! (1982)

Scarface (1983)

Revolution (1985)

Sea of Love (1989)

The Godfather Part III (1990)

Dick Tracy (1990)

The Local Stigmatic (1990)

Frankie and Johnny (1991)

Glengarry Glen Ross (1992)

Scent of a Woman (1992)

Carlito's Way (1993)

Two Bits (1995)

Heat (1995)

City Hall (1996)
Looking for Richard (1996)
Donnie Brasco (1997)
The Devil's Advocate (1997)
The Insider (1999)
Any Given Sunday (1999)
Chinese Coffee (2000)
S1mOne (2002)
Insomnia (2002)
Gigli (2003)
People I Know (2003)
The Recruit (2003)
Angels in America (2003)
The Merchant of Venice (2004)
Two for the Money (2005)
88 Minutes (2006)

THE PLAYS

The Adventures of High Jump (Children's Theater, 1962)

Jack and the Beanstalk (Children's Theater, 1962)

Hello Out There (William Saroyan; 1963)

A Brick and a Rose (Louis John Carlino; 1964)

The Creditors (August Strindberg; 1965)

Why Is a Crooked Letter (Fred Vassi; 1966)

The Indian Wants the Bronx (Israel Horovitz; 1966, 1968)

The Peace Creeps (John Wolfson; 1966)

Awake and Sing! (Clifford Odets; 1967)

America, Hurrah (Jean-Claude Van Itallie; 1967)

Does a Tiger Wear a Necktie? (Don Petersen; 1969)

The Local Stigmatic (Heathcote Williams; 1969, 1976)

Camino Real (Tennessee Williams; 1970)

Rats (Israel Horovitz; 1970)

The Basic Training of Pavlo Hummel (David Rabe; 1972, 1977)

Richard III (William Shakespeare; 1972 & 1979)

The Resistible Rise of Arturo Ui (Bretolt Brecht; 1975, 2002)

Hamlet (William Shakespeare, workshop; 1979)

The Jungle of the Cities (Bretolt Brecht; 1979)

Othello (William Shakespeare, rehearsals; 1979)

American Buffalo (David Mamet; 1980, '82, '83, '84)

The Hairy Ape (Eugene O'Neill; 1982)

Julius Caesar (William Shakespeare; 1986)

Crystal Clear (workshop; 1987)

National Anthem (Dennis McIntyre; 1988)
Chinese Coffee (Ira Lewis; 1989–90, 1992)
Salome (Oscar Wilde; 1990–1, 2002–3)
The Father (August Strindberg; reading, early 1990s)
Hughie (Eugene O'Neill; 1996, 1999)
Oedipus Rex (Sophocles; 2002)
Orphans (Lyle Kessler; 2005)

ACKNOWLEDGMENTS

My initial thought was simply to thank Al for our talks, because let's face it, these conversations wouldn't exist if he wasn't up for them. So, first and foremost, thank you, Al. I'm glad we've been able to record as much as we have; but even more, I value the private time, when I get to tell *you* things.

I also want to single out Noah Lukeman. Noah is more than just my agent: He's a good sounding board, and he puts in the time. He's the one who got Ryan Fischer-Harbage, my editor for this project, to come on board, and I'm thankful for that, because Ryan made some astute suggestions, which I at first resisted but then came around to realizing he was right. So thank you, Ryan. I've enjoyed the process. And thank you, Roberta, for your contributions—no brother has ever had a more supportive sister. Or a more knowledgeable brother-in-law than Ethan Intrater. Or a better companion than Zach. I should also thank Al's assistant, Tim Judge, because every time I needed to check a date or someone's name, I'd e-mail Tim, and he'd find the answer. My wife, Hiromi, and my daughters, Maya and Hana, have to be thanked, for understanding my complicated relationship with Al—and for accepting him not as a movie star but as a person (albeit, an eccentric one) into our family. And Maya dear, a special thank-you, because you are my constant reality check. You are the one who said, "Dad, if not now, when?" And, for a change, I listened.

INDEX